Birder's
Mexico

———

NUMBER TWELVE:
THE LOUISE LINDSEY MERRICK
NATURAL ENVIRONMENT SERIES

ROLAND H. WAUER

Birder's Mexico

TEXAS A&M
UNIVERSITY PRESS
College Station

Previously published as *Naturalist's Mexico.*

The paper used in this book meets the minimum requirements
of the American National Standard for Permanence
of Paper for Printed Library Materials, Z39.48-1984.
Binding materials have been chosen for durability.

Library of Congress Cataloging-in-Publication Data

Wauer, Roland H.
    Birder's Mexico / Roland H. Wauer.
       p.   cm. — (Louise Lindsey Merrick natural environment series;
no. 12)
    Rev. ed. of: Naturalist's Mexico, c1992.
    Includes bibliographical references (p.).
    ISBN 0-89096-918-3 (p)
    1. Natural history—Mexico. 2. Birds—Mexico. 3. Birds—
Mexico—Habitat. 4. Mexico—Description and travel.
5. Naturalists—United States—Anecdotes. I. Wauer, Roland H.
Naturalist's Mexico. II. Title. III. Series.
QH107.W38   1999
508.72—dc21   99-40623
                                                    CIP

TO BILL SCHALDACH,
and all the other early-day naturalists
who got there before me.
Among them are:
Vernon Bailey
Frank Blair
Archie Carr
Irby Davis
Edmund Jaeger
Edgar Kinkaid
George Miksch Sutton
Francis Sumichrast
John Xantus

Contents

PART IV. TROPICAL MEXICO

Illustrations

(All photos, except the Worthen's sparrow on page 41,
are by Roland H. Wauer.)

MAPS

Foreword

Years ago Frank Chapman, the great ornithologist, wrote that one develops a deep affection for nature in our northern climes, but falls hopelessly in love with her in the tropics. So it has been for me and judging by the enthusiasm Ro Wauer expresses for Mexico in his excellent book, *Birder's Mexico,* the same was true for him.

Like Ro's, my first encounter with the tropical world was in Mexico. One of my childhood mentors was a remarkable naturalist and conservationist named Manuel Armand Yramategui. Like me, he was born in Houston, but his parents were both immigrants from Mexico. On that memorable first trip in December, 1954, we drove his parents to Monterrey and then continued south to Tamanzunchale. I'll never forget the excitement of waking up in an entirely new natural environment. We participated in the Xilitla Christmas Bird Census. On count day I was walking through the forest when I spotted a Blue-crowned Motmot perched at eye-level just thirty feet away. It was a breathtakingly beautiful creature with an iridescent blue crown, soft green wings, and a bright red eye. From that moment on I was in love with tropical nature. Since that initial visit I have returned to Mexico every year. I have visited every region and been fortunate to have seen many wild and beautiful places.

And so I relate very well to *Birder's Mexico.* It brings back many wonderful memories of that country's diverse natural environment. It is one of a kind, a treasure house of information. This book fills an important gap in the natural history of Mexico.

Until Roger Tory Peterson completed *A Field Guide to the Birds of Mexico* in 1973, there was no adequate book on Mexican birds. How well I remember trying to identify a Golden-crowned Warbler on my first trip in Mexico using Emmet Reid Blake's *Birds of Mexico,* and then opening for the first time the Peterson guide. I had waited a long time for that book.

I first met Ro Wauer in the summer of 1970. He had found the first
Black-vented Oriole ever recorded in the United States in 1968, and it
had returned in 1969 and 1970. I stopped by Big Bend National Park to
meet Ro and see the oriole. From the onset I was impressed by Ro's keen
enthusiasm for birds and his overall natural history expertise. Later I
read the two books he wrote about the Big Bend region: *Birds of Big
Bend National Park and Vicinity* and *Naturalist's Big Bend*. Both represent valuable pieces of natural history literature. *Naturalist's Big Bend* is
remarkable in its treatment of such a large subject with such a concise
and readable text. Every time I use this superb book I appreciate the
natural world of the Big Bend more deeply. In *Birder's Mexico,* Ro has
done for an entire country what he did for Big Bend.

The United States is unique among developed countries in bordering
a less developed country that has a culture and natural landscape so different from our own. For decades Americans have journeyed south in search
for many things, including exotic scenery, a chance to view the ruins of
ancient cultures, winter warmth and sun, and attractive places to relax.
Most travelers have flocked to the major cities and tourist destinations
such as Mexico City, Guadalajara, Acapulco, and Cancun. Recently a
new type of tourist—the "eco-tourist"—has emerged on the scene. The
eco-tourist wants to see wild places, natural landscapes, and a rich diversity of birds, butterflies, plants, and animals. Mexico provides all of that.
But until now there has not been an adequate guide. *Birder's Mexico* will
undoubtedly become the handbook for Mexico's greatly increasing numbers of eco-tourists.

Costa Rica has already become a popular destination for eco-tourists.
Costa Rica is known for its stable government, friendly people, and its
rich, varied natural landscape. It also is renowned for its extensive national park system. Many lodges have been built to accommodate eco-
tourists. Costa Rica's economy depends upon tourism, and eco-tourism
is becoming increasingly important.

Recently the Mexican government has also begun to recognize the
value of eco-tourism and has expanded its efforts to protect its remaining natural areas. A host of young Mexican biologists are working to
study their natural world and to help preserve it. Mexican entrepreneurs
are starting to develop attractive lodges designed for travelers who prefer
a natural setting for their vacations.

With the proximity to the United States and its rich natural diversity, Mexico will increasingly be a prime destination for nature-oriented travelers. This superb book by Ro Wauer will be invaluable to such travelers, in preparing for their journey and also for its use on-site. *Birder's Mexico* will go a long way to helping first-time visitors to Mexico as well as veteran travelers to understand and appreciate what awaits them just across the border. In addition, it will impart to both visitors and locals the conservation imperatives that confront us all.

—Victor Emanuel

Preface

Mexico! It is one of the world's most fascinating countries. To the nature-lover, it is a biological paradise of enormous natural diversity. Although Mexico is only one-fourth the size of the United States, it possesses as many plant species—approximately 20,000—and significantly more kinds of animals. One major reason for this great biological diversity is its complex topography. Mexico is as much a vertical country as it is a horizontal one. Elevations vary from sea level to more than three miles, or 18,851 feet at the summit of Pico de Orizaba. That is more than 4,300 feet higher than the tallest mountain in the continental United States; California's Mount Whitney is 14,494 feet. Mexico's huge central plateau, the *altiplano,* is the third highest inhabited area in the world, after Tibet and Bolivia.

There is an often told story about a sixteenth-century description of Mexico's landscapes. When the Spanish king asked a returning conquistador for a description of this new land, the visitor seized a piece of paper, crushed it into a crinkled ball, and then laid it in front of the king. "There, your Majesty," he said, "is a map of your New Spain." The crinkled ball, indeed, was a good representation of Mexico's contrasting peaks, ridges, slopes, and valleys.

Ever since I took my first trip to Mexico I have searched both the popular and technical literature for information about the country's rich natural resources. I discovered that there is a paucity of information about Mexico's outdoors. Prior to each trip, I read everything I could find about the region I planned to visit. Consistently, I unearthed a considerable amount of information about the cities and towns, including hotels and restaurants, good up-to-date material on the numerous archeological sites, and fairly good background on Mexico's fascinating history, customs and philosophy. Only rarely did I come across even meager details about what I consider the country's most valuable assets: its natural resources.

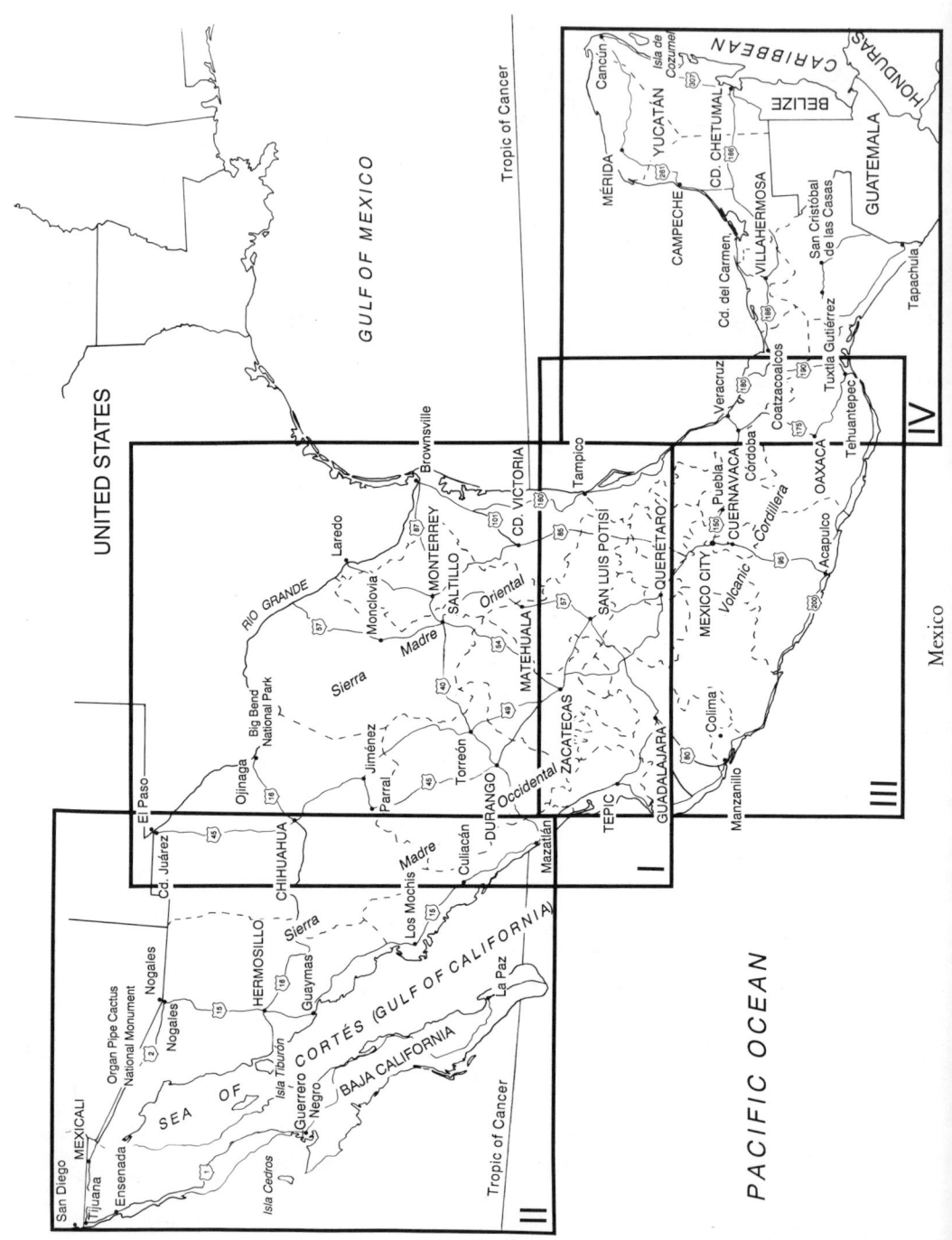

This book is designed partially to fill that void. Although it is primarily about my numerous trips and experiences within a variety of Mexico's natural areas, it also includes much information about the flora and fauna and the interrelationships between them. I found long ago that the two ingredients of nature I enjoyed most were encounters with new birds and seeing the remote habitats where they occur. I have tried to express that dual interest here. I have not tried to make this book a scientific thesis on the ecology of the various areas. My principal hope is that it provides the kind of information that people with a sincere interest in their natural surroundings might find helpful to better enjoy a trip to Mexico.

Personal Concerns

Since 1966, I have spent from five to thirty-five days in Mexico almost every year. I have visited every one of its thirty-one states and the federal district (Mexico City). And in all that travel I have not experienced a life-threatening or serious incident. Accidents, both on the highways and elsewhere, do occur, and there are plenty of crosses along Mexican highways to mark the more serious ones. However, very few Americans are part of those statistics. Unfortunate episodes in Mexico are a lot like airplane accidents: whenever a U.S. citizen is involved in any way, American newspapers pick it up and give it plenty of play. In all of my trips to Mexico, only once—Dick Russell and I were stopped and our vehicle was carefully searched at the Jalisco-Colima border in 1976—did I ever feel even slightly threatened. In fact, I have felt much more secure in the interior of Mexico than I have in many places in the United States. I would in no way feel comfortable roaming the back streets of Mexico City or Juárez, Tijuana, or, for that matter, any of the border towns after dark. But I feel exactly the same about New York City, Chicago, and dozens of other cities in the United States. Old-fashioned horsesense is indispensable wherever you are.

Entry

Getting into Mexico, like entering any foreign country, usually involves some formalities. Obtaining the required entry permit is one of those facts of life for visitors. However, difficulties can be kept at a minimum if you possess appropriate papers. Proof of citizenship is an absolute necessity. The best proof is a passport. The original or a copy (preferable) of a birth certificate or voter's registration card will also suffice. Those are the documents most often utilized and therefore will cause the least confusion. For a vehicle, some proof of ownership is required. The vehicle title is best and is readily accepted. If all of your papers are in order, you can usually get through the border and be on your way in thirty minutes to one hour, depending upon the number of people in line front of you.

Traveling by air usually offers the least hassle, although there is always some necessary paperwork and baggage scrutiny at the port of entry. This can be exasperating on holidays, especially Christmas, New Year's, and Easter, when airports and flights are packed. Mexico City's international airport can be bulging with people traveling somewhere for the holidays. I have purposely scheduled around those special times of the year. But at the very least, flight reservations are absolutely essential. The major advantage of air travel, of course, is time saved. It is much faster to fly to Mexico City and then rent a car to drive on to Villahermosa, Merida, or most other parts of the country than it is to drive from the border. There is another more subtle advantage, as well. I have found that renting a vehicle in Mexico can be advantageous, since one is less reluctant to drive a rental vehicle to places where one might worry about taking a personal vehicle. And in many cases, Mexican vehicles are better able to utilize a cheaper brand of gasoline that may be the only gasoline available in some out-of-the-way places. Bob Burleson and David Riskind (1986) have written an excellent book on backcountry travel in Mexico that is well worth obtaining and reading prior to extensive backcountry exploration.

Money Exchange

Exchanging money can be done at almost any bank, large hotel, or airport throughout Mexico. But I always try to secure enough pesos before leaving the United States to get by for the first several days. At the border, find a *cambio* before crossing that will offer a competitive rate. At the airport, one can change money at the bank kiosk. Although traveler's checks are worthwhile if staying at popular resorts, many establishments will not accept them, or at best will prefer U.S. currency. Mexican banks close at what seem to us the most inappropriate times. So think ahead, and make sure that the day you plan to pass through a place where you want to exchange money is not a Sunday or a holiday, when banks will definitely be closed. When open, expect long lines. The exchange rates at most hotels or markets are much less favorable than at banks, so you are better of exchanging your money at banks or airports. Exchange rates vary from one day to the next.

Road Conditions and Fuel

Highway conditions in Mexico vary greatly. Major routes are for the most part comparable to major state highways in the United States. Toll roads usually are excellent. Backcountry roads, however, are another story. It is important to check locally about their condition before taking those routes that are shown on maps as anything other than a paved highway. When a road is signed as under construction—*en construcción*—it is best to check these out as well. Although most Mexican detours are safe, they can be unbelievably rough and dusty. All of the federal highways, called *rutas federales,* are marked by signs with "Mex" and the appropriate highway number. Other highways are maintained by the individual states.

Good maps of Mexico are now available. Although the free maps provided by your insurance or car rental agencies may be appropriate for the main highways, they usually are inadequate for backcountry driving. However, there are better maps, with good information on less traveled routes, available at reasonable costs. And, topographical maps at 1:250,000 scale are also usable for backcountry exploration.

Many of Mexico's major highways are patrolled by vehicles designed for providing special assistance to motorists. These vehicles, usually white and green covered pickups called *angeles verde,* or green angels, and operated by the Ministry of Tourism, carry all kinds of equipment. The drivers are most helpful and courteous. Travelers in need of help are charged only for parts.

Gasoline can be found throughout the country, although a few basic precautions are necessary. First, buy only the first-class unleaded gasoline, called *sin plomo,* from the silver pumps, for your personal vehicle. Second, take extra care that you do not run out of gasoline. There can be long stretches of highway where stations are few and far between. If your map does not include towns along your route, particularly if you plan to drive into the backcountry, you may need to carry an addi-

tional supply of gasoline. But if you are traveling only the paved routes
this will not be necessary. Although I have run out of gas three or four
times in Mexico, each time it could be attributed either to carelessness—
not filling up when I should have—or to taking an extra side trip to
explore one place too many without adequate planning. On each occasion that I did run out of gasoline I got almost immediate help from
passing motorists.

Mexican service stations are usually located at major road junc-
tions and at each end of every town and are usually numerous within
the larger cities. Most are operated by the federal government under
the "Pemex" name, but private stations of various kinds are increasing. Since Mexico is a major oil producer, gasoline prices are reasonably low.

Restrooms and Accommodations

The restrooms in the majority of service stations are poor to unbear-
able. I have made a habit of stopping at the more modern hotels,
such as Holiday Inns and the like, along the highways because their
restrooms are so much more pleasant. Many of these hotels or motels
also provide excellent places to eat, and the overnight costs of these
highway accommodations are only a little more than at some of the
better known places in towns. They also provide for faster get-aways
in the mornings. However, generally the center of town offers a mood
and a window on Mexican culture that are missing if one stays on
the outskirts.

I have paid anything from three to forty-five dollars a night in
Mexican hotels and motels. The three-dollar room was little more
than four walls and a cot, but that was all I required at the time.
I have also stayed at very beautiful places, complete with private
patios and swimming pools, for as little as twelve dollars a night.

The Language

The language has never been a real problem for me, despite the
fact that I speak only enough Spanish to order beer and food, fill
the car with gasoline, acquire a room for the night, and ask some
very simple directions. The price of gasoline is displayed on pumps.
Most restaurants have menus and provide bills. And one can always
use enough sign language to ask a waiter or clerk to write out the
price of a meal or other purchase. Besides, it is amazing how many

Mexicans speak a little English. In that English is mandatory in Mexico's schools, everyone with the equivalent of a junior high education has learned some English.

Like the United States, Mexico contains a melting pot of peoples. Indian blood predominates; nearly thirty percent of the inhabitants are racially and culturally Indian. About sixty percent are considered mestizos, people of mixed Spanish and Indian descent. And some ten percent are settlers from other countries.

Approximately four million Americans travel to Mexico every year. Mexico's tourist business is second only to its oil industry, and U.S. tourists make up more than seventy percent of the foreign travelers. According to the U.S. State Department, Mexico's Ministry of Tourism operates a hotline twenty-four hours a day that "is accessible from anywhere in Mexico for visitors seeking immediate assistance or guidance." In 1985 a tourist guide told me that Mexico City police also respond to all telephone calls to numbers 06 or 07 regarding any harassment; he said Mexico City police were well paid and not permitted to badger visitors or accept any money on site. If any Mexico City police officer takes advantage of or puts pressure on a tourist, one should note the badge number and report the incident immediately.

Food and Drink

The questions most often asked about Mexico by friends north of the border involve the water and food. The answer on water is simple: don't drink any untreated water, and if you are not sure, don't chance it! Diarrhea—"Montezuma's revenge"—is a reality in Mexico, as in most developing countries. But sickness can be avoided. I usually drink soft drinks or juices during the day and *cerveza*—beer—in the evenings. My favorite beer in all the world is Tres Equis (XXX), with Tecate *y limon* (with lime) in second place. These are both excellent Mexican beers. I always carry a canteen of purified or treated water. Bottled water can be purchased throughout Mexico at grocery stores and most service stations. And all the better hotels and motels provide safe drinking water. A few, such as the Mexico City Airport Holiday Inn, have a water treatment plant on the premises and you can drink water directly from the tap. Iodine tablets or drops are the best and safest method of treating questionable water. Again, don't take a chance!

Food is another matter, and I may take too many precautions.

But since my system seems to work for me, I haven't changed it since I first started going to Mexico. First, there are some good, safe things to eat, that are acceptable almost without exception. Then there are a number of things that can be eaten with care. And lastly, there are foods I will not eat under any circumstance.

I have never had a bad bowl of Mexican soup; *sopa* of almost any kind can be a meal in itself or a major part of a meal. I have eaten some fish soups that included a quarter-pound of fish. Vegetable soups are just as good and filling, and they are safe. So are tortillas and most fried or broiled foods, like seafoods and steaks, chicken (*pollo*), ham (*jamón*) and eggs. Many restaurants serve some strange concoctions of "Mexican food" that they have developed at the suggestion of visiting gringos. Although I have yet to find any that taste much like the typical Mexican dishes of southern Arizona, New Mexico, or Texas, most of these, if they aren't too greasy, are safe. And many of the true Mexican dishes are perfectly safe as well — *carne asada, huevos rancheros, pollo ala méxicana, ceviche, camarone* and *pozole.*

One of my greatest gastronomic joys in Mexico is *pan dulce,* sweet bread. Mexican breads are, to me, some of the finest in the world. I can easily make an entire meal from several pieces of fresh Mexican bread and a bowl of sopa, with a couple cervezas to accompany the meal.

My habits of eating seem a little strange to friends expecting three meals daily. I discovered long ago that the only way to find birds was to be where they are when they are most active, and that is at dawn. This means either camping at the site or driving there very early in the morning. And since few Mexican restaurants are open before dawn, my breakfast usually consists of a can of juice and a granola bar brought from the United States, or one or two pieces of pan dulce. Pan dulce can be purchased at *panaderías* (bakeries) at even the smallest village almost anywhere in Mexico, and the price of a huge sack of it, enough to last for about two days, is usually less than four or five dollars. Since Mexican pan dulce does not contain preservatives, like most of the sweet breads in the United States, I buy only enough at one time to last for two days. Besides, panaderías are some of the best smelling and most enjoyable places to shop in all of Mexico.

When traveling in out-of-the-way areas, I usually carry some canned foods that can be eaten in late morning or early afternoon, once the initial birding activities decline. This also is a good time to travel to the next location or to stop at a restaurant for something more substantial.

Then there are the foods that I never, absolutely never, eat in Mexico. Lettuce heads the list; pardon the pun. Although most Mexican restaurants use lettuce to decorate the plate, I always scrape it away and try not to eat any part. I must admit that I begin to long for a good salad, but I'd rather be safe than sorry. Fresh uncooked vegetables, fruit that can't be peeled, and ice are also on my list of nonedibles in Mexico.

Fruits that can be peeled are safe, and are readily available and inexpensive throughout Mexico. A couple of dozen oranges or tangerines usually cost only a few cents. Bananas in season are cheap as well. In many areas fruit is readily available directly from the trees. But the easy access to it can be hazardous as well. I ate so many small, fresh and delicious bananas right from the trees during a three-day stay at San Blas, Nayarit, that Montezuma's revenge caught up with me from overindulgence, rather than from bacteria or a virus.

Mexico's eating establishments are difficult to judge. Although there are a few that cater to the "upper class," some of my best meals in Mexico have been in the less impressive settings. I would rate a fish dinner at a tiny three-table place on the outskirts of Córdoba and huge filets of shrimp at an ancient restaurant in San Blas as two of my most memorable.

General

It is never a good idea to drive Mexico's highways after dark. There are several reasons for this, but the most important is that numerous trucks and buses utilize the roads then, usually traveling faster than I prefer to drive, faster than passenger vehicles are driven in the United States. It is a combination of this type of traffic, the narrowness of all but the key highways, loose livestock, and one's inability to see the countryside that eliminate any enjoyment from driving at night. On the other hand I have driven after dark when it was necessary. I remember one eighteen-hundred-mile return trip from Catemaco to Brownsville, Texas, all in one long rush, that I would not want to repeat. Jim and Cilla Tucker, Benton Basham, Arnold Small, my wife, Betty, and I all took turns driving and sleeping. We arrived at Santa Ana National Wildlife

Refuge in Texas just after dawn, in time to see a hook-billed kite. It was a new U.S. bird for each of us.

I have experienced occasional mechanical problems in Mexico, but each time I found help that was friendly, courteous, and inexpensive. One time was in Villahermosa, Tabasco, a city of two hundred thousand people, located in the Gulf lowlands about halfway between Catemaco and Palenque. We were driving Jim Tucker's Ford station wagon. It had been serviced last in Austin, Texas, just before leaving for Mexico, and Jim had also purchased new tires for the trip. Everything had gone fine for the first two thousand plus miles, but just as we entered Villahermosa, on a Saturday morning at about 10 A.M., the right front wheel began to wobble and make a very loud grinding noise. We immediately stopped and checked the tire, and discovered that the Texas tire people had not tightened the lug nuts well enough, and the long drive had stripped the screws that held the wheel on. We asked some questions and found out about a Ford garage just ahead two or three miles.

We reached the Ford garage at about 11:30 in the morning to find it was to close at noon. I know that there are exceptions, but I know all too well what would happen in the United States if you were to pull in just before closing time. You would be invited to return on Monday morning. But here we were, en route to Palenque with a disabled vehicle on a Saturday morning. The man at the Ford garage immediately took us in and put the vehicle on the rack to evaluate the full extent of the problem. He then gave us the required parts to take down the street to have another mechanic complete the job. We drove to the designated shop, explained the situation to the mechanic there, and within another hour we were on our way to Palenque. The total cost of that stop, including the part, was fifteen dollars.

Another example of Mexican kindness and ingenuity occurred in the tiny village of Zaragoza, Coahuila. Five of us were en route to the Maderas del Carmen, via Musquiz, and had stopped at a small café on a dirt street in the middle of town to drink a Coke. We were driving Grainger Hunt's Dodge power wagon. As Grainger prepared to restart the vehicle, he placed the wrong key in the ignition cylinder and it became stuck. Extracting that key somehow damaged the inner combination of the cylinder so that the correct key would not work.

As we sat there trying to figure out what to do next, the woman from the café approached us and asked what was wrong. When we explained what had happened she immediately offered to call her brother, a mechanic, to help us. In about twenty minutes, riding a bicycle down the middle of the street, he appeared. He looked the situation over, both at the steering wheel and under the hood, and soon had the cylinder out. He then informed us that he knew where he could obtain another cylinder, and off he rode on his bicycle. Soon he returned with a replacement cylinder taken from a friend's Dodge power wagon.

We watched as he tried to fit this piece into the empty slot where he had extracted the original cylinder. But after several minutes he decided it would not fit properly and said he had another friend with a power wagon, and would go and get that cylinder. Off he pedaled again on his bicycle. This time he did not return for almost an hour. We had begun to worry that he couldn't find the vehicle or that his friend wouldn't let him take the cylinder. But he did return with a third cylinder. Once again we watched as he tried to make it fit. Once again it would not.

He then announced that he had no other friends with Dodge power wagons, and would have to fix it so that we could start the vehicle by sticking a finger into the slot and pushing a little lever. We had no idea that it would be so easy. Within just a few minutes he had the motor humming and whatever he had done under the hood back in order. He informed us that he was terribly sorry that he had been unable to fix it properly. We, of course, were jubilant! We had begun to fear we would be there until a new part could be acquired from elsewhere. And when we tried to pay him for the three to four hours of work he had done, on a warm May day in a dusty street in a hot little desert town, he would not take any payment. We ended up insisting that his sister accept ten dollars for their help.

Attitude

Mexico's people and their ways, the fascinating ruins of the ancients, the spectacular scenery, and the unique habitats and wildlife combine to make the country a very special place. To appreciate those values, remember that in Mexico you are a visitor to a foreign country. Just as you would expect a foreign visitor anywhere to behave with consideration, treat Mexicans you meet with courtesy and respect. Do not come across as "the ugly American" by pushing your views and taking advantage of their hospitality and honesty. Their culture is different from ours north of the border. Delays must be expected. You will be a happier traveler if you give yourself time to unwind and "smell the roses." Show appreciation for the distinctiveness of the country and its people. That attitude will pay handsome dividends in the long run.

Acknowledgments

A project of this kind requires the help of many friends and colleagues. Without their assistance this project would include many more errors that it currently does; I thank them one and all. Any errors that might still exist are the fault of the author.

I want to acknowledge the following individuals, alphabetically, for their kind assistance: Jim Carrico for up-to-date information on the status of the Maderas del Carmen park project; Mark Elwonger for review of the preface and "The Northeastern Corner"; Victor Emanuel for his help with bird identifying and for his many comments on aspects of travel in Mexico; Bill Graber for help on visiting Alta Cima and review of that chapter; Greg Lasley for being an enjoyable traveling companion and for reviewing "Alta Cima"; Gil Lusk for his review of the preface, "The Northern Deserts," and "Maderas del Carmen"; Allan Phillips for many helpful comments about the birds of Mexico over the years; David Riskind for his very thorough review of the whole manuscript, and particularly of common and scientific plant names; Roseann Rowlett for her assistance with bird identity and for being an enjoyable companion on a Maderas del Carmen trip; Dick Russell for being an enjoyable field companion and for his review of and comments on four chapters: "Tiburón," "The Jalisco-Colima Circle," "The Yucatán," and "Island of Swallows"; Andres Sada for help in locating Worthen's sparrow; Dr. A. J. Sharp for help with identifying several plants photographed at El Triunfo; Arnold Small for suggestions on "Baja Norte"; Bo and Woody West for their companionship on several Mexican adventures; Peter White for his comments on "Jungle" and other comments relative to plant ecology; David Wolff for comments regarding Mexican birds in general. And last but certainly not least, I thank Betty Wauer, my wife, for her general support, help with the manuscript, and putting up with the long hours that I was away from home wandering the wilds of Old Mexico.

PART I

Northern Mexico

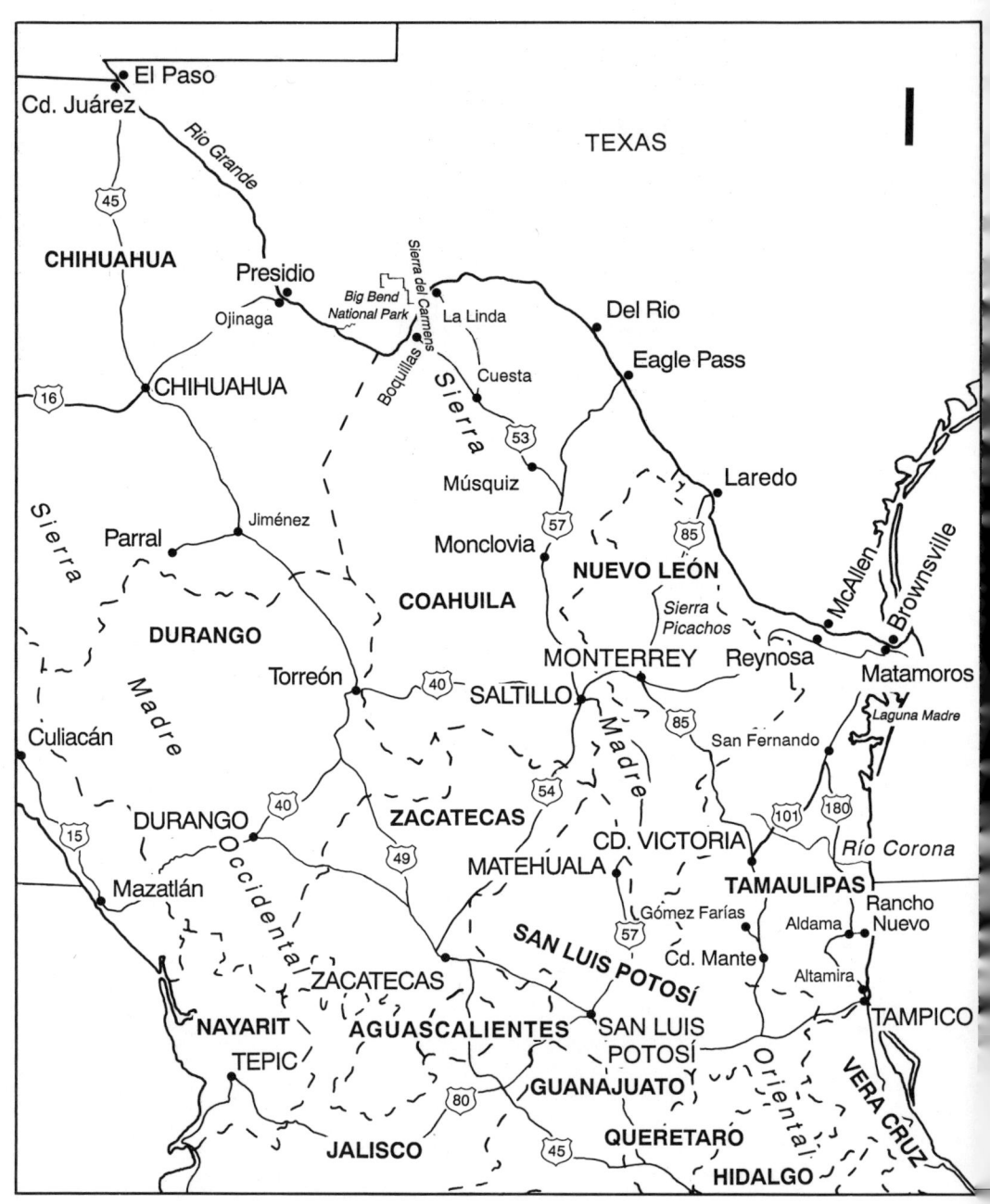

Northern Mexico

1

The Northeastern Corner

Brownsville, Texas, by virtue of being the southernmost city in the continental United States and situated in a subtropical setting, seems to me to provide the most appropriate of all the entry points to Mexico. And Matamoros, Brownsville's sister city across the Rio Grande in the Mexican state of Tamaulipas, is a border town to whet the appetite of the neophyte visitor to Mexico. Matamoros still possesses a bit of the "Old Mexico flavor" missing from so many of Mexico's more commercial frontier towns and villages. I have found Matamoros to be a friendly and enjoyable city. It has more than a few good restaurants and an excellent *mercado* (market).

Matamoros is a city of approximately two hundred thousand people who seem to possess a very strong tie to their counterparts just north of the border. That relationship is probably related to the agricultural interests in Texas that are dependent upon Mexican workers. But Matamoros has long been a significant agricultural area in its own right. Cotton was farmed extensively within the Rio Grande floodplain during earlier years, enough to make the Matamoros area Mexico's most important cotton production region. During the U.S. Civil War, Matamoros became an important source point for contraband cotton for the Confederates. Founded in 1765 and originally named Herioc, Matamoros was burned and pillaged several times before it became the stable and progressive city that it is today.

Lower Rio Grande

Long before the sister cities came into existence, the Rio Grande formed a broad and meandering waterway that produced numerous *resacas* or oxbows within its broad floodplain, and an extensive marshy environment at its mouth. Some of the earliest Spanish explorers called the lower river Río de las Palmas, because of the abundant palm trees that grew along its banks. Arthur Schott of the First Boundary Survey reported that these Texas palms extended upriver as much as eighty miles, according to Fred Gehlbach (*Mountain Islands and Desert Seas*). Today, the Valley's only remaining native palm grove is the Sabal Palm Grove Sanctuary, a 172-acre preserve that was established in 1971. This area is owned and operated by the National Audubon Society. Most of the Rio Grande floodplain has been cleared by bulldozers and cutters to make way for agriculture, grazing and a wide variety of construction projects.

There are but three protected areas in the lower Valley: the Sabal Palm Grove Sanctuary, Santa Ana National Wildlife Refuge, and Bentsen–Rio Grande Valley State Park, all on the U.S. side of the border. Beginning in the 1980s, the Texas Parks and Wildlife Department and the U.S. Fish and Wildlife Service began buying more land to protect additional remnants of riparian habitat. The concept of protecting a wildlife corridor along the Rio Grande is extremely important if this valuable habitat with its many threatened and endangered species is to be saved.

The landscape east of the sister cities, toward the nearby Gulf of Mexico, also has changed considerably. Both banks of the Rio Grande are now crowded with homes, businesses, and farms. The only remaining natural areas south of the river are the salt marshes and mud flats that dominate the scene east of Matamoros. This playa area can best be reached by Mexican Highway 2, which runs thirty-eight miles east from the center of town to the coast. The last twenty miles cross wetlands that contain a few ponds, roadside ditches, and a habitat of coastal marshes and estuarine backwater. The drier sites are grazed by goats, cows and horses. Although this area can be terribly hot and dull in summer, I found it to be a lively area during winter.

Playa Road Birdlife

I spent a winter day along the playa road (Highway 2) in January, 1985. I was curious about the area and the birdlife that might occur there in winter. There are several birds that are fairly common in Texas just north of the Rio Grande, but have only rarely been reported in Mexico along the northern border. I figured that if I spent a complete day along the Mexican side of the Rio Grande I would stand a pretty good chance of seeing at least a few of those. Although I had an extremely enjoyable day, and I did find several interesting species, I saw only two of the birds that I had hoped to find, the masked booby and northern gannet.

One of my most wanted Mexican birds was, and still is, the masked duck. It is a tropical species that is not only rare in occurrence but is elusive and shy, as well. Although I have recorded it in Texas, at Santa Ana Wildlife Refuge, I have never seen it in Mexico. It is similar in appearance to the ruddy duck; it is in fact the same genus — *Oxyura.* The major difference in appearance between the species in winter is the more extensive white cheeks of the ruddy compared to the black-banded cheeks of the masked duck. Also, ruddys usually are found in open water, while masked ducks prefer the edges of ponds close to vegetation and rarely venture too far away from easy cover and protection. I searched the various ponds along Highway 2 to no avail.

One pond in particular, at kilometer post 18, did provide habitat that was certain to be good for masked ducks. This pond, actually a set of two ponds side by side and approximately two acres in size, possessed a rather extensive cattail marsh that circled the open water. I spent more than an hour there on two occasions that day watching for a masked duck to venture out of the cattail concealment into the open. None did. Nor did I see any of the other three species I was searching for that could have utilized this same habitat: hooded merganser, least bittern, and common grackle.

I did record American bittern, sora and Virginia rail, marsh wren, common yellowthroat, and swamp sparrow there among the cattails, and seven species of ducks, least grebe, and common moorhen on the open water. A variety of other species were found in the immediate area, including olivaceous cormorant; great blue, little blue and tricolored herons; great, snowy and cattle egrets; white-faced ibis, greater yellowlegs, black-necked stilt, meadowlark (probably eastern), and great-tailed grackle.

The last eight or ten miles of Highway 2 were built above the saltgrass flats that extend for miles along the roadway. Much of this area was flooded, although slightly elevated dry pastureland occurred here and there. I scoped the drier flats for sparrows that I thought might include longspurs, northern fringillids that winter south of the frost line. Finding McCown's and chestnut-collared longspurs in this kind of habitat was unlikely, but until someone looks, who knows? I have discovered some exciting birds, reptiles, and mammals in out-of-the-normal locations, just because I bothered to look. Wildlife doesn't necessarily stay where the literature says it should be.

Although I saw no longspurs that day, the grasslands did contain several other birds of interest. Most noticeable of these was the long-billed curlew; I counted more than 250 of these buffy shorebirds. Early in the morning they all were moving in a northwesterly direction, in small groups of two to eight birds, and at dusk I found them flying east as if they were moving back to a roost along the coast. They settled down here and there on the grasslands rather than along the beach or in estuarine sites. Their flight, particularly early in the morning, was most interesting. They would fly straight ahead for several hundred feet and then suddenly, almost as if to elude a predator, twist and turn and dive, and even make some fancy rolls, and then fly straight ahead again. I saw several groups of two or three birds do the twist-roll-and-dive flight in unison. Although I had seen long-billed curlews many times before, I did not recall such spectacular flying.

I did find a predator, a lone peregrine falcon, perched on a small dead shrub. It was only five hundred feet away from the road when I first saw it, but flew off when I stopped for a better look. It flew north very low over the grassy flats, flapping and gliding, to another perch about a mile away. I did not see it again the rest of the day, in spite of watching for it.

The greatest number of birds I found that day was at the little bay just behind the very low duneline next to the beach. I stopped on the adjacent roadway and photographed eight roseate spoonbills that were preening themselves behind a small flock of black-necked stilts. A couple of dozen laughing gulls, mixed with a few herring and ring-billed gulls, and a lone great blue heron provided a pleasing foreground. And a large flock of shorebirds, including greater and lesser yellowlegs, both long-billed and short-billed dowitchers, killdeer, black-bellied plover, willet, and a dozen or so least sandpipers, filled in the background. Further on were several more waders, including a reddish egret (I counted five during the day) and a white ibis. On the opposite side of the causeway were a few additional species, including eight American avocets and a pair of red-breasted mergansers. The mergansers appeared to be feeding on small fish or arthropods along the very shallow shoreline; they spent more of their time out of the water than afloat.

The beach and offshore habitats provided few birds, at least at first. The ubiquitous sanderling was the only species on the beach when I first arrived; willets and a pair of ruddy turnstones appeared a little later. Except for a few gulls and some Forster's terns, little else was present over the surf and Gulf waters.

I spent about an hour walking along the beach when I first arrived, then decided to drive back toward Matamoros and search the grasslands further. I added three snow geese that were flying south. But by noon I was back at the beach staring out to sea. I remained there until midafternoon, scoping the horizon. Almost immediately I found my first record bird, a lone northern gannet! Although I had seen this northern pelagic several times in winter from jetties at Galveston and Freeport, Texas, this was my first Mexican record, and one of the species I had hoped to find that day. At 1:10 P.M., a lone, southbound common loon flew by a couple hundred feet off the beach. And at 1:25 P.M., I started watching a tiny dot on the horizon that, when it finally came close enough to identify, turned into a magnificent frigatebird.

The bird of the day, however, (actually four individuals appeared between 2:10 and 2:25 P.M.), was masked booby. One adult and three immatures flew by several hundred feet off the beach going south. This pelagic species is listed by Peterson and Chalif in their *A Field Guide to Mexican Birds* as "casual" for Tamaulipas. It represented only the second new Mexican bird I had seen that day, but it made the entire day worthwhile.

I made a late-afternoon drive toward Matamoros, as far as the cattail ponds, and found two more birds of interest. Just east of the cattail ponds is a small residence with a couple of mesquite trees in the front yard and a small thornscrub thicket behind the house. A medium-sized hawk was perched on the open mesquite in front of the house, and sat there for several minutes while I identified it as a roadside hawk. This is a common hawk a hundred miles further south in Mexico, but rare this close to the border. And sitting on top of the adjacent mesquite was a Couch's kingbird, a species only recently (1983) considered separate from the tropical kingbird. Couch's kingbird is restricted to eastern Mexico and southeast Texas; I have recorded it as far west as Big Bend National Park.

Early evening found me back at the beach staring out to sea once again. Suddenly, I was watching three scoters flying north several hundred feet off the beach. I could not detect any facial markings or white wing patches, but I couldn't be positive. I believe that they were black scoters; this would have been another Mexican "lifer."

I waited at the beach until the sun started to sink below the western horizon before starting back to Matamoros. I drove slowly and scanned the sky, expecting to see some late birds going to roost, or perhaps an owl. One of my most wanted Mexican birds was a short-eared owl. I had found it in similar habitats near Galveston on several earlier occasions, and so I searched the sky for the butterfly flight of this crepuscular species, but without success. I did add three horned larks for the day that I found along the roadside just as it was becoming almost too dark to see. This species was number ninety-eight for the day.

I couldn't help but feel that some of the birds I had wanted to see could have been found, given enough time. Although some species would be more readily detected during spring, and others would be more numerous during migration, potential resident species, such as the masked duck, least bittern and short-eared owl, would probably only take additional searching.

South of Matamoros

Highway 101 runs south of Matamoros through rather arid flatlands that have been cleared of native vegetation for agriculture and grazing. One agricultural product that I have never seen in the United States but I found growing only a few dozen miles south of the border is henequen. The henequen fields looked like rows of succulent green daggers pointing skyward. This plant is a source of fiber used for rope, hammocks and a large number of other products, including a high grade paper (it takes eighteen tons of raw green leaves to produce one ton of pulp).

Very little of the native plantlife still existed, and then only on steep and rocky hillsides and in less accessible arroyos. The native vegetation type covering much of northeastern Mexico is mesquite-grassland or *pastizal,* an important element in the region classified by plant ecologists as the Tamaulipian biotic province.

Dr. W. Frank Blair described this biotic province in a 1950 *Texas Journal of Science* article. He stated that "a few species of plants account for the bulk of the brush vegetation and give it a characteristic aspect throughout the Tamaulipian" (p. 103). The most important of these plants include: honey mesquite, various species of acacia and mimosa, desert hackberry or *granjeno, guayacán,* javelina bush, *cenizo* (sometimes called purple sage), common bee-brush or white brush, Texas prickly pear, and *tasajillo* or desert Christmas cactus (it produces bright red berries in winter).

The idea of biotic provinces is a useful one in trying to identify various geographic units by their principal characteristics. It helps ecologists to separate biotic units by their specific flora, fauna, soil and climate. In fact, all the biotic provinces of North America were mapped by Dr. Lee R. Dice in 1943.

The Tamaulipian province extends south of the border for almost two hundred miles between the coast and the deciduous woodlands on the slopes of the Sierra Madre Oriental. The only exceptions to the rather arid shrub-covered landscapes are the lines of riparian vegetation within the few river valleys.

Río Corona

One of Tamaulipas' major riverine systems is the Río Soto la Marina, which includes the Río Purificación and Río Corona. Highway 101 crosses both of these rivers just above their confluences with the Soto la Marina. The Río Purificación crossing occurs just below the town of Guemez. The riverbanks there have been heavily utilized by the citizens of Guemez and their goats and cattle for many decades; little natural vegetation remains. On the other hand, the Río Corona floodplain still possesses considerable natural habitat that generally is considered to be the northernmost tropical birding habitat in Mexico.

Until recent years the Río Corona floodplain was very much intact, but some of the adjacent lands were cleared for agriculture in 1979 and 1980. Since then the floodplain has begun to suffer a fate similar to that of the Río Purificación — increased erosion, pollution from chemicals used in agriculture, an increase of exotic nonproductive plant species, and general loss of native wildlife. However, since the Río Corona is only 170 miles south of the border, it has long attracted attention of nature enthusiasts from the United States.

The vegetation adjacent to the Río Corona is surprisingly similar to that which occurs at Santa Ana and Bentsen preserves on the Rio Grande. However, the dominant tree that lines the banks of the Río Corona — Montezuma bald cypress — is rare along the Rio Grande.

Wash day in the Río Purificación in central Tamaulipas, from
the Highway 1 bridge.

That was not always the case. According to William Emory's 1857
report of his exploration of the Mexican–U.S. borderlands, the species was then present for approximately one hundred miles up the
Rio Grande from the Gulf. Correll and Johnston, in *Manual of the
Vascular Plants of Texas,* reported it only as "occasionally along resacas" in the Rio Grande Valley. This species should not be confused
with a second, more northerly cypress, bald cypress, which occurs
from east Texas to Missouri and Arkansas.

In Mexico, Montezuma bald cypress is called *Sabino* or *Ahuehuete;*
ahuehuete means "old man of the water." This tree differs from its
closest relatives (pines, firs and junipers) by dropping its needles in
winter. Ahuehuete occurs along river courses and in other wet places
throughout Mexico south to Guatemala. One individual specimen,
the gigantic "Tree of Santa Maria del Tule" in Oaxaca, is more than

two thousand years old and has a trunk circumference of 170 feet, according to Correll and Johnston.

Two other large and noticeable trees that grow on the riverbanks and send their branches out over the waters of the Río Corona are Texas ebony, locally called *ebano,* and sycamore. In places, this habitat of cypress, ebony and sycamore forms a gallery that covers the stream to form cathedral-like passageways beneath the tropical greenery. It is this habitat that apparently attracts birds of more southern affinity.

The natural environment of the Río Corona has drawn a good deal of biological attention for many years, and a list of naturalists who have visited the area in the past would be most impressive. One of these was Dr. Fred Gehlbach, a professor of biology at Baylor University in Texas. It was he who made a careful survey of the Río Corona birdlife in 1973 and 1974, and compared these populations with those found in the Rio Grande Valley.

Gehlbach and colleagues published a summary of his research in the January, 1976 volume of the *Auk,* North America's major ornithological journal. He summarized his findings as follows: "On the Rio Corona we found at least 48 breeding species. About half of these (48%) reach their northeastern breeding limits in the Rio Grande Valley or south coastal region of Texas and so provide a definite aspect to that regional avifauna; 35% are at their northeastern breeding limits in the Río Soto la Marina basin, and 17% are widespread in North America" (pp. 57–58). The most interesting group of birds is that which is known to breed only so far northeast in North America as the Río Corona.

Parrots are everyone's idea of tropical birds. Gehlbach reported four breeding species for the Río Corona, green and olive-throated parakeets and red-crowned and yellow-headed parrots. My idea of tropical birds must include the trogon and motmot. Both occur on the Río Corona. And the name "elegant" trogon is perfect for this gorgeous bird. The male has a brilliant rose-red belly and greenish-gold chest, back, neck and head. A white line crosses the gold between the chest and belly. Its bill is yellow and eye-ring is orange-red. The female is more subtly colored in browns and also has a rosy belly; she has a distinct white ear-patch that is missing on the male.

Although elegant trogons occur as far north as Texas, New Mexico and Arizona, they cannot survive the colder winters there and must migrate south each year. Fruit is undoubtedly the key to their range, because trogons rely on fruit for their principal food. Mashed insects are fed to their young, but their survival depends upon the availability of fruiting trees, shrubs and vines.

My first-ever blue-crowned motmot sighting occurred just below the Highway 101 bridge at the Río Corona. My memory of that event is as distinct as if it happened yesterday. Jim and Cilla Tucker, Benton Basham and I had crossed the border at Brownsville on December 26, 1974, en route to Catemaco. Except for one stop for gas and pan dulce, our first long pause was at the Río Corona at midday. We had walked down a narrow dirt track to the riverbank, and then followed a grassy trail upriver, skirting huge cypress buttresses. I took a photograph of Jim wearing his "birding cape," a Christmas present from Cilla that showed a Count Dracula-like figure, binoculars in hand, and ready for whatever might appear.

Actually, the photograph included the blue-crowned motmot, but we did not see the bird, perched on a cypress branch over the waterway, until after taking the slide. My first impression of the bird was that it was much larger than its Pacific Coast analog, the russet-crowned motmot, which I had seen in Nayarit several years earlier. But actually the blue-crowned bird is larger by four or five inches. It was in full view and indulging in the unique motmot habit of slowly swinging its long tail from side to side. The tail looks like a pendulum because the bird strips the feathers off the shaft except for an inch or two on the end, thus giving it a racket-like appearance. Watching a seventeen-inch, bright blue and green bird with such a strange and swinging tail not more than fifty feet away was an occurrence not easily forgotten.

Gehlbach reported five species of hawks along the Río Corona. Two of these—the gray hawk and collared forest-falcon—breed there. Gray hawks occur as far north as Texas and Arizona. The collared forest-falcon, on the other hand, is truly a tropical species of heavy forests, including thickets and mangroves. It is a remarkable bird, because its behavior is nothing like that of any of the birds of prey in the United States.

Although the collared forest-falcon is never common, it can be quite obvious. My first encounter with this raptor was in a rather dense oak forest near El Naranjo, in nearby Nuevo León. A tawny phase bird suddenly flew out of nowhere and landed on a large oak limb some twenty feet from where I stood searching the canopy for warblers. The hawk, perched on the limb horizontally, with its long tail hanging off to one side, cocked its head and stared at me as if to inquire: "What right do you have in my territory?" It walked along the limb for several feet, stopped twice and looked at me, and then, just as suddenly as it had arrived, dropped from the limb in a kind of awkward dive, and disappeared into the foliage of an adjacent oak. I heard it call twice just afterwards; two loud and single *haah* notes that seemed ventriloquistic in quality.

The collared forest-falcon is a large bird, about two feet in length, with a long, barred tail. It can occur in three distinct color patterns. The bird I saw at El Naranjo had a tawny breast, but birds can also be very light, almost white, or black. The melanistic phase is rare, and I would think that melanistic birds would be difficult to identify unless one could observe their behavior; one key character of this species is the very distinct dark collar that extends out on the neck just behind the white or tawny cheeks. Young birds are barred with sooty brown streaks.

Crane, common black and roadside hawks also breed in the area, but Gehlbach considered these birds to be only visitors within his study plots. The crane hawk is another of those species that seems of obvious tropical affinity rather than of the temperate climes. I have seen this bird only once on the Río Corona. On December 30, 1984, at dusk, a lone bird flew into one of the huge cypress trees under which several of us were camping. It seemed surprised to find a reception of enthusiastic observers and remained for a few minutes only. Even then its behavior was very typical for the species; it "crawled" around one of the huge limbs, apparently searching for lizards or amphibians. Crane hawks possess a very small outer toe complete with claw on each foot that gives them extra capability for the arboreal acrobatics that they perform in search of food.

Other raptors recorded by Gehlbach, but not considered to be breeding within the area, were hook-billed kite, Harris' and red-shouldered hawks, and crested caracara. And I added the sharp-shinned and zone-tailed hawks, which were present during my December, 1984 visit.

Other tropical species included within Gehlbach's list of those birds that reach the northeastern edge of their breeding range on the Río Corona are bronze-winged and lineated woodpeckers, sulphur-bellied flycatcher, Mexican crow, spot-breasted wren, clay-colored robin, crimson-collared grosbeak, and blue bunting. The crow, robin and bunting have since been recorded along the Rio Grande, and at least the crow and robin are known to nest there.

I did not see the spot-breasted wren during my first visit to the Río Corona in 1974, presumably because of its shy habits. But it is virtually impossible to spend much time during the morning and evening hours along the Río Corona without hearing this wren's very distinct and beautiful song. It has a clear but loud, melodic song that reminds me a little of the flute-like song of the western meadow-lark of our western grasslands. But hearing the song of one or a dueting pair of these little wrens from a dense thicket along the banks of the Río Corona is most memorable.

George Miksch Sutton, one of America's most renowned ornithologists and bird artists, as well as a fine nature writer, also found the spot-breasted wren song impressive. Dr. Sutton wrote, in his very enjoyable book, *Mexican Birds: First Impressions,* "It was elusive, to be sure — elusive to the point of being utterly unseen and un-heard most of the time; but one is not apt to remember the elusive-ness of any creature whose song makes one literally jump with sur-prise; one is apt to remember, rather, its canny temerity, its ability to see without itself being seen, its almost physic way of waiting by the trail until one is very close (and, of course, very much wrapped up in one's own thought) before hurling from the thicket its little bombshell of song" (p. 125–26).

Of all the tropical birds that occur along the Río Corona, none are as appealing as the owls. There are two species in particular — the tiny, diurnal ferruginous pygmy-owl, and the larger, nocturnal mottled owl. The pygmy-owl is not one of Gehlbach's thirty-five per-cent reaching the northeastern edge of its range there, because it also is known to breed in the southeast corner of Texas. But for most birders, at least for those who enter Mexico from Tamaulipas, the Río Corona provides their introduction to this little owl. And it is not a difficult bird to find.

My first Tamaulipian observation of the ferruginous pygmy-owl occurred just below the Río Corona bridge. We heard its call as we walked down the trail from the highway in 1974. Peterson and Chalif describe the call as a "mellow staccato whistle, *poop* or *purp* or *poip,* often repeated rapidly and monotonously 2–3 times per second."

Irby Davis, whom I consider the most astute recorder of bird sounds, described the call in his annotated checklist of northeastern Mexican birds in this way: "Song phase is a series of clear, fairly loud and mellow 'whistled' figures. If one tries to whistle 'wuh' a very good imitation will result; pitch F3. Usually from ten to sixty figures in a phase. The tempo is the fastest of any of the genus, with a rate of 150 figures per minute" (p. 18).

We discovered the tiny owl perched on an acacia tree in full view from less than fifty feet. It remained there for fully ten minutes while we edged closer and closer, until we were standing beneath the tree staring up at our diminutive attractant. Not only did it continue to call, with an occasional break of silence now and then, but it turned around once so that we were able to see it from both sides. It was undoubtedly one of the best views I have had of this dynamic little owl.

In December, 1984 and again in 1989, I participated in Christmas bird counts on the Río Corona. Although both counts documented several ferruginous pygmy-owls, other bird species were missing. In 1984 I spent all day with Mark Elwonger of Victoria, Texas, surveying the birdlife downriver from the bridge; our list of seventy-two species was far below what we expected. In 1989 Joan Holt, of Port Aransas, and I recorded only eighty species. The most obvious miss both years was a blue-crowned motmot.

I did record mottled owl on the 1984 count day. In fact, I was awakened at about 5:00 A.M. by a pair of these tropical owls calling from the large cypress tree above me. I am not sure if calling is the right word, because these birds have a repertoire of song that ranges from a typical *hoot hoot* to a whistling screech. It seemed to me they were practicing everything they knew that morning. I lay there thoroughly enjoying their vocalizations. And twice during the mottled owl chorus, a common barn-owl joined in with its obnoxious rasping shriek. I couldn't help but wonder how many of the larger owls nest along this stretch of the Río Corona. The abundant cypress trees, with their many holes and crevices, must provide plenty of roosting and nesting spaces. This type of habitat is one of the reasons that the Río Corona riparian zone is so valuable as the northernmost tropical bird mecca in Mexico.

But changes are taking place that could eliminate the various requirements of the numerous species that use the area. The presence

of the common barn-owl might hint at such a change. Gehlbach
did not record it during his study of the area. And barn-owls are
much more numerous in rural areas than they are in wild lands.
As indicated, Mark and I could not find the blue-crowned motmot
during the Christmas count day when we walked more than eight
miles along the river and in the adjacent woods. As for parrots, fewer
and fewer are being reported; I saw only one throughout that day.
Are these our first indicators of the changes that are taking place
within the Río Soto la Marina drainage of Tamaulipas?

I hope that the Mexican people realize the importance of retaining some natural areas within their landscapes. These are vitally important to their long-term existence, providing life support systems
that are crucial to their lives, and those of their neighbors and loved
ones. They serve as storehouses for an incredible variety of wild seeds
and vegetable matter, wildlife and fish, as well as fresh water, pollinators for plants, and hundreds of other less obvious functions. These
last remaining refuges also attract foreign visitors whose sojourns contribute to the tourism economy. Options are still available, but they
are decreasing rapidly.

2

The Northern Deserts

There is nowhere I'd rather be in early morning than in the desert. Nowhere else have I felt so at one with nature. The desert possesses a great silence: there is no wind among the trees, no stream noise, no sound of surf. One hears only the members of the desert community. Bird songs can be abundant, and the final calls of night animals resound across the landscape. The great horned owl and coyote are everywhere. And when the sunlight touches the desert floor, there in the sandy arroyo are clear telltale signs of the wildlife that prowled there overnight. The signs often are one upon another; the experienced eye can read and understand.

The Deserts

About one-fifth of the world's land surface is desert, an environment known for abundant sunshine, high temperatures in summer but usually pleasant in winter, and consistently low humidity. Although this definition is usually reliable, the only sure thing about deserts is the low annual rainfall, which may range from less than two to as much as ten inches.

In Mexico more than 175,000 square miles—almost one-quarter of the total land surface—are covered by desert. This arid region is called *matorral xerofilo* (dry scrub). Although Mexico's deserts sometimes are considered only southern extensions of the Sonoran and Chihuahuan Deserts of the United States, the opposite is actually the case: these two U.S. desert regions are northern extensions of Mexico's larger and more developed matorral xerofilo.

More than two-thirds of the Sonoran Desert and three-fourths of the Chihuahuan Desert are in Mexico, according to Robert Schmidt of the University of Texas at El Paso. Schmidt defined the border of the Sonoran Desert in a 1989 paper published in *Journal of Arid Environments,* saying that the Sierra Madre Occidental clearly separates the Sonoran and Chihuahuan Deserts. The inland boundary of the Sonoran Desert follows the three-thousand-foot contour. The southern border "includes the narrow coastal strip along Topolobampo and on to the area just south of the mouth of the Río Culiacán at about 24 degrees N" on the mainland. All of Baja California but the northwestern corner is also considered Sonoran Desert.

If the Sierra Madre Occidental separates the two deserts, it stands to reason that these mountains form the western border of Mexico's Chihuahuan Desert. And the Sierra Madre Oriental to the east forms the eastern border. However, the three-thousand-foot contour line does not apply for the Chihuahuan Desert which generally is higher in elevation. Its southern boundary extends south of Saltillo and Torreón to San Luis Potosí, to about 22 degrees North.

To me, the more interesting geographic facts about Mexico's two major deserts are their differences. The most obvious is in the drainage of the two regions. The entire drainage of the Sonoran Desert is westward into the Pacific. All drainage of the Chihuahuan Desert flows into the Atlantic or into enclosed basins. Most important, perhaps, is the higher average elevation of the Chihuahuan Desert, resulting in cooler temperatures (by ten to twenty degrees Fahrenheit) and a shorter growing season. The Sonoran Desert lies chiefly below 2,000 feet while more than half of the Chihuahuan Desert is above 4,600 feet in elevation. According to Forrest Shreve, often considered the "dean of desert botany," Chihuahuan Desert plants may frequently be found up to 7,000 to 8,500 feet. Therefore, the Chihuahuan Desert, especially the northern portion, is more susceptible to wintertime "northers."

The number of mild or frost-free days greatly affects plant distribution, and is one reason that the Chihuahuan Desert does not possess the large tree cacti that are common within and symbolic of the Sonoran Desert. Rainfall amounts and patterns are quite different, too. Average annual precipitation is generally greater in the Chihuahuan Desert, and seventy percent of the rainfall occurs from May through October; January to May is usually dry. By contrast, the winter months provide the greatest rainfall within the Sonoran Desert.

Desert Vegetation

Botanists tell us that the affinity for most of the desert's dominant plants is south of the border, not within the United States. The best

Río Grande at Boquillas, Mexico. The background is the Sierra
del Carmen range, the northern extension of the Sierra Madre
Oriental.

example is creosote bush, of the genus *Larrea,* which is South American in origin, according to paleobotanist Philip Wells. There are four very different species of *Larrea* in South America, but only one (*L. divaricata*) reaches the northern Mexico deserts.

On lists of the twelve most common and characteristic plants of the Sonoran and Chihuahuan deserts respectively, there are only three species in common: creosote bush, ocotillo, and honey mesquite.

Creosote bush can undoubtedly be considered the best indicator plant of all. It is the most successful and widespread of all the dry-land plants. Its range is almost identical with the boundaries of the North American deserts. Thus the common Mexican name for creosote bush, *gobernadora,* which literally means governor, probably refers to the widespread character of the plant. It is often mistakenly called greasewood, but greasewood (or antelope bush) is a different plant altogether and occurs only in upland desert communities, not in the creosote bush-dominated lowlands.

Creosote bush usually grows in an evenly spaced pattern on the landscape. Its roots put out a chemical that limits most other plants from growing nearby, thus reducing competition for moisture and nutrients. A member of the caltrop family, creosote bush is an evergreen shrub that may grow to eight or ten feet in height, but usually is four to six feet tall. The shrubs are exceptionally aromatic, and the characteristic scent of the desert after summer showers comes from this species. After living for several years in the desert, the two things I missed most when I moved away were the songs of the coyote and the scent of creosote.

Creosote bush possesses very small shiny green leaves and blackish-grey bark on its thin woody branches and stems. Small, bright yellow flowers appear after each spring, summer and fall rainstorm. In Mexico, both the foliage and stems are utilized for medicinal purposes, as a cure for rheumatism, tuberculosis, and gastric problems. A concoction made from the leaves is used as an antiseptic for wounds and burns, and as a most effective cure for athlete's foot. In addition, desert Indians used a gummy "creosote" residue derived from the plant for waterproofing baskets and mending pots.

Apparently, some of these same characteristics that people learned to utilize for their own well-being help to protect the plants from native wildlife. Creosote bush leaves and bark are eaten by very few desert creatures. Several animals use the plants for shade, a few rodents and insects harvest the rather large and nutritious seeds, and I have watched black-tailed jackrabbits gnaw on the hard, brittle branches. But creosote bush is off-limits as food to all of today's browsers. This may not always have been the case, however. Some paleobotanists—scientists who study the prehistoric evidence about plant ecology—believe that ancient creosote bush was consumed by such extinct browsers as Pleistocene ground sloths.

Ocotillo, in spite of the fact that it bears numerous sharp spines, is not a cactus. It belongs to the distinctive family Fouquieriacae, which includes seven species in Mexico, among them the boojum of northern Baja California (see chapter seven, "Baja Norte"). The ocotillo can be one of the desert's most beautiful plants. After rainstorms it produces bright green leaves along its long spindly stems and the tips become adorned with tubular scarlet flowers. The bril-

Greater roadrunner on an ocotillo stalk in the Chihuahuan Desert.

liant flowers are very attractive to the numerous resident and migrant hummingbirds. In sharp contrast, the plant can be little more than a bunch of long, spiny, very dry sticks between rainy seasons.

Mexicans use the spiny stalks for fencing as well as walls for houses and pens. The cut stalks have an ability to root and grow in soil where it seems impossible to sustain life, and in some of the harshest conditions. Living house walls and fences of ocotillo possess a certain appeal when they are covered by bright green leaves and topped off with flame-colored flowers.

Honey mesquite is probably the desert tree that evokes the greatest range of human emotions. There are four species of mesquite of the genus *Prosopis* in northern Mexico, but the most common is honey mesquite. This is the well-known invader of pastures and grasslands, the one that usurps valuable groundwater, a plant that many people believe must somehow be controlled. Others consider

it extremely valuable for its nutritious beans, shade, and wood—
recently popular for barbecues; its thick gum is used for candy, as
a cement for pottery, and as a black dye; and the tree is valued for
soil stabilization, and for its aesthetic appeal. It seems that almost
everyone takes one side or the other, for or against mesquite.

Mexico's earliest desert inhabitants depended upon mesquite for
their very existence. Edmund Jaeger wrote in *Desert Wild Flowers*
that for "certain of the Cahuilla Indians the eight seasons of the
year were named in relation to the development of the bean" (p.
96). Jaeger quotes Dr. C. C. Parry, a nineteenth-century desert botanist, who described the food made from the bean as follows:

> A due mixture of animal and vegetable diet is also secured in
> the mesquite bean, the pods of which are largely occupied with
> a species of weevil. The whole pod and its contents are pounded
> into a fine powder, only the woody husk of the seed being re-
> jected. The process of baking is equally primitive. A squaw
> takes, generally from her head, a cone-shaped basket of close
> texture; the meal, slightly sprinkled with water is packed of
> close layers into this hat or pot as the case may be; when full
> it is carefully smoothed off and then buried in the sand ex-
> posed to a hot sun. The baking process goes on for several hours,
> till the mass acquires the consistency of a soft brick, when it
> is turned out, and the hat resumes its proper position on the
> head. The solid cake so made is sufficiently palatable, contain-
> ing a gummy sugar which dissolves in the mouth and is un-
> questionably nutritious.

Mesquite is one of the few trees that can thrive in sand dunes,
because its taproot is capable of penetrating as deep as fifty to sixty
feet in search of water. The trees turn bright green in early spring
when the new leaves appear, and soon produce catkin-like clusters
of yellow flowers which seem to attract every bee for miles around.
The fruit produced are green and tender at first, and are favorite
"sweet-sticks" for the local children. Mature beans look like knobby
stringbeans four to eight inches in length. These can be picked for
the meal as described above, or they fall to the ground and are consumed by a myriad of desert creatures, ranging from ants to coyotes.
In a sense, the desert mesquite can be considered the finest of nature's smorgasbord.

Other Plants of Interest

Although some plants are common to both of Mexico's deserts, many species are restricted to only one region. Some of the plants that have limited range serve as good indicator species because they are consistently present in one area but never occur in the other. For example, the tall columnar cacti of the Sonoran Desert do not occur east of the Sierra Madre Occidental. On the other hand, lechuguilla and guayule are good Chihuahuan Desert representatives because they never occur west of the Sierra Madre Occidental. It goes even beyond that. It would be possible to blindfold someone who knew desert plants well enough, transport that individual to any of a million desert localities, and upon having the blindfold removed, that person could identify the location to within a few dozen miles simply by identifying the plants growing nearby.

This example implies that Mexico's northern deserts contain a wide and varied assortment of plants. That is unquestionably the case. Some of the very best indicator plants of Mexico's western (Sonoran) desert include three of the large columnar cacti that also occur in southern Arizona: the saguaro, organ pipe cactus, and senita. A fourth indicator is cardon, another tall columnar cactus that is restricted to the arid landscapes south of the border. In places, such as along the Sonoran gulf coast, all four species occur together, although cardon and senita are more numerous on the open and deeper soils while saguaro and organ pipe prefer the rocky hillsides. The well-known barrel cactus or *bisnaga* is present in the Sonoran Desert area, more common on rocky hillsides than on deeper soils. These same desert areas usually contain a dozen or more additional species of cacti, particularly the *Opuntia,* a genus which includes both prickly pears and chollas.

The Sonoran Desert also contains a number of small trees and shrubs that are unique to various regions of this desert. One of the most noticeable of these is elephant tree or *torote* (little bull), a short, fat tree with soft, whitish bark and reddish-brown twigs that possess exceptionally small, green leaves only during the rainy season. Among them, this plant and the palo verde, brittlebush, ocotillo, desert lavender, creosote bush, ironwood, and jojoba, and a variety of cacti dominate many parts of the Sonoran Desert landscape.

Ironwood and jojoba have received considerable attention in re-

cent years. Ironwood, called *palo fierro* in Mexico, is a member of
the pea family, which has numerous representatives in the Mexican
deserts. Ironwood is a mesquite-like tree best known for its exceptionally hard wood, which is used for woodcarving by the Seri Indians (see chapter ten, "Tiburón"). Ironwood seeds are also utilized
by the native people, who roast the mature seeds in late summer
for food; they have a peanut-like taste.

Jojoba, sometimes called coffeeberry, a goat-nut or wild hazel,
is another unique native plant of the Sonoran Desert. It is a low-
growing, evergreen shrub with gray-green, notched, smooth but thick
leaves that are eaten by several desert animals. The seed is an oblong
berry, dark red outside and white inside, that tastes a little like a
filbert when dried and roasted. Utilized for a variety of medicinal
purposes, the seeds are rich in protein and oil. Considerable research
is currently under way to find a better way to commercially produce
this plant for its valuable products.

Instead of the tall columnar cacti, the Chihuahuan Desert landscape is dominated by numerous succulents, especially yuccas, tall,
green members of the lily family. Although yuccas also occur in the
Sonoran Desert, they reach their greatest abundance and height in
the Chihuahuan. One of these, the giant or Spanish dagger can be
particularly dominant wherever it occurs and occasionally forms a
true yucca "forest" that is as grand as the tall cactus forest. The
Chihauhuan Desert has as many kinds of cacti as the Sonoran, although they are smaller in stature and bulk.

Three of the best indicator plants of the Chihuahuan Desert region are lechuguilla, guayule, and tarbush or *hojase.* All three are
partial to the abundant calcareous (limy) soils. The most widespread
is lechuguilla, a low-growing succulent that occurs on the very driest
slopes imaginable, and extends south as far as the state of México.
The plant looks like a rosette of fleshy, spiked leaves, and can be
so abundant that plants can number in the hundreds within an acre.

Like most agaves, lechuguilla blooms only once and then dies.
The flower stalk, usually five to ten feet in height, grows out of the
center of the rosette, produces small yellow to reddish flowers in a
few weeks, and then dies and dries up. The stalk is the only place
where the Lucifer hummingbird will nest. This little hummer is restricted to the arid, agave-covered slopes of the Chihuahuan Desert
for nesting.

Agave lechuguilla, the best indicator of the Chihuahuan Desert,
a region that covers thirteen percent of Mexico's total land mass.

Guayule (pronounced "y-oo-lee") is a rather unobtrusive, low-growing shrub of the sunflower family; its leaves and branches are often silvery and its small yellowish flowers can be quite aromatic. Guayule commanded a great deal of attention during the First World War because its latex-like resin can be utilized as a rubber substitute. Large patches of Chihuahuan Desert were cleared of guayule from 1916 to 1919 and the plants were taken to processing plants in Texas. Although there was minor success, the idea of using guayule as a practical substitute for making rubber was pretty well given up by the middle of the 1940s.

Tarbush, another member of the sunflower family, is sometimes called blackbrush because of its very dark trunk and branches. It is also sometimes confused with creosote bush which has gray bark, but tarbush is a low-growing, compact plant. Both plants possess small green leaves and yellow flowers, and they often occur together, usually on desert flats or valley bottoms. Tarbush leaves and flowers are dried and sold under the name of *hojasen* to relieve indigestion in Mexico.

Another desert plant restricted to limestone soils along the northern border is candelilla or wax plant. This low-growing plant, that appears for all the world like thin, gray-green candles, has been an important economic resource in northern Mexico for more than a hundred years. The Mexican government is now planting large areas with candelilla in an effort to increase its importance as an economic base within the northern Chihuahuan Desert.

Candelilla is utilized in making candles, commercial waxes and polishes, phonograph records, and chewing gum. The processing is rather interesting. The thin waxy stems are pulled from the ground, along with the roots, bundled on burros, and taken to a crude processing plant. Since water is required in the production of candelilla wax, camps are almost always located on a river or at a spring or *tinaja* (pothole). Water is boiled in large metal vats before handfuls of the candelilla are thrown in. A little sulphuric acid is added to the mixture to render the natural wax from the plants. When the wax foams to the top of the boiling water, it is skimmed off and placed in cooling tanks. The cooled wax, relatively lightweight and yellow-tan in color, is then broken into small chunks, dumped into gunny sacks (usually made from the fiber of lechuguilla), and hauled by burros to buyers who further process it to take out impurities. It is then resold to producers like Wrigley's where it is used in chewing gum.

There are hundreds of other fascinating plants that occur on Mexico's northern deserts. And many of these are represented in both deserts by slightly different forms. For example, both deserts possess a plant known as leather stem or *sangre de drago*. Both are leathery-stemmed and reach only two or three feet in height, produce small fleshy leaves after rainstorms, and exude a clear sap that dries to a blood-red color when the bark is damaged; hence the name *sangre de drago,* or "blood of the dragon."

Joint-firs, Mexican tea or Mormon tea belong to another group of plants represented in both deserts by numerous species. In a few places in some of the most arid parts of the deserts, joint-firs are the dominant shrub. But wherever it occurs, and some grow at quite high elevations, it is utilized by local residents for its tannin content for making tea. I have made sun tea on numerous occasions by placing a small handful of dried joint-fir stems in a quart of water and letting them steep in the sun for about half a day. I have also used boiled water and four or five joints of the plant to speed up the process. However, don't leave it for more than fifteen minutes or it becomes too strong. The right brew produces a wonderful native beverage.

Palo verdes also occur in both deserts. These rather small trees can be abundant along drainages or on deeper desert soils. Palo verde means "green stick" in Spanish, referring to the green branches of this very pretty tree. All have delicate foliage and produce yellow or white flowers. I have seen several of the yellow-flowering palo verdes festooned with so many large, showy flowers that the trees looked like huge patches of yellow from a distance. Palo verdes bear bean-like seeds, and possess either straight or decurved spines, typical characteristics of most members of the pea (legume) family. Some of the more abundant examples of this family that can be found in the northern deserts include the numerous mesquites, acacias, and mimosas.

Two desert plants that are sometimes confused with legumes, because of their pod-like beans, but instead are members of the catalpa family, are yellow trumpet and desert willow. These are two of my personal favorites. Both are attractive flowering shrubs that occur in some of the most unexpected places. Yellow trumpet, called *esperanza* or *tronadora* in Spanish, is common in desert washes, but can also be expected in drier places as far south as South America. Desert willow is more restricted to desert washes, and I have discovered that it is a real favorite of hummingbirds. One warm May day in Coahuila, while eating lunch in the shade of an adjacent honey mesquite, I watched four species of hummingbirds—broad-billed, Lucifer, black-chinned, and broad-tail—feeding at its large purplish-red blossoms.

Many desert plants have evolved special characteristics that permit them to go for longer than normal periods of time without water.

These adaptions may include special water retention methods, such as those utilized by the cacti and other succulents. Several plants possess the special ability to drop their leaves during dry periods and to grow leaves and produce flowers very fast when rain does occur: ocotillo is an excellent example of this. And other species, such as creosote bush, are able to space themselves out over the desert terrain to ensure minimal competition with their neighbors.

Desert Wildlife

The ability to get along with minimal moisture is not limited to plants. Desert animals have also been able to adapt to arid conditions. Spadefoot toads dig down into moist soils and secrete a gelatinous material around themselves in which they can live until the next rainstorm. They then breed and lay very fast-hatching eggs that grow into tiny adults before their puddle dries out once again. Other wildlife, such as lizards, snakes and rodents, lie up during the warmer hours of the day, and are active only during the cooler and less demanding hours. Several desert rodents, including kangaroo rats, are able to manufacture their entire supply of water from the seeds of various desert plants. They may never in their lives touch standing drinking water.

Many desert birds are able to survive by moving from place to place to nest in response to local weather conditions. There are a few desert sparrows — rufous-winged, Botteri's, Cassin's, and Worthen's sparrows — that follow patterns of precipitation within Mexico's northern deserts. They can be expected only in areas that have had adequate moisture, and may be completely absent elsewhere, even though they may have been common there the previous year. This may also be true for grasshopper and lark sparrows, which nest within Mexico's northern grasslands.

Two of Mexico's desert grassland sparrows may be considered true desert endemics. The rufous-winged sparrow is known only in the Sonoran Desert region from south-central Arizona south to southeastern Sonora and to central Sinaloa. And the Worthen's sparrow has an even smaller range, from southern New Mexico south to southwestern Tamaulipas and western Zacatecas (see chapter three, regarding Worthen's sparrow). The latter species is one of the rarest of Mexico's more than one thousand known bird species, probably because of the isolated localities where it breeds.

Of birds that are restricted to the combined deserts of northern Mexico and the adjacent southwestern United States, two are endemic to Mexico. Both of these, Xantus' hummingbird and gray thrasher, occur only within the desert of the southern Baja Peninsula (see chapter eight, "South of La Paz").

Large desert mammals are rarely seen by the average visitor. Although tracks and other evidence of coyotes, gray and kit foxes, badgers, skunks, javelinas, bobcats, and even mountain lions can usually be found during the early mornings, before the desert breezes or numerous lizards erase the telltale signs, sightings of the animals themselves are few and far between. The best chance to see any of the desert mammals would entail a dawn walk into the desert, away from roads and villages. Early morning is when you are most likely to hear the dawn chorus of coyotes or surprise a small band of foraging javelinas.

My favorite desert mammal is, without question, the javelina, properly called the collared peccary. It looks like a small, blackish-gray razorback hog, complete with snout and pig-like eyes. Javelinas are North America's smallest hoofed animal, but the hoof is little more than a modified toe. Both sexes, particularly the boars, develop tusks that can be rather dangerous weapons. And both sexes have a large musk gland on the rump. They utilize this gland to mark their territories as well as to rub their scent onto other members of their band. On numerous occasions I have watched a pair stand nose to tail, each rubbing the side of its head against the other's rump gland. Sometimes the smell is so strong that it lingers for several hours in the vicinity. It is a little like diluted skunk aroma.

Javelinas eat almost anything. I have seen them tear apart lechuguilla plants to reach the softer, inner portion of the leaves. I have watched them chew the edges of prickly pear pads. I have watched them eat the remains of a roadkilled jackrabbit. And I have fed them extra spaghetti, which they feasted on with great relish. On one memorable occasion, at Rio Grande Village Campground in Big Bend National Park, Texas, I returned from a nature walk to discover that one of the women on my walk had lost her Chihuahua (dog). She had tied the dog to a tree in the campground while she was away. We returned to find an empty leash and a satisfied javelina stretched out on the grass nearby finishing a meal of fresh Chihuahua.

On another early morning in the northern Chihuahuan Desert,

I found myself in the middle of a band of thirty to forty javelinas that had been quietly feeding along an open arroyo. We discovered each other at about the same time. Although the majority of the band fled, in all directions, two or three of the largest and most aggressive boars remained behind. I could tell that they were having a difficult time detecting my exact whereabouts, in spite of the fact that one was within twenty to twenty-five feet of me. He just stood there staring in my direction, while the hair on his back stood straight up, and he sniffed the breeze for my scent. I stood perfectly still, watching for what would happen next. The nearest javelina remained rooted to the spot, but a second boar, thirty to thirty-feet away, began to circle. He suddenly appeared to catch my scent, because he snorted, ran a few yards, stopped, turned in my direction with bristles rising and falling on his back, and snorted once again. Then, as if he had lost my scent, he continued to circle. In fact, he made an entire circle, not just once, but three times. Each time when he appeared to get my scent, he went through the same act, snorting and running a short distance, only to stop and sniff and snort again. The nearest javelina had immediately left when the circling boar first caught my scent. The entire episode lasted for about fifteen minutes. And the scent from that band of javelinas remained in the vicinity for another half-hour at least.

Javelina eyesight is poor at best. They largely depend upon smell for feeding as well as for detecting danger. Many of the javelinas that live in the Chihuahuan Desert, where lechuguilla is so dominant, have lost their sight in one or both eyes. But in spite of this loss of a sense that is so important to humans, the peccaries seem to continue about their business with little change. One cannot help but be impressed with the toughness and flexibility of some of the desert creatures, like the javelina and coyote. Both have survived in spite of human persecution. They are good cases for the adaptions that are necessary for both plants and animals to persist within Mexico's northern deserts.

3

Monterrey's Unique Highlands

Their loud, raucous calls were almost overwhelming. We reached a place at the base of the high cliffs where we could sit and watch. Fourteen maroon-fronted parrots were perched only 125 to 150 feet away from us. But in less than a half-hour that number increased to twenty-four, and soon after that there were thirty-eight individuals, more than three dozen very loud and highly vocal birds.

They appeared as curious about us as we were about them. It seemed to me that the newcomers had joined the first group to assess our presence. They openly gawked at us, shuffled a bit, and squawked with each other. A few individuals, probably paired birds, preened one another as we watched. They were perfectly safe even at only 125 feet away: their perch was on two scraggly Arizona cypress trees growing out of a deep crack at the base of the eighteen-hundred-foot cliff face. Between us was a very steep but narrow canyon and eighty feet or so of cliff. We could hear two to three dozen more parrots higher up on the precipitous cliff to our right. Occasionally a pair or a whole flock of thirty-five to eighty birds wheeled overhead, and then settled on the cliff face. Many of them perched in crevices where we assumed they were nesting. Once we had reached the base of the cliff, after a two-hour-long scramble from the valley below, we had from fourteen to as many as two hundred birds continuously in sight at any one time. It was a phenomenal experience, one that I will never forget, being with what was probably the largest concentration of maroon-fronted parrots anywhere in the world.

These parrots (*Rhynchopsitta terrisi*) occur only within the northernmost highlands of Mexico's Sierra Madre Oriental, in the tri-state area of Nuevo León, western Tamaulipas and Coahuila. Their only close relative is the thick-billed parrot (*R. pachyrhyncha*) of the Sierra Madre Occidental highlands to the west. The two populations are physically separated by several hundred miles of arid country.

Some ornithologists believe they are one and the same, but the American Ornithologists' Union (the governing body for avian taxonomy) has split the two populations into distinct species. Both, however, are considered threatened by habitat loss due to logging, grazing, land clearing for orchards and other crops, and their capture for the pet trade. The International Council for Bird Protection (Mountfort, 1988) lists the maroon-fronted parrot as endangered, with only about two thousand birds still in existence. We were observing one-tenth of the world's remaining population.

They are gorgeous birds, and I could well understand their appeal as pets. But they seemed so secure in their mountain fortress that I found the idea of capturing these birds not only impractical but impossible. They seemed so very aware of their situation, so close and yet so far away from us, that I imagined they were truly masters of their environment. We two mere humans—Greg Lasley and I—could only watch and admire these incredible creatures. How did they discover the security of nesting on these impenetrable cliffs, develop a social system that so enhanced their chances of survival, and what about their amazing curiosity?

From close up, their large size was obvious. Although not as large as macaws, they are larger than any of the round-tailed *Amazona* parrots. *Rhynchopsitta* parrots have long tails and very large, greatly compressed bills. My on-site description of the maroon-fronts that day reads: "Body is all green, but bend of wing is bright red; shows well when perched but not evident in flight. Breast is green but with dull grayish patches. Head has deep maroon on forehead and extends above eye like eyebrow. Yellow skin patch around eye. Bill is gray-black. Calls are reminiscent of laughing gulls; sometimes like acorn woodpeckers. The 2 note 'bark' is half duck and half dog."

Joseph Forshaw, in *Parrots of the World,* described their calls as "a harsh, raucous *kurr-rak . . . kurr-rak* and a loud *kuk-kuk-kuk-kuk-kuk.*" Roger Tory Peterson and Edward L. Chalif, in *A Field Guide to Mexican Birds,* stated that the bird's squawks and screeches are audible for more than a mile. He also pointed out that the two species differ in that thick-bills possess a "bright yellow stripe on underwing" that is not present on maroon-fronts, and that the western thick-bills differ from their eastern cousins by possessing a red instead of a maroon forehead.

We remained along the base of the parrot cliffs for most of the day, although we were able to move laterally for only a couple of hundred yards. Greg photographed parrots perched on the cypress trees and on several other trees, perched in crevices above us, and birds in flight. Their flight silhouette high up reminded me of that of a peregrine falcon. We watched parrots soar, twist, and then suddenly dive much like peregrines. We wondered aloud about predation, and agreed that a peregrine would meet its match in a maroon-front.

As the morning progressed it seemed that new birds were arriving from elsewhere, some approaching from so high above the cliff that they were little more than dots at first. Even those, probably over a mile above us, could still be heard as they communicated with others, perhaps with the birds that we were watching. We assumed that the arriving birds had departed these same cliffs earlier that morning, probably at dawn when we first detected their activities, to go elsewhere to feed. Maroon-fronted parrots feed almost exclusively on conifer seeds from several species of pines and firs, and so most cover hundreds of square miles to find a continuous and adequate supply.

Although our view from the base of the cliffs could not compare with that which the high-flying parrots could experience, the scene eastward into the narrow and winding canyon and the steep ridges beyond was spectacular. The air was sparkling clear at our elevation of about 7,100 feet, but on the far horizon to the southeast we could detect some of the ugly smog that envelopes much of the Monterrey area. After Mexico City, Monterrey is one of the dirtiest cities in all Mexico. Yet to the south, upwind and away from the influence of belching smokestacks and exhaust-filled streets and highways, the air was clean and clear.

The sudden song of a redstart, a little below us to the left, attracted us away from our contemplations. We had seen painted redstarts around our campsite in the canyon below, but this was a very different song. The bird moved upward and into the oak and hickory trees between us and the cliff. It sang again. Then Greg found it briefly—black back and orange-red breast, and no wingbars. A slate-throated redstart! For only a second he saw the chestnut cap. Then the bird disappeared. Although we heard it sing a couple more times, we were never able to get close enough for another good look or to photograph the bird. Later, we listened to taped songs, and were able to reconfirm its identity.

Slate-throated redstarts are not only incredibly beautiful birds, but this one, according to our field guides, was seemingly "out-of-range." Its expected range is south of the Monterrey mountains, from San Luis Potosí south to Bolivia, South America. Yet here it was in Nuevo León. Its presence underscored that these Monterrey highlands have had very little study, and probably contain many more southern species than are credited in the field guides. We were less than 150 airline miles from the Texas border, but in an entirely different world. No wonder birders in southwestern and southeastern Texas have discovered so many Mexican species. The birds need only cross some eighty-five miles of desertscrub, between the northern end of the Sierra Madre Oriental and the lush riparian vegetation of the Rio Grande Valley. Such a feat is quite possible for most species. The reported sightings of slate-throated redstarts in the Chisos Mountains of Big Bend National Park make much more sense if the bird is resident in the forested highlands just south of Monterrey.

The vegetation directly below the parrot cliffs was extremely lush and thick. The northern slope of the canyon, shaded for most of the day, was considerably different than the more arid south slopes at eye-level a quarter of a mile away. Some of the arid species on the south side also were present on the open cliff face above us; agave and sotol were most obvious. But lower down, in the crevices and along the edge of the cliffs where the moist soils begin, was an entirely different habitat. The tallest trees were firs (*Abies coahuilensis*). Their cones, near the treetops, stood upright and oozed whitish sap. I picked one up that had fallen on the ground and got sticky sap on my hand for my efforts.

On one of the large boulders that had fallen off the cliff face sometime in the past I found pieces of fir cones and attributed the remains to the tree squirrel that I had encountered among the foliage while I had been parrot-watching earlier in the morning. It was reminiscent of the eastern fox squirrel of the United States. After searching through Hall and Kelson's *Mammals of North America,* I believe that the squirrel which left the deposit of fir cone bits was none other than Allen's squirrel (*Sciurus alleni*), another of Mexico's endemics. This species is restricted to the high mountains at the northern end of the Sierra Madre Oriental, another indicator of the unique environment in which we were exploring.

Hickory trees were the most numerous of the midlevel woody plants, and hop-hornbeam, with its furrowed bark, double-toothed leaves and scaled buds, was common as well. But the most interesting tree there was Mexican yew, with its flat-needled foliage and unique fruits: red, fleshy and cup-shaped with interior seeds. It is a rather low-growing tree that seemed to fit nicely into the montane habitat there at the base of the cliff. That was my first encounter with this species, although Jerzy Rzedowski, in *Vegetación de México,* lists it as being occasionally present in the "montane mesic forest" habitat in the northern Sierra Madre Oriental. The shrub layer below the trees contained a shiny-leafed sumac, a very prickly holly-like shrub, and mountain sage.

A little further down the slope, in less mesic conditions, were numerous oaks and pines. Based upon C. H. Muller's 1939 paper in the *American Midland Naturalist,* "Relations of the Vegetation and Climatic Types in Nuevo Leon, Mexico," the oaks included *Quercus clivicola, Q. canbyi,* and *Q. porphyrogenita.* Pines listed for this zone included *Pinus rudis, P. montezumae,* and *P. arizonica.* Still further down the slope near our camp I discovered a lone Aztec pine; its bright green drooping foliage has earned it the appropriate Mexican name of *pino barba caída,* or drooping beard pine.

A few other bird species were found along the base of the parrot cliffs. Blue-throated hummingbirds were fairly common, feeding on the bright red flowers of mountain sage and providing high-pitched squeaks as they zipped by us en route to other nectar-rich flowers. We heard the loud descending whistles of canyon wrens several times; it was a perfect habitat for this crevice-lover. And four or five brown-backed solitaires flitted among the trees; one immature bird still had a spotted head. Another surprise at this northern avian frontier was rufous-capped brush-finches. Their high-pitched *zeet* calls were more common than were our few sightings of this secretive species. This is another example of the lack of knowledge about what birds occur in these mountains; all the field guides indicate that this species should be further south. We wondered what other mysteries are yet to be found in these seldom studied highlands.

This northermost portion of the Sierra Madre Oriental contains some outstanding geological features. The whole region is an anticline where Mexico's great eastern range makes an abrupt westerly turn to form a biotic corridor to the Sierra Madre Occidental of western Mexico. Our trip into these mountains south of Monterrey was oriented toward visiting the parrot cliffs, a location where Greg had gone with Andres Sada the previous year, and also to search out the little known Worthen's sparrow. Both species are considered endangered and finding them can be most difficult.

We had crossed into Mexico at Nuevo Laredo, on October 3, 1990, and had spent our first night camping out north of Monterrey, above Sombreretillo in the Sierra Picachos. This relatively low mountain range, usually visible from Falcon Dam, is less than sixty airline miles from Texas. We found the lowlands dominated by vegetation with many Tamaulipian scrub species, but we could see a rather extensive forest on the northern slopes of the highest peaks. David Riskind informed me that the northern slopes contain some of the largest Coahuila firs he has ever seen. And yet, except for brief investigations of these mountains during the 1970s by John Arvin, Gene Blacklock, Edgar Kincaid, Roseann Rowlett and Suzanne Winkler, the area has had little biological attention. Nevertheless, we found ferruginous pygmy-owl, spot-breasted wren and clay-colored robin — three typical Mexican species — within a couple of hours the following morning. The most surprising of the three was the spot-breasted wren; there are no records for the United States in spite of this Sierra Picachos population existing so close by. Birders in the Rio Grande Valley may one day add this species to the list of U.S. avifauna.

Worthen's Sparrows

I will forevermore associate Worthen's sparrows with prairie dogs. Following directions provided by Andres Sada, we drove south from Saltillo, Coahuila, on Highway 54. Twenty-five miles south of the city we turned off the highway and drove eastward into the tiny village of Tanque de Emergencia. It contained a dozen or so adobe houses and hundreds of huge agaves, bordering each yard and serving as very adequate fencing for livestock. We passed through the village and followed the unpaved roadway for about four more miles to an old and broken stone watertank situated at the top of a little rise within the open grasslands. It commanded a marvelous view of the surrounding valley. All around us were high plains grasslands, kept

Coahuila grasslands south of Saltillo, home of Mexican prairie
dogs and Worthen's sparrows.

short by the multitude of prairie dogs that barked at us from all
directions. We had arrived at our destination.

Prairie dog habitat looks the same wherever these chubby rodents
occur in numbers, from Canada to central Mexico. They once numbered in the millions, but our so-called progress — cities, agriculture
and cattle — have today eliminated most populations. They remain
only in remnants of the shortgrass prairies that once covered one-
quarter of western North America. Describing the once thriving
prairie dog populations in Texas in his 1966 book, *The Mammals
of Texas,* William Davis wrote: "Vernon Bailey recorded that at the
turn of the century an almost continuous and thickly inhabited dog
town extended in a strip approximately 100 miles wide and 250 miles
long on the high plains of Texas. This 'city' had an estimated population of 400,000,000 prairie dogs" (p. 139).

Mexico's prairie dog populations are now limited to some of the
high grasslands used only by subsistence cattle herds, in the states

of Chihuahua, Coahuila, Zacatecas and San Luis Potosí. The area
that we visited, between Tanque de Emergencia and El Cercado, in
southeastern Coahuila, contained hundreds of prairie dogs. Bare
mounds and their prairie dog guardians were visible up and down
the broad valley as far as we could see. I at first identified them as
the black-tailed prairie dogs, because of their blackish tails. Con-
sulting Hall and Kelson's indispensable two-volume *Mammals of
North America,* however, indicated that we had found another Mexican endemic, the Mexican prairie dog (*Cynomys mexicanus*). According to Hall and Kelson, this species is similar to the more northerly "black-tailed" form, but is "more grayish and vinaceous-buff;
black hairs more numerous, giving more grizzled effect" (p. 412).

Like prairie dogs everywhere, these live in randomly spaced family groups that defend territories with much verbosity and little action. Underground is a labyrinth of passageways that are connected
to three or four mounded entrances. On the surface, the mounds
and surrounding areas are bare of vegetation, kept clean by the ten-
ants so that grasses and shrubs will not hinder their views. Prairie
dogs stay close to their entrance holes whenever a predator or stranger
appears, and will bark shrill, two-note, dog-like warnings to their
neighbors at the slightest hint of danger. They depend almost totally upon vegetation, particularly grasses, for their food.

Andres had suggested during our visit with him in Monterrey that
we search for Worthen's sparrows near the broken watertank. But
in spite of a two-hour search in all directions that afternoon, we were
unsuccessful. We did find a few savannah sparrows, which we tracked
down to be sure, and a lone lark sparrow. Curve-billed thrashers were
fairly common, as were western meadowlarks and a few western blue-
birds, all representatives of western avifauna. But the bird of the
day was an adult ferruginous hawk seen cruising over the terrain.
Early October seemed very early in the season for this northern species.

While searching for the sparrows, we came suddenly upon another resident of the prairie dog town, a prairie rattlesnake (*Crotalus
viridis*). Its greenish-brown coloration blended extremely well with
the grasses and low herbs through which we were walking. We approached this poisonous reptile to within less than three feet before
it warned us of its presence. The stark, hollow rattle of a rattlesnake
must be one of the most conspicuous sounds in nature. This rattler
was only about thirty inches in length, and had just four rattles,

but that was enough to startle us. It drew back and rattled its warning, and then moved into the protection of a thorny shrub. It never did strike at us, nor did we provoke it. In the wilds, the policy must always be to live and let live.

Rain clouds had been building over the surrounding ridges throughout the afternoon, and by 4:30 a hard rain enveloped the valley. Temperatures dropped by twenty or more degrees; at 8:00 P.M. we recorded fifty-seven degrees Fahrenheit, and that temperature stayed constant throughout the night. Just before dark the rain stopped, and we walked out into the grasslands again to stretch our legs before bedtime. Three hours in my Volkswagen camper had dampened our spirits somewhat. But they were rekindled as we listened to the evening songs of coyotes and the mellow calls of common poorwills.

Our evening walk also provided an opportunity to examine the vegetation more closely. And for me it was like visiting an old homeplace, because the great majority of plants examined I recognized as Chihuahuan Desert species. The tallest were two yucca species: Torrey yucca and a larger, heavier species that I identified as giant dagger or Spanish dagger, locally called *palma samandoca*. Mexican huts are sometimes constructed from the yucca's tough trunk and leaves. According to Robert Vines in his excellent book, *Trees, Shrubs and Woody Vines of the Southwest*, the specific name of giant dagger (*carnerosana*) was derived from Carneros Pass, Coahuila, where it was first collected; Carneros Pass is located on Highway 54 just north of the Tanque de Emergencia turnoff.

Cacti were scattered throughout the grasslands, in both the grazed grassland habitat as well as the desertscrub. The most obvious ones were the tall tree or cane cholla, sometimes eight or more feet tall. The shorter prickly pears with rounded, prickly pads were one form of the widespread Engelmann's prickly pear. But the biggest surprise was the finding of a few lechuguilla plants, an *Agave*, the very best indicator of true Chihuahuan Desert.

Beyond the open grasslands, in the adjacent desertscrub habitat, I found tarbush, squaw-bush, desert hackberry, *agarito* or barberry, a couple species of acacias, mariola, and resin-bush. Further up the slope was a sparse and very short pinyon-juniper woodland. I identified Mexican pinyon, redberry juniper, a stunted little fragrant ash, and a scrub oak.

I was well aware that Chihuahuan Desert flora extend far south into Mexico, but I did not expect to find this highland valley of 6,200 feet elevation dominated by Chihuahuan Desert plantlife. David Schmidly (1977) included mesquite-grassland habitat in his discussion of factors governing the distribution of mammals in the Chihuahuan Desert region, and pointed out that Mexico's high grasslands are refugia in danger of being absorbed by drier desert habitats. He regards the Mexican prairie dog as a "geographic isolate," one of the species that "reached the sites of their present occurrence by range extensions of the main body of their respective genera when environmental conditions were more mesic than now" (pp. 180–81). The black-tailed prairie dog of the United States is their nearest relative in both a physical and genetic sense.

Dawn found us searching again for the elusive Worthen's sparrow. It was a cool morning with no breeze. The sky was reddening to the east as we passed through the prairie dog town en route to the desertscrub habitat beyond. The prairie dogs were still underground; none acknowledged our presence. Except for a lone killdeer call and two northern flickers in the distance, all was still.

But things began to change as we approached the thicker vegetation. As we walked north into the desertscrub we began to see sparrows flitting about the shrubs. And in less than half an hour we had found the bird of our quest! Our first good sighting of a Worthen's sparrow—a pair, in fact—was of birds perched atop a yucca several hundred feet north of the roadway. At first glance they could have passed for field sparrows. But closer study revealed a more obvious white eye-ring and the lack of the dark streak behind the eye. Otherwise, the birds appeared identical. They suddenly took flight and we followed them to a shrub a hundred feet or so further west. We found one individual perched in the center of the shrub, and we watched it preen itself.

Although Andres Sada was already aware of this Worthen's sparrow site, it apparently is not well known. Emil Urban reported only one Coahuila record in his extensive 1959 paper, "Birds from Coahuila, México." He stated: "The single specimen of Worthen's Sparrow" is from "just outside the limits of Saltillo on April 16, and represents the only record of occurrence of this species for Coahuila" (p. 512).

As soon as we had assured ourselves of the bird's identity, Greg

Worthen's sparrow held by the author in high desert grasslands south of Saltillo, Coahuila. *Photo by Greg Lasley*

returned to the van for the poles and mist nets we had brought along with us for this occasion. We set up the six nets in front of shrubs on which we expected the birds to perch, and after walking two broad semicircles, we began to walk back through the habitat in an attempt to drive any birds ahead of us into the nets positioned against the early morning sunrise. We were successful on our first drive! We captured three sparrows: a vesper and clay-colored, neither of which we had previously seen, and a Worthen's.

We immediately released the vesper and clay-colored, but carefully examined and photographed the Worthen's sparrow before releasing it. Greg took more than fifty close-up photographs, from all angles. We wondered if anyone had ever before handled a live Worthen's sparrow. Not only is it a rare Mexican bird now, but it apparently has always been hard to find and identify. Oddly enough, the type specimen was taken by C. W. Worthen on June 16, 1884, at Silver City, New Mexico. Since then, however, the only positive records of the species have been in Mexico.

It wasn't until we had examined the bird thoroughly and were in the process of photographing our captured one that it dawned on us that this bird, as well as at least three of the eight or ten we had observed earlier, had blackish legs. The look-alike field sparrows possess pink legs. Greg's photographs clearly show the dark leg color. Could this characteristic be the key to easier field identification?

With this in mind we made a second drive in an attempt to capture another bird, but without success. We moved the nets to a new location and tried a third sweep toward the nets, but without capturing a single bird. By now a wind was blowing, making the nets puff out and thus more obvious, and the sun was higher in the sky. Our sparrows had suddenly disappeared. We searched the surrounding vegetation, but the birds had for all intents and purposes completely vanished. We folded our nets and moved on.

4

Maderas del Carmen

We heard the peregrine tiercel (male) calling to his mate long before we saw him. We also heard the responsive cries of the peregrine haggard (female) somewhere on the face of the gigantic cliff directly across from our lofty perch. I turned my binoculars toward the deep canyon below and searched for an invisible dot that would be the eyrie-bound hunter. Another call from the depths below somehow directed my search a little to the left. There he was! The tiercel was flying swiftly in a direct course towards the eyrie and his waiting mate.

I watched that incredible bird with all of the respect he so well deserved. He was returning to his eyrie with food that he had caught in the desert far below. His flight upward was at an angle of at least forty-five degrees. Yet the weight of a bird almost his own size—either a white-winged or mourning dove, I couldn't be certain—did not seem to hamper him. The peregrine's powerful wing strokes drove him upward.

Three of us watched the tiercel every stroke of the way after my first discovery. We knew when he was nearing the eyrie because of the increased calling of both birds. Then suddenly he disappeared from view into a hidden crevice within the rhyolitic fortress. We understood what was taking place as he shared his kill with his mate and, perhaps, three to four downy youngsters.

A few minutes later the tiercel reappeared, flying out and upward toward the top of the cliff, another six hundred feet or so. There, in full view and perched on an old weathered snag, he rested. We watched him preen, ruffle his feathers, and finally settle down as if to stand guard on his Maderas del Carmen homeland.

We had hiked from our camp at Los Cohos Spring to the summit of Loomis Peak earlier that morning. Roseann Rowlett, David Ligon and I had been standing in awe admiring the grand scene before us when our attention was caught by the peregrine's calls. And we continued to admire that incredible bird from afar for some time before we again turned our eyes to the scenery around us.

View from the Summit

The view from the top of Loomis Peak (8,960 feet) may be one of the finest in North America. The desert lies to the west, below the 5,500-foot escarpment. On a clear day the Chisos Mountains stand out to the northwest. They seem almost touchable although more than fifty miles away. On dusty days they glimmer like a mirage against the far horizon. To the north are the other peaks of the Maderas del Carmen, and the flatland that lies beyond is the uplifted limestone portion of the range.

More of the Maderas del Carmen stretch out in a wide semicircle northeast to southeast from Loomis Peak. A dozen or more plateaus and canyons form parallel lines, one after another, all the way to the shimmering desert beyond. Because of the distance involved, one cannot pick out details in the desertscape below the cliffs on the west. The eastern side of the Maderas del Carmen forms a series of gradually descending steps that eventually terminate on the desert floor.

The high peaks to the south of Loomis Peak fall sharply off toward the west. And there below the southern rampart are the white scratches of Los Cohos Mine (at 6,300 feet elevation). Until 1976, western access to the highlands was available only by trail from the mine. A rough ore road provided access to that point.

Sierra del Carmen Geography

The Sierra del Carmen forms a massive limestone and volcanic mountain range east and south of Big Bend National Park, Texas. That range arose from the same geologic past that created the prominent topographic structures that jut out of Big Bend's desert landscape. In about the center of the 801,000-acre park is a volcanic mountain range known as the Chisos. To the west is a broad limestone mesa that was sliced in half by the Rio Grande to form spectacular Santa Elena Canyon. South is Mariscal Canyon that forms the elbow of the Texas Big Bend Country. And to the east are the Sierra del Carmen and Boquillas Canyon.

The Sierra del Carmen comprises three rather distinct units. The northern end of the range forms the east side of Big Bend National

Park and usually is called the Dead Horse Mountains or, in Spanish, Cabrillo Muerto. This region is a series of extremely arid limestone ridges and valleys. South of Boquillas Canyon in Mexico the uplifted limestone ridge forms gigantic horizontal layers that provide a magnificent backdrop to the park's Rio Grande Village and the settlement of Boquillas in Mexico. South and slightly to the east of these limestone slopes is a higher series of volcanic peaks that run north-south for about twenty-five miles. This portion of the Sierra del Carmen range is known as the Maderas del Carmen.

The Maderas del Carmen contains seven peaks over 8,000 feet in elevation. Approximately 115 square miles lie above 5,500 feet. By contrast, just ten square miles of the Chisos lie above 5,500 feet; Emory Peak, the highest point in the Chisos Mountains, is only 7,835 feet elevation. An important difference between the Maderas del Carmen and Chisos Mountains is in the amount of annual precipitation the two areas receive. More than twenty inches is rarely recorded in the Chisos, but the Maderas del Carmen usually receives forty inches or more. This mountain mass is closer to the Gulf of Mexico and storms often diminish over the del Carmen before reaching the Chisos.

Mexico's Sierra del Carmen is more than an extension of the Texas Big Bend country. It contains all of the same ingredients that have made Big Bend National Park one of the world's greatest wilderness preserves—and then some. The park was dedicated in 1984 as one of North America's first international biosphere reserves, a status bestowed upon it by the Man and the Biosphere program (MAB) of the United Nations Environmental Program (UNEP). Yet the mountains south of the Rio Grande, which have received only minimal recognition, contain an even greater assortment of wildland flora and fauna, and spectacular scenery.

Plantlife

The desert that surrounds the Sierra del Carmen is typical of the arid lowlands throughout most of the Chihuahuan Desert region of Coahuila and eastern Chihuahua. For those who understand the desert it is a gentle and exciting place to be. But for the uninformed it can be harsh and deadly; daily summer temperatures can easily exceed one hundred degrees Fahrenheit. The desert is more than a transition zone between the Rio Grande's line of greenery and the

Aerial view of rugged landscape of Sierra del Carmen range. The Maderas del Carmen rise above striped limestone cliffs near the Rio Grande.

grasslands of the del Carmen foothills. It is the start of the mountains, the bottom of the pyramid.

On the warmer southern slopes, grasslands occur between 3,500 and 6,500 feet elevation, but the same habitat occurs at somewhat lower elevations on the cooler north-facing slopes. This habitat is relatively indistinct on the west side of the Sierra del Carmen where the escarpment rises rather abruptly from the desert to the sheer cliffs of the mountain tops. The western escarpment ascends 5,500 feet in less than two miles. But on the east side of the del Carmen mountains the same elevational change is stretched out to approximately twelve miles. The eastern side, therefore not only provides easier access to the highlands but allows greater use by ranchers, loggers and hunters.

Chisos agave is one of the unique succulents found within the del Carmen grasslands; until the 1960s it was considered endemic to the Chisos Mountains of Big Bend National Park. A second and even rarer agave occurs above the grasslands on the rocky cliffs and ridges of the Maderas del Carmen. It is known to occur only within the mountains of northern Coahuila — the del Carmen, Encantada and Santa Rosa ranges. This is *Agave potrerana,* a heavy-stemmed plant with a beautiful rosette leaf base. Yellow flowers appear in late July and, like all agaves, the plant dies at the end of the first flowering season. It takes agaves from fifteen to thirty-five years to bloom.

A woodland of pinyon pine, junipers, and oaks occurs above the grasslands. This pinyon-juniper-oak habitat forms rather extensive woodlands on the eastern slopes of the numerous ridges and mesas and within the midelevation valleys. On drier slopes this habitat may reach up to 7,000 feet. Fingers of oak, hackberry and other broadleaf trees follow canyon bottoms to about 4,000 feet elevation. But somewhere between 6,500 and 7,000 feet begins a more extensive montane forest that runs to the very tops of the highest pinnacles.

The real treasures of the Maderas del Carmen occur in the highlands. The forest crowns the rhyolitic castles and hides the fragile meadows and clear streams. Southwestern white and ponderosa pines blend with an amazing variety of oaks on open flats and ridges, and Douglas-fir and Arizona cypress are more common in narrow canyons and other protected niches. Coahuila fir grows in some of the highest and most out-of-the-way canyons.

Visit to the Maderas del Carmen Highland

The new road, which is unpaved and extremely rough, climbs above Los Cohos Spring and crosses the divide into Madera Canyon (locally called Cañon Cinco). From that point, an old road follows the canyon bottom eastward all the way to the desert.

Near the top of Madera Canyon is a peaceful, straw-colored meadow set in a cathedral-like setting. Except for an assortment of wildflowers at various seasons, needlegrass is by far the most common groundcover. A slight breeze ripples the tawny stems like a field of summer wheat. But this field was not planted by farmers. It is a product of the rains, the soils, and wildfires. The meadow grass

feeds deer, pocket gophers, and a variety of rodents. One of these —
the yellow-nosed cotton rat — occurs only in meadows of needlegrass,
in places left unabused, and where nature is still in control.

I was awakened one very early morning in a nearby meadow to
the low whistles (a descending call that sounded as if it might come
from a canyon wren–eastern screech-owl hybrid) of Montezuma quail.
Nowhere have I found this beautiful *Cyrtonyx* as abundant as it was
in the Maderas del Carmen. The theory that this species does better
on ranchlands in the United States is certainly refuted by the del
Carmen population. It must reach its greatest abundance in these
native mountain grasslands.

Sierra del Carmen Whitetails. I surprised a mountain lion stalk-
ing a deer in the Madera Canyon meadow on one trip. My sudden
appearance frightened the lion from its venison meal. The deer of
the Sierra del Carmen is a small race of whitetail named after these
mountains and occurring only in the del Carmen and Chisos mountains and adjacent wooded "islands," usually above 4,500 feet elevation. The various populations once were contiguous, but desert now
separates these upland areas.

Philip Wells studied woodrat middens (dens) found within dry
overhangs in the foothills of the Chisos and Dead Horse mountains.
His 1966 report on his research described pieces of pinyon foliage
more than 20,000 years old found in the middens. According to
Wells's chronology, until about 10,000 years ago, the woodrats lived
in a woodland environment quite similar to that found in the mountains today. Then the vegetation began to change to a more xeric
type and finally to true desert. These studies suggest that the Chihuahuan Desert invaded northern Mexico as recently as 9,000 or so
years ago.

The Sierra del Carmen whitetail deer apparently followed the treeline upward when the desert became established. Today, the Chisos
and del Carmen mountains are like islands surrounded by an ocean
of desert. And sometime in the last few thousand years mule deer
have moved into the lowlands.

Cañon del Oso. My favorite place in all the Sierra del Carmen
is Cañon del Oso (Bear Canyon). It is the greenest and most peaceful of all the beautiful canyons within the Maderas del Carmen. On
the canyon floor is a stream that flows between grassy banks and
trickles over rocky ledges. Numerous pools are spaced here and there

where mossy boulders have lodged on some previous high water to dam a place or form a new meander. We bathed in some of the deeper pools in Cañon del Oso. The temperature of the water was almost too cold for us to stay submerged for more than a few moments. But the sunshine was warm and relaxing.

We were not the first people to use the delicious waters. At the head of Cañon del Oso is Cañon Tres, which contained remnants of an old logging camp. Weathered board houses still lined a relic roadway in one part of the canyon, and a pile of decaying slash marked the site of a long-forgotten mill. Beyond the pile of waste were narrow gauge tracks that led away from the mill site into a side canyon that still showed scars from logs dragged off the hillside to be torn apart and cut into boards.

It seemed incredible that such a place really existed within Cañon del Oso, incongruous, given the wild character of the canyon and the wilderness setting. The logging camp took on an almost surrealistic character as I wandered about. A rusty tool here and a piece of glass there brought ghosts back to that tiny village for a while. I was amazed at the idea that timber was so valuable during the 1930s that this remote sanctuary was breached. And the route used to transport machinery and equipment to the site, and to haul boards and logs away from the mill, was just as unreal. The roadway followed the canyon bottom for more than ten miles, over boulders and rockfalls, around narrow bends and down steep grades. In places a log road had been constructed within the canyon bottom but high above the cascading water.

Only remnants of the roadway still existed, where huge planks were high enough above the canyon for a flash flood to pass underneath without disturbing the roadbed. In other places the rushing waters had totally torn away the roadbed and no sign of human endeavor remained.

The logging camp itself — Campo Tres — had been built at the end of the roadway in a little valley that lies between a high rocky cliff to the north and a high plateau to the south. A spring flowed from a grassy bank at the head of the valley and followed a shallow gully past two rows of houses and a tremendous pile of slash and sawdust. In one side of this pile was a deep hole where a black bear had recently dug for either shelter or food. Bear tracks led toward the high plateau via a steep side canyon.

Birdlife

I spent almost an entire day wandering on that forested plateau. The timber was tall once again, but I could not help imagining what it might have been like before the loggers came and changed things. I searched that day for trees that had been used by a woodpecker larger than those I already had seen throughout the forest. Acorn woodpeckers were common within the lower woodlands and ponderosa pine stands, and an occasional hairy woodpecker was found, too. Northern flickers were present in the highlands, as well. But I was looking for evidence that the imperial woodpecker, North America's largest, existed within the Maderas del Carmen.

The initial idea of these mountains containing imperials began on my first visit to the Maderas del Carmen in 1969. The Mexico highlands had enticed me ever since 1966, when I first went to Big Bend National Park as chief park naturalist. My hopes of seeing the del Carmen highlands finally transpired when six of us climbed the steep burro trail above Los Cohos Mine into a different world. We camped at Los Cohos Spring and hiked out each day to explore the scenic wonders and learn what we could about the local flora and fauna.

One afternoon, high above camp on the western rim, I found three ponderosa pine snags with large, oblong holes in the trunks twenty-five feet above the ground. I was surprised at the size of the holes and took several photographs. I assumed at the time that the holes were remains of pileated woodpecker activities. Since that bird had never before been recorded in these mountains, I intended to document its presence. It was not until later that I learned that pileated woodpeckers do not occur in Mexico. The only large woodpecker that frequents habitat like that of the Maderas del Carmen was the endangered imperial, a bird known only from the Sierra Madre Occidental highlands, far to the west. Like the ivory-billed woodpecker of the southeastern U.S. lowlands, the Mexican imperial is more of an enigma than a reality. And yet, there in the Maderas del Carmen was possible evidence of its existence far out of its previously known range.

Three weeks later I returned to the Maderas del Carmen highlands to try to find the bird or hard evidence of its existence. I found additional nesting trees, although every one was old and not adequate proof. I attempted to climb to one of the nest holes, hoping that an ancient feather had been left behind, but a near fall reduced my enthusiam for that method of discovery. If I had known then that those trees were the last bit of nesting evidence I was to find, I would have risked my neck again and again until I retrieved any clues that remained in the nesting cavities.

One more piece of circumstantial evidence came my way on that second trip. I met a bear hunter wandering along Madera Canyon early one morning. We struck up a conversation and he soon was telling me about the local wildlife. I learned about the bears and *panteras,* as well as the deer and fox. I opened my Peterson field guide to the plate on hawks and falcons and asked him if any one of those birds lived in these mountains. With only a moment's hesitation he pointed to the Cooper's hawk, goshawk, and peregrine falcon. Although I was a little uncertain of the goshawk then, I later found it nesting in Madera Canyon. I next turned to the plate on western warblers. Again, he was correct. He pointed only at the painted redstart and Colima and olive warblers.

The only picture I had found of the imperial woodpecker at that time was in Ernest Edwards's 1968 bird-finding book. I had photocopied that plate and it had reproduced quite well. I took that copy from the back of my book, unfolded it, and asked the bear hunter if any of the birds on that plate lived in the Maderas del Carmen. He looked at all of the illustrations. Then he pointed at only one, the imperial woodpecker.

I asked him how recently he had seen one. He said it had been a long time, maybe four or five years ago; he said he used to shoot them for food because they made a very good dinner.

I have returned to the Maderas del Carmen seven times to search for the imperial woodpecker, but since 1970 have found no new evidence. My last visit to the Maderas del Carmen was in 1976 and with the same amount of anticipation as I had experienced on that second trip. Two friends—Joan Fryzell and Grainger Hunt—had told me of seeing a "large crested woodpecker" in Cañon del Oso the previous year. Joan, Grainger, and I revisited the site in 1976, but I again returned without proof.

However, the highlands of the Maderas del Carmen were once again being invaded by wood cutters. The old logging camp in Madera Canyon had undergone a complete restoration. I counted thirty-four

Mexicans busy with their projects of cutting the timber, dragging it off the hillsides and down the canyons to newly constructed roads, and trucking the logs to the mill to be cut into boards for transportation to Musquiz and Sabinas.

It is impossible to know what the Maderas del Carmen were like during the centuries before the first loggers cut the forest. I believe that the imperial woodpecker lived within these forested highlands. And I cannot help but wonder what other forms of life will be destroyed by new logging activities.

Over the years, the birdlife of the Sierra del Carmen has commanded greater attention from scientists than any of the other wildlife. However, no investigations were done before the area was first logged. Alden Miller was first to describe the del Carmen birdlife, in 1955. Dave Ligon and I compared the area's breeding birds with those of the Chisos, Davis and Guadalupe mountains in the 1970s. Although the Maderas del Carmen bird population is similar to that of the Chisos Mountains, there are several significant differences.

The greater variety of breeding raptors, undoubtedly the result of the much larger land mass, is most important. Golden eagles, redtails, zone-tails, goshawks, sharp-shinned and Cooper's hawks, peregrines and prairie falcons, and American kestrels are known to nest. One night at Los Cohos Spring I heard four kinds of owls calling: eastern screech, flammulated, northern pygmy and northern saw-whet. Great horned and elf owls nest lower down the mountain.

I found the Maderas del Carmen montane forest habitat to be very similar to that of the Chiricahuas of southern Arizona. The brown-throated race of the house wren was abundant and seemed to sing from every pile of downed logs and brush. If behavior and vocalizations are any criterion for being a separate species, this bird deserves that status. Yellow-eyed juncos (earlier called Mexican junco) were just as numerous within the forest. Pygmy nuthatches were common in the stands of ponderosa pines. And high in the foliage of the pine and fir communities were olive warblers. In more open places, painted redstarts busied themselves flycatching in typical redstart manner.

Plans for Resource Protection

During the pre–Big Bend National Park days of the 1930s, a grand plan for an international park that would include the mountains and desert on both sides of the Rio Grande was encouraged by U.S. officials and other interested persons. Early park planners made a serious attempt to include the Sierra del Carmen in the planning process. The U.S. National Park Service sent biologists to both sides of the river to make initial surveys. Botanist Ernest G. Marsh, Jr., visited the del Carmen mountains and prepared a 1936 report on his findings, encouraging the establishment of a comprehensive national park comprising the best of both countries.

After Big Bend National Park was designated in 1944, biological surveys continued. As part of an ecological study of the new Texas park, a team of scientists including Walter P. Taylor, Walter B. Mc-Dougall, Clifford C. Presnall, and Karl P. Schmidt visited the northern half of the Sierra del Carmen in spring, 1945, and reported on this survey the following year.

A Mexican "national park" was finally identified during the 1970s, and several Mexican maps included a park boundary line for the Maderas del Carmen park. However, the area received no administration or management and only minimal protection; and I discovered that local residents were unaware of park status.

Throughout the 1980s there was considerable communication about a "companion park" across the Rio Grande from Big Bend. According to Jim Carrico, Big Bend National Park Superintendent at the time, Coahuila governor Eliseo Mendoza Berrueto was very supportive of the establishment of a major park for the Sierra del Carmen. The governor or his staff "discussed designation proposals and their implications" of a companion park with U.S. Park Service officials five times during 1988.

Superintendent Carrico presented a paper on this issue at the November, 1988 Triennial Conference of the George Wright Society, in which he reported that much of the initiative for a Sierra del Carmen park is now coming from Mexico. He said that "members of the Coahuila Governor's staff have indicated that an area of approximately 1.6 million acres will make up the study area" in Coahuila. On September 7, 1989, an official program document, called "Programa de Desarrollo de Boquillas y Maderas del Carmen," complete with an exhibit of photographs and small scale models, was presented to Mexico's minister of tourism.

U.S. officials informed me that they believe that "high level SEDUE officials have personal interests in seeing the Sierra del Carmens receive protected status as well as proper management." SEDUE (Secretariat for Urban and Ecological Affairs) is analogous to the Department of Interior or Agriculture in the United States. However, only time will tell whether or not the good intentions expressed will become reality.

I hope that Mexico's policy makers will soon realize that the resources of the Sierra del Carmen are more important to the Mexican people if they are retained in their wild character rather than logged and hunted and mined. Mexico has a gold mine of another kind! A well planned national reserve can do more for the economy and opening up of the northern frontier than any logging operation or hunting program could possibly accomplish.

It may someday be possible for people from all parts of the world to enjoy the beauty and resources of the Sierra del Carmen. More than one million visitors annually travel thousands of miles to see Big Bend National Park. These same people may someday visit a companion park across the Rio Grande. And, perhaps, a few of them may stand on top of one of the massive cliffs of the Maderas del Carmen's west side and marvel at the kind of view that raises mind and spirit above the routine concerns of our petty world.

5

Alta Cima

Alta Cima will hereafter be synonymous with the golden-browed warbler. I found it almost everywhere in the Alta Cima area. Although I had seen this tropical warbler on numerous other occasions, throughout much of its range in Mexico, the Alta Cima birds seemed to be more colorful and more obvious than any of those I had seen earlier. Nowhere had its bright yellow eye-line, throat, and brow, contrasting with its deep chestnut cheeks and crown, been as evident. And in the right light its olive-green back and yellow underparts were also richer in color.

During the three days that I camped at the tiny Tamaulipian village of Alta Cima, I explored the forested slopes above the village along the higher eastern slopes of the Sierra Madre Oriental, as well as the canyons below. Wherever I went near Alta Cima, I was attracted to various bird parties because of the obvious *zi-zi-zi* calls of the little golden-browed warblers; in the vast majority of cases, initial detection of golden-brows led to seeing a larger bird party of several species. Golden-brow calls were more obvious than those of any of their companions. I found the best description of their call in Edwards's book, *A Field Guide to the Birds of Mexico*. He described it as "a very rasping metallic *zi-zi-zi,* much like the call of a Katydid, but weaker" (p. 221).

I never did find golden-brows very high in the vegetation; they were always at lower levels within the shrubs and smaller trees, and always with five or more other golden-brows. Their constant activity and almost continuous *zi-zi-zi* calls made them easy to track as they moved through the forest. Their most constant companions were two or more rufous-capped warblers. Crescent-chested warblers were usually members of the party, as well, but they feed higher in the trees. On one occasion I watched a fan-tailed warbler as it foraged near the ground. Its distinct "tail-fanning" behavior, very much like

that of an American redstart, was conspicuous. And the brilliant
blue color of the blue bunting was also part of the Alta Cima scene.
Finally, several North American passerines were usually found with
each party. These included (in order of abundance) ruby-crowned
kinglet; Wilson's, orange-crowned and black-throated green warblers;
solitary vireo, hermit thrush, black-and-white warbler, western tanager, house wren, and magnolia warbler.

Alta Cima, Tamaulipas

Alta Cima is situated at the end of a rough, eight-mile-long mountain road that begins at Gómez Farías, a small hillside town at the
end of the paved roadway. This is the same region of the Sierra Madre
Oriental that George Miksch Sutton tells about in his beautiful book,
At a Bend in a Mexican River. Sutton and Olin Pettingill wrote a
more scholarly account of their bird studies in the region for *The
Auk,* published in 1942. However, the majority of their bird records
were derived from the Río Sabinas lowlands east of the mountains.

Sutton and Pettingill were the first scientists to recognize and write
about the influence of the area's cloud cover. The almost perpetual
clouds produce a tropical climate that is similar to cloud forest habitat much further south. Their list of bird records was more typical
of the tropics than of northeastern Mexico. We now know that the
Gómez Farías region contains what is considered to be America's
northernmost cloud forest habitat. That was what I had gone there
to see, and that special environment was most accessible from Alta
Cima.

I was one of seven gringo visitors to Alta Cima. The idea for the
trip came from Bill Graber, who had visited Alta Cima the year before
and been so impressed that he decided to return to see the area more
extensively and to write a bird-finding article for ABA's *Birding* magazine. Our party planned to spend a few days at Alta Cima just prior
to our participation in the Río Corona Christmas bird count. Gene
Blacklock, the Río Corona count coordinator, and friends Sharon
Bartels, Mark Elmonger, Dave Hirch and Les Lacy were the other
members of our party.

The village of Alta Cima lies within a beautiful little valley at
approximately 5,500 feet elevation. The high ridge above the village to the west is the same ridge visible from along the Río Sabinas
at the base of the mountain. Locally known as Sierra de Guatemala,

this ridge runs north to south for more than twenty miles, its highest points are more than 7,000 feet in elevation.

The village itself contained only a couple of dozen houses and outbuildings. Each family's land was surrounded by low stone walls that kept the burros, cows, pigs, goats, chickens, and turkeys more or less sorted, at least overnight. During the days they all seemed to wander at will, although the goats were daily herded down and back up the road to various feeding sites. The Alta Cima residents did not mind us camping within a little grassy meadow below their houses.

To say that Alta Cima marked the end of the road is not entirely correct, because two roads actually continue beyond the village from a fork in the center. The right fork goes down-canyon (this was the first entrance route), while the left fork crosses the upper part of the village and enters the forest. It then switchbacks upward for about four miles to where it crosses the Sierra de Guatemala ridge before descending a long canyon to the village of San José. A rough map of the area is included in Edwards's *1985 Supplement to Finding Birds in Mexico*. That map represents the count circle utilized for the Gómez Farías Christmas bird count.

Vegetation

The count circle includes five distinct zones of vegetation, mapped by Paul Martin for his study of the herpetofauna of the Gómez Farías area, published in 1958. Many of the terms Martin used to describe the vegetation were borrowed from earlier papers by either Leopold in 1950 or Beard in 1955. Later, in 1983, Jerzy Rzedowski utilized Martin's vegetation map in his *Vegetación de México*. Accordingly, the base of the mountains is dominated by tropical deciduous forest. This zone is called *bosque tropical caducifolio* by Rzedowski, who listed four principal plant species (reported by Puig in 1970) for this area: gumbo limbo and lysiloma (often codominant), and Mexican laurel and Texas ebony.

Within the tropical deciduous forest is a narrow riparian habitat that follows the Río Sabinas. Although this environment is minimal in scope, it is an important habitat for wildlife. The dominant tree species there is the beautiful Montezuma bald cypress, a tall stately tree with drooping foliage.

Just above the tropical deciduous forest is a narrow band of semievergreen forest or, according to Rzedowski, *bosque tropical sub-caducifolio.*" Rzedowski referred to Puig's 1974 description of this area, and listed the following plant species: gumbo limbo, figs, hackberry, *Nec-tandra* sp., *Robinsonella* sp., *Drypetes lateriflora,* and *Sargentia greggii.*

Above these on the eastern slope is cloud forest, Rzedowski's *bosque mesolfilo de montana.* This is the habitat that is so distinctive because it represents an important northern extension of the Neotropics. It forms a narrow band between approximately three thousand and five thousand feet elevation. Rzedowski referred to Sharp's 1950 description of this area, and listed the following tree species: sweet gum and two oaks (*Quercus sartorii* and *Q. germana*) were dominants, and wild cherry, podocarp (a native member of the gymnosperm family Podocarpaceae), a beautiful magnolia known locally as *corpus,* Mexican alder, maple, hickory, and a fir (identified only as *Abies* sp.) were common.

Above the band of cloud forest is a humid pine-oak forest, which Rzedowski calls *bosque de quercus.* He once again refers to Martin's plant list for this habitat which is dominated by Montezuma pine and three oak species (*Quercus affinis, Q. diversifolia* and *Q. reticulata*). The latter species is netleaf oak, which also occurs north of the border from Texas to Arizona. Rzedowski points out that pine stands in the highlands often include both Montezuma and Aztec pines in association with weeping juniper, Texas madrone, and walnut.

The western slope of the highlands contains two additional vegetation zones: a large area of drier pine-oak woodlands that is interspersed with chaparral. I did not visit these habitats during my 1989 visit to the area.

A simplified description of the vegetation zones of the Gómez Farías region appears in Fred Webster's 1974 article in *American Birds,* where he lists five zones as follows: "*Lowland tropical*—Riverside forest; cultivated fields; tropical deciduous forest to lower slopes of the Sierra. *Mountainside tropical*—Upper portions of tropical deciduous forest; tropical semi-evergreen or mountainside tropical forest to about 3,000 feet. *Cloud forest*—Oak-sweet gum and oak-sweet gum-beech cloud forests between about 3,000 and 5,000 feet. *Humid pine-oak*—Humid pine-oak forest mainly on eastern flank of the sierra from about 5,000 to 7,000 feet. *Dry oak-pine*—Dry oak-pine woodland and savannah on the western slope of the sierra (p. 5).

Alta Cima Birdlife

Dawn of December 27, 1989 was clear and cold at Alta Cima. Frost had formed overnight on the grass. Birds were evident only by their calls and songs that rang out around the clearing. The loudest and most obvious were those of the spot-breasted wrens; at least four individuals sang from the undergrowth. A blue mockingbird sang briefly, I detected songs of brown-backed solitaires and gray silky-flycatchers further up the hillside, and an Altamira oriole contributed to the morning chorus. Then a flock of twenty-five to thirty red-billed pigeons suddenly flew across the clearing toward the upper village, where I later learned there was a favorite watering hole.

As the sunlight reached the valley treetops it triggered further activities, and a few additional bird species made themselves known, the most obvious being the social flycatchers. These gregarious little birds lived up to their names; their constant *chee cheechee cheechee* echoed across the clearing. A Couch's kingbird added to the songfest. Several clay-colored robins flew into the open branches of an adjacent snag; they were accompanied by two American robins. And from the nearest vegetation I could hear the familiar notes of ruby-crowned kinglets and orange-crowned and Wilson's warblers. Our day at Alta Cima had begun.

Mark and I left camp first. We wandered through the village, across the upper pasture, and followed the left fork trail into the forest. Almost immediately new sounds greeted us. The first was the mournful whistle-call of the dusky-capped flycatcher; I still prefer the old name, olivaceous flycatcher. Plain chachalacas, three I think, were next detected in the upper foliage; these large birds were surprisingly adept at moving through the canopy with minimal disturbance. A white-tipped dove glided silently across the roadway from a nearby perch and disappeared into the forest. Below us along the densely wooded slope we could hear a rufescent tinamou. Its call was a plaintive double-note whistle, like *whooo-ooo* with the second note slightly higher in pitch than the first. It had such a ventriloquistic quality that we couldn't be sure of the distance or direction.

As we progressed higher along the track, we heard green and brown jays on several occasions, and caught sight of one or two individuals as they flew ahead of us. We stopped several times to sort out the species within a bird party. We added two yellow-winged tanagers

Alta Cima village in central Tamaulipas, on eastern slopes of
Sierra Madre Oriental.

at one stop, and a lone rufous-browed peppershrike a little further
on. It had been more than three years since I had last seen a peppershrike, and I took time to examine this unique species. Until recently
it was classified within the New World family of Cyclarhidae that
included only two members, the Mexican rufous-browed peppershrike and the Andean black-billed peppershrike. The 1983 AOU
Check-list, however, includes these two species as members of a sub-
family (Cyclarhinae) of the larger family Vireonidae. Although its
yellow, greenish, and gray colors and rufous brow provide it with
excellent camouflage among the foliage, its rather sluggish characteristics make it a fairly easy bird to observe once it is spotted.

A thousand feet or so below the ridgetop we began to find an
increasing number of sweet gums, trees characteristic of cloud forest
habitat. The scientific name of this species is *Liquidambar styraciflua;*
the genus name seems most appropriate. A clear amber is secreted

by the tree when injured. That material was used as soap and incense by the highland Indians.

Suddenly we detected a raptor at about eye level a quarter of a mile to the east. As soon as we got our binoculars on the bird we recognized it as a peregrine, and then realized that we were watching a pair of these magnificent birds. We gazed with fascination as they rolled and dove together time and again. They put on a wonderful exhibition of aerial maneuvering for us. Such a sighting of this endangered species made me appreciate our visit to Alta Cima even more.

Montezuma pine and an assortment of oaks dominated the ridgetop. There, too, were the ever-present golden-browed warblers. We heard a least pygmy-owl calling reasonably close by, but we never did locate this elusive little predator. At the very top of a tall pine was a greater pewee. A flock of black-headed siskins was present nearby, and very near the pass we watched a pair of pine flycatchers busy in the upper foliage of pines at the edge of a clearing.

Had time allowed this, we would have continued down the road to the west, maybe as far as San José. It appeared that the western roadway was in much better condition than the route we had followed above Alta Cima. I couldn't help but wonder if the western slope might have produced some additional birdlife.

We started back toward Alta Cima by 2:00 P.M. We added summer and western tanagers, bronze-winged woodpecker, and mountain trogon before we got back down to the sweet gums. Then just ahead of us at the very top of a tall snag was a bat falcon. We approached slowly so as not to frighten it, and I was able to work my way into a position directly below the dead tree from where I took several photographs. It was a marvelous bird, its contrasting colors of black, white and rufous very obvious. After about fifteen minutes I went on, leaving the bat falcon still perched atop the snag.

The Lower Canyon

Before dawn the next day I walked along the entrance road for about a mile listening to the night sounds and anticipating the dawn chorus. The previous night had been cold, but I could find no frost as I had the previous morning. A pair of tawny-collared nightjars was active along the roadway fairly close to camp. One perched briefly in a small tree along the roadway, and I was able to see it well in the bright beam of my flashlight. I heard at least one additional bird calling further down the slope; all were singing a *chip-willow* song that was first described by Sutton.

After a brief breakfast, Mark, David, Lee, Gene and I hiked down the canyon, via the right fork. Once we passed through the village, the road became very steep and rough; I understood why the newer route that we had taken to Alta Cima was most popular. The lower canyon road would have been next to impassable. However, the bird-life along this route was outstanding.

"Trip birds" (those not already seen in the area) included smoky-brown woodpecker, spot-crowned woodcreeper, blue-crowned motmot, masked tityra, white-throated robin, long-billed thrasher, black-headed nightingale-thrush, Hutton's vireo, bananaquit, black-headed and crimson-collared grosbeaks, and yellow-billed cacique.

Of all the birds seen within the lower canyon, none was as surprising as the bananaquit. Although we saw it for only a few seconds, at approximately forty-five feet and in good light, there is no mistaking a bananaquit, especially after spending three years in the Caribbean where it is the most common bird species. It is a very striking yellow, black and white bird. The interesting thing about this sighting is that it represents a significant range extension. The bananaquit normally is found only north to Veracruz on Mexico's Gulf Coast. What it was doing at about 3,500 feet elevation in the Sierra Madre Oriental of southwestern Tamaulipas is anyone's guess.

Many of the birds seen within the lower canyon were feeding on berries from small trees with long, dark green leaves; I later identified them as wild cherry. They were among the few that apparently had not been damaged by a recent cold spell. Most of the trees and shrubs showed some evidence of stress; millions of dead leaves were still falling. These lower elevations, such as the canyon below Alta Cima, contained many more birds than I had found higher up. Throughout our stay I did not see one hummingbird. Many birds must have been affected by the extreme cold weather that reached far south into Mexico that year.

El Cielo Biosphere Reserve

A mile and a quarter below Alta Cima is a side road to the north that goes to Rancho del Cielo. A large sign had been placed at the junction by the Mexican government. It read:

"Reserva De La Biostera
EL CIELO
ESTRICTAMENTE PROHIBIDO CAZAR
CAPTURAR EX TREAR SIN PERMISO
LA FLORA Y FAUNA SILVESTES."

The sign also contained the name and symbol of the government organization responsible for its protection and operation, SEDUE (Mexico's principal natural resource agency).

Rancho del Cielo is one of two sites where Texas Southmost College has biological research stations. The use and operation of this station within the biosphere reserve is under special permit from SEDUE. Rancho del Cielo is situated at 3,800 feet elevation in the Sierra de Guatemala, part of the Sierra Madre Oriental. Rancho Cielito, the second site, is in the lowlands on the banks of the Río Sabinas. The lowland site is easily accessible by car, just off Mexico Highway 85 at Encino, but Rancho del Cielo requires four-wheel-drive capability even during the best of seasons.

A total of 357,134 acres of the El Cielo area was established as a biosphere reserve, under the auspices of the United Nations' Man and the Biosphere program (MAB). Such an international designation gives the area greater recognition as a significant natural system, and also provides emphasis for programs of sustainable development throughout. The MAB program objectives for biosphere reserves are most appropriate for this unique area. They include:

"1) to conserve for present and future use the diversity and integrity of biotic communities of plants and animals within natural ecosystems, and to safeguard the genetic diversity of species on which their continuing evolution depends.
2) to provide areas for ecological and environmental research including, particularly, baseline studies, both within and adjacent to such reserves, such research to be consistent with objective (1) above.
3) to provide facilities for education and training" (p. 11).

Biosphere reserves are established through the United Nations Charter but are the responsibility of the country in which they occur. The Mexican government has established several biosphere reserves in various parts of the country, and is to be commended for its efforts. It is therefore most important that visitors to this area be aware of the global importance of its resources. Precautions must be exercised to preserve the natural integrity of the wild lands and at the same time to understand and support the interrelationships between nature and the people who live on the land. Their continued existence depends upon the care they give their homelands.

6

Rancho Nuevo

The loudest of the bird songs was coming from a thicket where a spot-breasted wren repeated its song over and over again. Another spot-breast was singing further ahead along the centerline of my transect. Off to the right was the drawn-out *who who wooo* of a red-billed pigeon, and I could hear another a hundred yards ahead to the left. Plain chachalacas, at least four individuals, were also calling somewhere beyond. Two brown jays were screeching in the trees just ahead. An olive sparrow sang from some shrubs a few yards to the left, and further to the left, maybe four hundred feet away, a ferruginous pygmy-owl added its repetitive single-noted whistle to the chorus. I also detected at least three masked tityras and a golden-fronted woodpecker calling from the same general area. The distinct call of a tufted titmouse, fairly close, was almost overlooked. Further off to the left I detected an elegant trogon; then I heard another at about the same distance to the right. And about three hundred feet ahead, a great kiskadee joined in the dawn chorus.

Early mornings in tropical forests are like nowhere else. Bird songs are by far the dominant sounds. The singing may last for as little as twenty minutes or more than an hour, depending upon the time of year and weather. Some birds sing their territorial song only during this brief period of the day, although they may call or sing other less expressive songs at various other times of day. Most bird songs are totally different than their calls. To hear the greatest number of bird songs at the peak activities, one must be out early to experience the dawn chorus.

Thorn Forest Transect

I had left camp at 5:00 A.M. and driven approximately six miles to an area of seemingly intact thorn forest habitat that I had found a couple days earlier. By 5:35 I was positioned at the start of my transect and ready to begin. The day was perfectly calm, although patches of ground fog occurred here and there. The temperature was exactly seventy degrees Farenheit. The forest was full of bird song. I had arrived in time to catch the dawn chorus.

All of the birds detected at the start of the transect, as well as all those I found elsewhere along the designated route, were noted on a field record sheet marked with squares representing specific locations in the study plot. The half-mile-long transect line was divided crosswise into twenty-six 100-foot intervals, with four 100-foot-deep intervals paralleling the centerline on either side. The resulting transect of $208 - (26 \times 8) - 100$-foot squares yielded a total coverage of fifty acres.

Besides those initial songs of the dawn chorus, I detected several additional birds by either sight or sound during the first few minutes of the transect. A yellow-headed parrot flew from a perch in a strangler fig tree early on, and was joined by two more individuals as it flew away. Three brown-headed cowbirds flew overhead in the same general direction I was moving, and I observed an olive sparrow scratching on the ground for seeds just off the centerline. The pecking of a large woodpecker attracted my attention ahead to the left; I found a lineated woodpecker working on a tall snag. Just beyond, a pair of green jays suddenly flew out from the foliage of a *ceron,* in hot pursuit of a passing roadside hawk that I had not seen until then. The hawk must have been perched nearby. A pair of brown jays joined in the chase for a short distance, and then disappeared into the heavy foliage. And four red-crowned parrots flew out of another huge fig tree, approximately 350 feet to the right, where they apparently had been silently feeding on fruit.

Slowly I progressed along the centerline of the transect, walking about one or two miles an hour, but stopping many times to observe or record the various birds. I heard the plaintive whistle of a thicket tinamou fairly close by to the right, and another called ahead of me to the left. I found a common black-hawk nest in a naked Indian tree; both birds had been near the nest when I first approached but flew silently off a couple hundred feet and perched in another tree. I left the transect line to inspect the nest more closely but found no evidence that young were present. When I returned to the centerline I observed four crimson-collared grosbeaks in a large patch of grapevine-like vegetation. Three Mexican crows called to one another as they flew right to left across the study plot. And I detected the distinct buzzing call of a migrant dickcissel flying overhead, as well.

Although it is important to progress slowly and carefully along a transect so as to detect all of the various birds present, it is difficult not to be distracted by other animals or unique plants along the way. I was once drawn away from the transect by a noisy family of coatis, sometimes called coatimundis and locally known as *Pisote*. They were feeding on fruit in a large fig tree about fifty to sixty feet off the centerline, and for a short time I watched their acrobatic antics in the upper canopy. I had seen this fox-sized mammal in southern Arizona on several occasions, usually feeding on the ground like a hog or armadillo. But this was the first time that I had had an opportunity to watch it in action in its more tropical habitat. Its prehensile tail was used like an extra hand, and I was amazed at its agility.

The transect itself, the detecting and recording of the birds in the field, is the most enjoyable part of this type of study. However, it is only a small part of the total project. The second step is to transpose information recorded in the field onto a second record. This summary sheet is a list of all the various species and the number of each recorded at various distances from the centerline of the transect. I also use it to summarize the totals. For example, I detected forty-nine bird species on the May 7 transect described above. I had recorded a total of forty-three individual red-billed pigeons. Only four of those had been detected within the 100-square-foot blocks next to the centerline; eighteen individuals had been in the second pairs of 100-foot squares just beyond; nineteen had been recorded in the next pairs of blocks; and two had been recorded in the pairs of 100-foot squares along the far edges of the transect.

The computations and analysis of all the collected data occur back in the office. Although it is sometimes possible to relive some of the memories of a field trip during this latter process, it is mostly a chore that is tedious and grueling. But the results of the computations and analysis can be extremely worthwhile, both in regard to a better understanding of the particular bird community being studied, and also for providing insight into the significance of the habitat. In the case of Mexico's thorn forest, I found it surprisingly productive and extremely important to the biological integrity of the entire region.

Thorn Forest

The term "thorn forest" comes from Dr. Starker Leopold's classic 1950 paper, "Vegetation Zones of Mexico," in which he first identified and described Mexico's many plant communities. Leopold's thorn forest habitat type was called "thorn woodland" by Beard in 1955. In 1971, Flores and his coworkers published a vegetation map of Mexico on which this same general habitat was called *selva baja caducifolio,* meaning short and dry woodlands. And Jerzy Rzedowski referred to thorn forest as *bosque espinosa,* or thorny woods, in *Vegetación de México.*

Whatever differences these botanists may have had about the name and distribution of Mexico's thorn forest, they all would agree with some basic characteristics. Thorn forest habitat is a scrubby, thicketlike woodland, forty to fifty feet in height, and dominated by thorny leguminous trees, particularly acacias. The diversity of the tree flora, however, is relatively poor with thirty or fewer species, and ground cover is usually absent or sparse.

Plant ecologists would also agree that the thorn forest habitat is the result of the natural forces exerted upon it, most notably the amount of annual rainfall. Annual rainfall in deserts is rarely more than sixteen inches, and that of mesquite-grasslands will vary from nine to thirty-six inches. Annual precipitation in thorn forests ranges from ten to thirty-four inches. Savannah habitat, a vegetative zone often associated with thorn forest, requires an annual rainfall of thirty-four to one hundred inches.

These four types of vegetation are more or less restricted to the Mexican lowlands, usually below 4,500 feet elevation. (The mesquite-grasslands can be the exception to this, also occurring in some of the more arid upland valleys in north-central Mexico.) Thorn forest habitat is often bordered by tropical deciduous forest vegetation on adjacent foothills. Tropical deciduous forest is taller, possesses fewer spiny plants, and requires more humid conditions. It often serves as a transition zone between the lowland thorn forests and savannah and the Mediterranean-type pine-oak woodlands higher up a slope.

There are three widely separated thorn forest areas in Mexico. All three strips of land are approximately fifty miles wide and fairly close to the coastlines. But the total acreage of the combined sites is less than 3.5 percent of Mexico's total land surface. The three areas occur along the west coast, the Gulf Coast, and near the tip of the Yucatán Peninsula.

Mexico's most extensive thorn forest region occurs on the Pacific slope. The northern border starts in southern Sonora, just south of Ciudad Obregón, and runs south along the coast through the states of Sinaloa, Nayarit, Jalisco, Colima, Michoacán, and Guerrero to just north of Acapulco. This elongated zone of thorn forest is interspersed by large "islands" of wetter savannah vegetation. On the Gulf Coast, thorn forest occupies a large area of east-central Tamaulipas and continues south along the coast to northern Veracruz, about one hundred miles south of Tampico. The third region of thorn forest occurs on the Yucatán Peninsula in a band along the north coast and situated between a coastal scrub zone and the inland tropical deciduous forest.

Rancho Nuevo Projects

I spent ten days within the Rancho Nuevo area of southern Tamaulipas (about forty miles north of Tampico) in May, 1978. The main purpose of my visit was to assist with a sea turtle project that I had helped design. Clyde Jones of the U.S. Fish and Wildlife Service and I (representing the National Park Service) had developed the idea, initiated a feasibility study that was done by Duke Campbell, and had invited several sea turtle scientists to participate. Drs. Archie Carr and Henry Hildebrand of the United States, and Rene Márquez of Mexico had been members of the initial advisory group that we established.

The purpose of the project was twofold: to provide increased protection to nesting Atlantic ridley turtles, and to restore a nesting population to Padre Island, Texas. Mexico's Rancho Nuevo was the only known location where this endangered species of sea turtle still nested in numbers. Its original nesting range probably included the entire Gulf Coast, but since 1947, when a movie film had been made of some forty-thousand ridleys nesting on the beach at Rancho Nuevo, their population had drastically declined. By 1977, the world's population was estimated at only twenty-five hundred. Padre Island Na-

Eggs taken from a laying Atlantic ridley turtle (lower right) during a project to restore this sea turtle to Padre Island, Texas.

tional Seashore was one of the few areas within their ancestral range where a nesting beach could be given complete protection.

Our plan was to increase protection of ridleys at Rancho Nuevo by focusing attention on the area during the nesting season, and to move some of the eggs from the natal beach to Padre Island for hatching and imprinting. We transported Padre Island sand in styrofoam boxes to Rancho Nuevo. A total of two thousand eggs were caught by hand as they were being laid by nesting females, and never touched Rancho Nuevo sand. The styrofoam boxes filled with ridley turtle eggs were then stored at Rancho Nuevo for forty days, until they were far enough along in their development to be moved. Not until then were they flown to Padre Island where they were held until they hatched.

On the fiftieth day they began to hatch. Each morning for five consecutive days the hatchlings of the previous day were released at

Atlantic ridley turtle being tagged at Rancho Nuevo, Tamaulipas, after egg laying is completed.

the high-tide line at Padre Island. The dollar-coin-sized youngsters
were allowed to crawl down the beach and into the surf. We believed that this was the way to be sure they would imprint on Padre
Island rather than further south.

The hatchlings were then collected from the surf, after they had
had the opportunity to swim in the Texas Gulf. Then they were flown
to Galveston and placed in large holding tanks maintained by the
National Marine Fisheries Service. They were fed high protein "trout
chow" throughout their stay at Galveston. Once they were large
enough (by the following spring they were plate-sized) to stand a
better chance in the wild, they were released into the Gulf along
Florida's west coast where they could continue their natural growth.
We hoped that when they reached maturity, in another twelve to
fifteen years, the adults would return to Padre Island to nest.

A total of nineteen hundred baby turtles survived the hatching and imprinting stages at Padre Island in July, 1978, an incredibly high hatching success of eighty-eight percent. A similar program has been undertaken each year since then. The number of eggs received at Padre Island from Rancho Nuevo annually has ranged from two thousand to three thousand and the number of hatchlings released into the wild has ranged between fourteen hundred and two thousand. Each individual released was tagged for later identification. A few of these have been discovered from the east coast of Florida to Chesapeake Bay. Further details of the ridley turtle project were published in the November, 1979 volume of *National Parks & Conservation Magazine* (Wauer, 1979). The final result of the program has not yet been determined.

Rancho Nuevo Plantlife

Although I was busy working with ridley turtles on the Rancho Nuevo beach every day after midmorning, early mornings were free. I had gone to Rancho Nuevo prepared to study the birdlife of the area, as well as to work with the other scientists on the ridley turtle project.

The native vegetation of the Rancho Nuevo area had been classified by Leopold into littoral and thorn forest types. For the sake of censusing the birdlife, I broke these two major zones into five reasonably distinct habitats. The one closest to the Gulf—in front of, between, and just behind the dunes was considered littoral habitat, much influenced by the tides and the salty air from the sea. Vegetation was sparse and usually only a few feet high, except for occasional shrubs. Glasswort, sea blite, and batis dominated the salt flats. Sea ox-eye daisy formed dense thickets in places that were less influenced by the tides. The occasional solitary shrubs were most often one of two acacias: huisache or bullhorn.

Beyond the littoral zone was a low scrubby habitat, little more than cut-over, secondary thorn forest, which I called thornscrub. The area was heavily utilized by cattle that kept much of the vegetation from recovering. Some of the common plants of this habitat included Spanish bayonet, huisache, bullhorn acacia and blackbrush, mesquite, goat-bush (a shrub with crooked spiny branches and reddish-purple flowers), desert yaupon, hackberry, two species of *Condalia*, tullidora (a shrub which has edible fruit but seeds that can paralyze wildlife and humans if swallowed), barreta and cenizo. Two large cactus species—*Lemaireocereus* and *Acantrocereus*—were also present throughout.

The "pure" thorn forest started a few hundred yards further inland. The best of this zone seemed to occur in patches of tall, mature woodland that showed no evidence of cutting. This habitat was the subject of a 1977 report by Martínez and Gonzáles, who listed several trees and shrubs for the Rancho Nuevo vicinity. The most numerous species, in descending order, included desert yaupon, barreta, and hackberry; naked Indian (a smooth, reddish-barked tree similar to Texas ebony); strangler fig (the tallest and most dominant tree in the community); *ceron* (a tall tree of the elm family); *jaboncillo* (another tall tree, with gray, fissured bark and seeds said to contain thirty-seven percent saponin, a plant glucoside that can be used as soap when mashed in water); cigarbox tree or *cedro* (another tall tree with smooth, gray bark and very durable and fragrant wood that is used for making cigar boxes); bread-nut tree or *moju* (which produces numerous small seeds that are utilized by the locals for their nutritious values); and phoebe (a tropical tree with long green leaves). Several of these species reach the northern edge of their range near Rancho Nuevo.

Lagoons were widely scattered along the coastline, usually where freshwater streams entered the gulf. One of these lagoons was located adjacent to our camp, and I discovered that it was the result of damming by shifting dunes. The outlet was only a few feet deep and very narrow, so narrow in fact that I was able to jump across. Fifty feet inland, however, was a deeper, brackish lagoon that widened to 250 to 300 feet at the widest place, and then narrowed again approximately 110–120 yards from the outlet to become more of a freshwater stream than a lagoon. The edges of the lagoon provided another habitat where I recorded three kinds of mangroves: small button (*Conocarpus erecta*), red (*Rhizophora mangle*), and black (*Avicennia nitida*). And I found several small blue bromeliads, a species Martínez and Gonzáles identified as *Tillandsia ionantha*, growing on the mangroves.

The freshwater streamsides provided an additional habitat of riparian vegetation that was the most luxuriant of the five. This plant community contained all of the same dominant tree species as occurred in the thorn forest, although strangler fig and naked Indian appeared to be more numerous. In a few places further up the stream, where it became quite narrow and intermittent, some of the tree trunks formed buttresses that dammed up the flowing stream to create miniature ponds surrounded by a truly jungle-like atmosphere.

Bird Census Results

Once the five vegetative units were adequately identified, I located sites within each that were large enough to permit me to survey the birdlife without too much influence from the adjacent habitats, although this was awkward in the riparian and mangrove areas because of their elongated character. All the vegetative types were then censused three or four times each, between one half-hour before dawn and about 10:00 A.M. By midmorning the days became too warm for the birds to remain fully active. I was able to run at least two double half-mile-long transects per day, amounting to twenty-eight censuses from May 2 to May 10.

I recorded a total of 146 bird species within the five study plots during the nine days. Only seventy-seven (53 percent) of those birds were considered to breed on site, however. The remaining sixty-nine species (47 percent) were considered as transients only; either migrants passing through en route to breeding grounds further north, or incidental visitors to the area. This group included birds that might nest nearby but for which I found no evidence of nesting within the five transects.

The thorn forest habitat possessed far and away the largest number of breeding birds. I found a total of fifty-three species nesting in that primary habitat. Forty-five species were found in the riparian zone, thirty-nine in the thorn scrub, twenty-six in the mangroves, and fourteen were found nesting in the littoral habitat. The richness of the thorn forest habitat was not too surprising because that is the principal habitat for that part of Mexico. This zone also contained the largest number of true Mexican birds (seventeen), those that do not reach the United States for nesting.

The five habitats censused supported a total of twenty-four Mexican specialities. The full list of those thorn forest Mexican species included the thicket tinamou, roadside hawk, red-crowned and yellow-headed parrots, squirrel cuckoo, mottled owl, blue-crowned motmot; the smoky-brown, lineated and pale-billed woodpeckers; ivory-billed woodcreeper, masked tityra, spot-breasted and white-bellied wrens, crimson-collared grosbeak, blue bunting, and melodious blackbird. Four additional Mexican species were recorded in the riparian habitat: bare-throated tiger-heron, boat-billed heron, Aztec parakeet and yellow-throated euphonia. One bird, the yellow-faced grassquit, was added in the thornscrub zone. The mangrove swallow was added in the mangroves, and the gray-crowned yellow-throat in the littoral zone.

Unfortunately the thorn forest is one of the regions of the country vulnerable to destruction. Tremendous areas of Mexico's flatlands are being cleared for either agricultural or grazing purposes. My study suggested that the loss of the thorn forest habitat could eliminate approximately twenty-three percent of the breeding birdlife of Mexico's northeastern corner. And there are numerous other resources, as yet unknown, that would also be lost.

Clearing of tropical thorn forest is directly related to the abundant demands upon the natural systems in Mexico made by U.S. consumers. Americans have become so dependent upon the fast food industry, where we can purchase everything from hamburgers to tacos, that extensive tracts of Mexico and Central America are being cleared of native forest for pastureland for beef cattle. It is a sad commentary about our way of life that we threaten key ecosystems for the temporary benefits that we are tempted to enjoy by the advertising minions of multinational corporations. How incongruous our world is when a television advertisement produced in New York City can threaten the thorn forest in southern Tamaulipas, Mexico.

PART II

Baja and Sea of Cortez

Baja and Sea of Cortez

7

Baja Norte

The word "Baja" evokes a broad range of images, from grueling desert auto races to exotic deep sea fishing, and from Tijuana nightlife to quiet desert solitude. In truth, the eight-hundred-mile-long Baja California Peninsula represents all of these and more. To naturalists, or anyone with a zeal for exploring and learning about the environment, Baja offers an exciting smorgasbord of natural treasures.

The topography is rugged in the extreme. Mountains dominate the peninsula, forming a jagged backbone that runs the entire length of it. The highest of these—the Sierra de Juárez and Sierra San Pedro Mártir—are in the north. They are continuous with the Sierra Nevada in southern California and extend approximately two hundred miles south of the border. Picacho del Diablo (Devil's Peak), located in the central Sierra San Pedro Mártir, rises to 10,126 feet elevation and is the highest point on the Baja California Peninsula.

The high dominating sierras serve as a natural barrier to the moist air of the west coast, creating a much drier environment on the eastern gulf slope. The winds of the cool Pacific keep the west slope at least nine degrees Fahrenheit cooler in summer and warmer in winter than the gulf slope. These factors produce a Mediterranean type climate in the northwest that supports a flora and fauna more like that of southern California than like the remainder of the Baja Peninsula. In fact, the northwestern corner of Baja, west of the high mountains, is classified by biogeographers as Californian province. The lowlands east and south of the high mountains are part of the Sonoran province.

The international boundary between the United States and Mexico is a straight line drawn across the terrain between the sister cities of San Diego and Tijuana east to Yuma, Arizona. At Yuma, the Colorado River serves as a more natural boundary between Baja Norte and Arizona for approximately twenty miles to the south.

A vegetation transect along the border would record chaparral on all of the western slopes, scattered pinyon-juniper woodlands at the higher elevations, desertscrub in the lowest and driest places, and a finger of riparian habitat along the Colorado River floodplain.

There are two popular Mexican border cities along the California–Baja Norte border, Tijuana and Mexicali. Tijuana receives many U.S. day (and night) visitors, but it is not very representative of Old Mexico. Mexicali, on the other hand, is more of a farming community, complete with several good restaurants, and in my opinion, provides the visitor with a better perspective on the real Mexico.

Most travelers to Baja Norte cross the border from San Diego to Tijuana, and then pick up new Mexico Highway 1 that runs the entire length of the peninsula. Highway 1 between Tijuana and Ensenada is an excellent four-lane toll road that follows the coastline for about seventy miles. It is built for speed and to transport lots of people into the Baja heartland. Old Highway 1, which follows the contours and crosses the newer highway numerous times, is also available to the traveler. It provides better access to the countryside and the various villages scattered along the coast.

Many of these northern villages have come into existence only during the last dozen years or so, since so many U.S. citizens have "discovered" northern Baja. The results are a series of fine homes built at strategic places overlooking the beautiful Pacific Ocean, and several housing developments scattered between Tijuana and Ensenada. There are places along Mexico Highway 1 where the scene is reminiscent of Malibu, California. This changing character of the northern portion of Baja Norte apparently has improved the local economy. The state of Baja Norte came into existence as recently as 1952; prior to then the area did not have the necessary population of eighty thousand people to be designated above district status in the Republic of Mexico. Don Belt's December, 1989, article in *National Geographic* provided a recent Baja Peninsula population estimate of 2.5 million persons, with approximately eighty percent crowded near the U.S. border.

Birding Baja Norte

I visited Baja Norte in January, 1983, for the express purpose of finding a number of birds that occur in Mexico only within the northwestern corner. Several months earlier I had made a list of every pos-

Dunes near Ensenada, Baja Norte; behind are foothills of Sierra de San Pedro Mártir.

sible bird that I had not yet seen in Mexico. I then classified each species by its most likely area of occurrence, and discovered that there was a possibility of finding as many as thirty-eight species new for me in Mexico within this northwestern region. Some of these, such as the pelagic species which only occur offshore, and then sometimes only during storms, were most unlikely. The chance of finding them on one trip was exceedingly poor. On the other hand, there were several land bird species of regular occurrence, those primarily of California or southwestern U.S. affinity. Several of these occur in Mexico only during wintertime. From experience or reading, I pretty well knew the proper habitat where each might be found. The plan was to visit those sites and try to find as many as possible.

A full list of "probables" included thirty-one species: red-throated and arctic loons; white-winged and black scoters; mountain quail; chukar (an introduced species); black rail; surfbird; the mew, Thayer's and glaucous-winged gulls; black-legged kittiwake, Lewis' and Nuttall's woodpeckers; Williamson's sapsucker; American crow; Clark's nutcracker; pinyon jay; mountain chickadee; plain titmouse; wrentit; California and LeConte's thrashers; varied thrush; tricolored blackbird; Abert's towhee; the sage, fox and golden-crowned sparrows; purple finch; and Lawrence's goldfinch. By the end of the five-day Baja Norte trip, I had found eighteen of the thirty-one species.

My traveling companions on this Mexican excursion were Woody and Bo West, from Los Alamos, New Mexico. We took the San Diego tram, a fast and painless method of transportation, from a downtown hotel where we had stayed overnight, to the border. Once in Mexico we hailed a taxi that took us to Tijuana's National Car Rental office. Two hours after crossing the border we were driving south on Highway 1 toward Ensenada.

We found the Baja Norte coastline almost as rugged as the mountains, and to me it was reminiscent of the Oregon coast. Our first stop was at a good pull-off along the highway at the El Rosario turn-off where we could scope the coastal area, including some rocky outcroppings just below the highway. We found surf and black scoters as well as a lone red-throated loon off the coast right away. The rocks below the road were busy with shorebirds and gulls, including both ruddy and black turnstones, wandering tattler, surfbird, marbled godwit, Heermann's and California gulls, and a lone glaucous-winged gull.

The Chaparral Habitat

Across the highway from the oceanside pull-off was a little canyon, filled with a covering of chaparral. Wrentit and California thrasher, Bewick's wren, brown towhee and song sparrow were common there, just as they are within this kind of environment throughout California's western lowlands. In a similar area nearby, among the abundant, wintering white-crowned sparrows, we later located another chaparral species, the golden-crowned sparrow.

Chaparral is the low-growing and very dense vegetation of southern California hillsides and is well known for its ability to burn hot and rapidly. Almost every year there are millions of dollars' worth of losses from fire that sweeps over the dry hills, destroying homes and other property. In truth, chaparral is a fire-dependent type of natural vegetation; it must burn on a regular basis if it is to persist. Without it as a natural stabilizer of the hillsides, a goodly part of the west coast slopes would long ago have been eroded into the ocean. Chaparral has taken millions of years to evolve into the unique and valuable habitat it is, and the occasional efforts to replace it with other more exotic forms of cover are illogical and a potentially serious threat to an area's many native plants and animals.

Typical chaparral habitat extends down the Baja Peninsula between the coast and the higher mountain slopes for approximately two hundred miles. Dr. A. Starker Leopold described it in his paper, "Vegetation Zones of Mexico," published in the scientific journal *Ecology* in 1950: "Chaparral is a well-known vegetational formation comprised of such genera as *Adenostoma* [chamise], *Rhus* [sumac], *Ceanothus* [wild lilacs], *Quercus* [oaks], *Artemisia* [sagebrush], *Prunus* [cherry], *Eriogonum* [buckwheat], *Arctostaphylos* [manzanita], and *Cercocarpus* [mountain mahogany]" (p. 512). In the United States, chaparral occurs from the west coast to the Texas Big Bend country. It always forms low, dense thickets of five or more of these nine genera of plants.

We followed Old Highway 1 south most of the way. It provided us with much better viewing of the coastline and the adjacent fields and croplands. Each time we came upon flocks of blackbirds we looked for the tricolored blackbird, a west coast endemic that occurs only from southern Oregon to central Baja. We found hundreds of redwings, thousands of Brewer's blackbirds, and finally just north of Ensenada, feeding in a cultivated field with many of the above, we observed three tricolored males.

Bahía de Todos Santos

Ensenada is a pleasant coastal community that caters to anglers. It is situated on a large, open bay known as Bahía de Todos Santos (Bay of All Saints), and the harbor is lined with fish canneries and charter fishing businesses. Fishing boats of all sizes and shapes filled the harbor when we arrived. These ranged from huge ocean-going cannery ships to modest single-family fishing boats. Ensenada also has an abundance of restaurants that advertise fresh seafood. After finding a room at Misión Santa Isabel, in the heart of Ensenada, we went out to continue my lifelong research on good restaurants.

And our selection of the Bahía Ensenada was a huge success. The three of us ate excellent seafood dinners, complete with plenty of tortillas, for a total of seventeen dollars.

Dawn found us along the Punta Banta road that circles Bahía de Todos Santos to the south and terminates at the little tourist village of La Bufadora. There were earlier sightings of short-eared owls along the bay, but in spite of being out at dawn in the right habitat, we found none that day. We did see common barn-owl and great horned owl just south of town, and I found a solitary sage sparrow (another bird of my quest) along a sandy flat area on the inner bay.

The road crossed a high promontory above the sea and then dropped into La Bufadora, nestled within the rocky shoreline of a little bay. The surf rushed in and out with tremendous force, and great surges of water splashed skyward where the tide met the rocky coastline. The road ended in a small parking area, from where a trail led to a viewing platform above a particularly rough and foaming cove that contained a spectacular display of sea power. Each wave forced a massive amount of seawater into a natural grotto with a hole at the top and created a huge geyser-like plume that erupted with a deafening roar. It was a fascinating sight, and we better understood the name of the place. *Bufar* is a Spanish word meaning to choke or snort, and La Bufadora identifies this as the place where the sea chokes and snorts—a most appropriate name.

There were only a few birds in the vicinity of the rough waters. Of most interest were the American and black oystercatchers feeding together on the rocky shoreline. In the United States, American oystercatchers are found only on the East Coast, while the black oystercatcher is a Pacific Coast species only. Both species utilize their large bills (bright red in color) for feeding. Henry Marion Hall best describes their feeding behavior in *A Gathering of Shore Birds*: "One plunged its bill into the wet sand as if groping for something and twitching out a small clam. In similar fashion they seize blood-worms, shrimp, and juicy sand-fleas. . . . Molluscs are their favorite food, although they also take sea-urchins, crabs, and small starfish. Their stout beaks make mince-meat of such creatures, but are equal to much harder work. They chip barnacles and mussells off shoreside rocks, and readily split open razor clams and other small shellfish" (p. 29).

The most common bird species at La Bufadora was the Heermann's gull. We watched with amazement as several fished within the very heavy surf. This gull is unique because it actually reverses the usual direction of migration. Adults breed along the Baja coastline and nearby islands, and post-nesting birds usually go north afterwards to spend their summer and fall along the California, Oregon, and Washington coasts.

Sierra de San Pedro Mártir

Our primary destination on this trip was the highlands of the Sierra de San Pedro Mártir. I wanted to visit the upper slopes of these mountains where we might find some birds of the coniferous forests. We turned off Highway 1 just south of the little village of Colonet, and headed east on a reasonably good gravel road. It followed the Río Lermo at first, and then began a series of ups and downs, in and out of rather large valleys with some impressive farmlands where wheat, barley, and beans were the dominant crops. It was an even fifty kilometers (thirty miles) to the Meling Ranch, where I had made reservations for us to stay three nights. We arrived in the early afternoon, and after checking in, we explored our surroundings.

The Meling Ranch is situated at approximately twenty-two hundred feet elevation within a rather arid valley that holds a shallow stream bordered for a mile or so by riparian vegetation. Cottonwoods and willows were the dominant woody plants along the stream. The surrounding hills were strewn with granitic boulders. The scene reminded me of the area along the eastern side of the Sierra Nevada near Lone Pine and Bishop, California. The geology and the vegetation of these two areas are similar. Chamise was the dominant plant species there, scattered between the abundant weathered boulders.

We found the birdlife at the Meling Ranch rather sparse. Only a few of the more than two dozen species we found there stand out as somewhat special. Two of these seemed out of place so far from a city, the European starling and house sparrow. These exotic but hardy species had found the Meling Ranch in spite of its isolated location. I also was surprised to find a pair of red-shouldered hawks there within the streamside vegetation, but I later learned that this area of Baja is the southwestern edge of their west coast range. Both mourning and white-winged doves were common there, as well.

I expected to find Nuttall's woodpeckers there and was not disappointed. This west coast species was common within the riparian

Meling Ranch, at twenty-two hundred feet elevation, in a little valley on western slopes of Baja's Sierra de San Pedro Mártir.

habitat, and represented another bird of my quest. The biggest surprise was a least flycatcher, a bird usually found only in the eastern half of North America. That night, as I walked alone along the stream, the "bounding ball" song of a western screech-owl vibrated across the little valley.

Beyond the Meling Ranch, the graveled road begins a steeper climb onto the western flank of the San Pedro Mártir. We found fox sparrows and more sage sparrows on the open sage flats ten miles or so above the ranch. Five miles further on we left the vehicle and wandered up an oak-filled canyon. It was there that we found a northern pygmy-owl — below its normal habitat of pines and other conifers — and a small flock of mountain quail, another quest bird. We also found a solitary Lawrence's goldfinch there; much higher in elevation than normally recorded.

The sprinkling of pines on these lower mountain slopes is Parry pinyon, a four-needled pinyon found only in northern Baja and in extreme southern California. The range of this little pine demonstrates the close relationship between southern California and the adjacent woodlands of Baja Norte.

Driving on, we finally reached the taller forest some twenty miles above the Meling Ranch, and just beyond this we entered Parque Nacional Sierra de San Pedro Mártir. This national park includes 157,500 acres of forest and chaparral. A second national park, Parque Nacional Constitución de 1857, is located approximately forty miles to the north in the Sierra Juárez. It is considerably smaller, covering only 12,375 acres, but contains a large lake. This northern park is most accessible from La Rumarosa, near the United States–Mexico border.

The road beyond the San Pedro Mártir park entrance continued to climb up through a very dense forest for another two or three miles to a pass, at about eighty-five hundred feet elevation. There we found a barrier; the road was blocked beyond with snow. We decided to leave our rental car there and to hike up the ridge to the north. We found the slope surprisingly steep and the forest heavier than expected. It took us the better part of two hours to reach an open area high enough up the ridge to offer a good view of our surroundings, but the view was truly spectacular.

We could see the higher ridges to the north and east—Picacho del Diablo is among a series of huge, rounded granite peaks—and we could see an observatory dome on the eastern ridge. The closed road continued to that observatory and then across the mountains to pavement at San Felipe. It is possible during warmer times of the year to cross the peninsula by this route as part of a circle trip that could include Mexicali or even Parque Nacional Constitución de 1857.

The view we had to the south provided the best perspective on the total San Pedro Mártir massif. We could see at least fifty miles of forested peaks. But the view west was best. I counted eleven ridges, one after the other, laid out in parallel lines. Backlighting made each stand out in various pinks and purples. Although we understood that we were still fifteen hundred feet or so below the highest peaks of the San Pedro Mártir, it was an impressive sight nonetheless.

The forest around us was equally impressive. The grandest of the trees there, as in California's Sierra Nevada, was the sugar pine. We found it fairly common along the highland slopes; it towered over most of the other pine species. I also identified knobcone and Jeffrey pines on the ridges, and ponderosa pine was abundant just below. Douglas-fir was present within the highland forest as well. And aspen and white fir have also been reported for these highlands, but I did not see any in the area above the park's west entrance. The shrub understory within this upland forest was surprisingly heavy, and consisted primarily of those plants listed above for the chaparral habitat.

During the better part of the day that we spent in the upland forests of the San Pedro Mártir, we recorded only twenty-one bird species. Two of those—Clark's nutcracker and mountain chickadee—represented new Mexico species for me. The additional species included: turkey vulture, sharp-shinned and red-tailed hawks, northern flicker, acorn woodpecker, yellow-bellied sapsucker, hairy woodpecker, scrub jay, plain titmouse, bushtit, pygmy nuthatch, Bewick's and canyon wrens, Townsend's solitaire, western bluebird, cedar waxwing, rufous-sided towhee, dark-eyed junco, and pine siskin.

All of the time I was in these mountains I watched the sky for a bird that I knew would not appear. But as a born optimist, it would have been against my character not to expect a California condor to come soaring over the ridge. None did, of course, in spite of the fact that these mountains are within the historic range of this endangered species. A California condor would have been easy to identify with its nine-foot wingspan and clear white patch along the underside of the black wings next to the shoulder. No one knows when these huge scavengers disappeared from the San Pedro Mártir, although a bird was reported as late as 1971.

Even though the United States and Mexico signed a natural resources treaty in 1942, to provide special protection to a number of wildlife species, key Mexican and U.S. wildlife continue to decline. The last of the natural population of this condor finally retreated to a tiny fragment of their original range in southern California. The U.S. Fish and Wildlife Service, in its *Endangered Species Technical Bulletin* of May, 1979, reported: "No more than 30 of the huge cathartids are believed to survive in mountainous areas north of Los Angeles, where their future is especially precarious because of increasing land development, diminution of food supplies, lingering pesticides, pollution, and other threats" (p. 1).

In his 1988 book, *Rare Birds of the World,* Guy Mountfort reported: "The last surviving wild birds have now all been taken into captivity, bringing the total in captivity to 27, and as a last resort captive breeding is being tried. Twelve condors have already been hatched successfully over the last few years but all from eggs taken from the wild, and it remains to be seen whether the captive condors can successfully rear young behind bars. The wild population can now be regarded as extinct" (p. 56). It is a sad commentary that a nation that can place an astronaut on the moon was not willing to take the steps necessary to save a wild population of one of the world's most magnificent birds.

The Meling Ranch was a comfortable and pleasant place to hang our hats during our three-day exploration of the western slopes of the Sierra de San Pedro Mártir. It lacked some of the essentials of our western society, such as electricity and telephones, but it was more than adequate for our needs. During much of the year it is filled with hunters and explorers of various kinds, but there was only one other family there during our stay; they told me they came annually during winter from southeast Alaska. The Meling Ranch undoubtedly provides a quiet getaway place for anyone seeking solitude and a dry upland environment.

I was not able to learn a great deal about this rustic hideaway. The present owner—Bertie Meling—is the granddaughter of the original owner. She operates the ranch with the help of three or four others. She told us one story about the early days of the Mexican revolution when her grandparents were forced to leave the ranch for safety in Ensenada. Revolutionaries appropriated the ranch for their own purposes for a couple years. However, at the close of the revolution, the family returned, rebuilt those structures that were damaged, and began life anew.

I later discovered a brief discussion of the Meling history in William Weber Johnson's *Baja California.* According to Johnson, the original Meling family came to Baja from Norway, attracted by the large land grants offered by the Mexican government during the nineteenth century. They survived as cattle ranchers, miners, and farmers. Bertie Meling is now the ruling "matriarch, not only of her own family but of a good part of northern Baja California as well—Mexicans, Indians and foreigners alike" (p. 78).

Boojum trees, which occur only in central Baja Norte within a
unique community of desert succulents.

The Boojum Forest

When we again reached Highway 1, we turned south and continued
to about twenty-five miles beyond the village of El Rosario. This was
the land of the boojum trees, the upside-down-carrot-shaped plant
that is called *cirio* (candle) in Spanish. The name boojum was derived from Lewis Carroll's imaginary inhabitants of "far, lonely, deso-
late coasts," in *The Hunting of the Snark,* according to naturalist
Joseph Wood Krutch. Boojum trees are restricted to a relatively small
area in central Baja and an even smaller area across the gulf on the
Sonoran mainland. Some plants reach sixty feet in height, but most
are less than twenty-five feet. It is closely related to ocotillo, a common plant of Mexico's northern deserts. Like ocotillo, it produces
leaves only during rainy periods; the entire plant can leaf out almost overnight. Red flowers appear at the very top.

This boojum-succulent desert habitat I found to be one of the most unusual places on earth. We walked out into the desert forest to get better acquainted. My first impression was that boojums were much more numerous than I had expected; there were several hundred per acre. Most of these were tall and thin, while others, probably much older ones, were short and fat. The texture of the trunks varied, too. Some were almost spongy, while others seemed hard and woody. Some grew in odd shapes and had tips that curved almost in circles; others actually trailed out on the ground.

The landscape was filled with the strange forms of true desert vegetation. I counted eighteen kinds of cactus. The large tree cactus cardon was present on the rocky ridges, while organ pipe, senita and barrel cactus were most obvious on deeper soils. I found some beautiful little *Mammallaria* cacti, and there must have been five different prickly pears. Shaw's agave and *Yucca valida* were also common throughout.

Baja's boojum environment seemed more like an arboretum display of succulents than a real-world desert scene. The unique, surrealistic-looking boojum forest provides a fitting transition zone between the Californian influence that so dominates Baja Norte and the desertscapes further south.

8

South of La Paz

Only three of Mexico's nearly one thousand bird species are restricted to the southern portion of the Baja Peninsula—Xantus' hummingbird, gray thrasher, and Belding's yellowthroat. None of the three has been found in northwestern Baja where the Californian environment is dominant or east of the Sea of Cortez on the Mexican mainland. Their limited ranges make them true endemics to Baja California. Therefore, for anyone striving to find all of Mexico's avifauna, a trip to Baja is an absolute necessity.

The Xantus' hummingbird (sometimes called black-fronted hummingbird) is a gorgeous little bird that can hold its own with any species in the animal kingdom. The male possesses a green back and chest, velvety black throat and face, distinct white ear-stripes, a deep chestnut belly and rufous tail, and a short but bright red bill tipped with black.

Baja's gray thrasher is a rather slender, brown-gray bird that looks very much like a dull long-billed thrasher of northeastern Mexico. Its breast spots are black and triangle-shaped; its tail, unlike that of long-bills, is tipped with grayish-white. It looks somewhat like the smaller sage thrasher that only winters in Mexico.

Southern Baja's third endemic is the Belding's yellowthroat; it was earlier called peninsula yellowthroat. This is a small warbler that can easily be confused with the common yellowthroat, and a few scientists believe they are one and the same. The color patterns of the two species differ only slightly; the stripe above the black mask and belly are yellowish on Belding's, not whitish as they are on the common yellowthroat.

The Mazatlán–La Paz Ferry Trip

The southern half of the Baja California Peninsula can be reached by air, by ferry boat from Topolobambo, Mazatalán or Puerto Vallarta, or by road from the California-Mexico border. Mexico Highway 1 begins at Tijuana and runs the entire length of the peninsula. Except after damage by occasional severe storms, which usually occur in late summer or fall, the complete route is paved. Highway 1 ends at Cabo San Lucas, the southern tip of the peninsula, more than a thousand miles from Tijuana. Guerrero Negro, the west coast town just south of the twenty-eighth parallel (the legal border of Baja Norte and Baja Sur), is almost halfway down the peninsula, and La Paz is 475 miles south of Guerrero Negro.

My visit to Baja Sur was designed for the primary purpose of finding Baja's three endemic birds. It actually was an extension of a longer trip to the Sierra Madre Occidental highlands near Mazatlán, in May, 1982 (see chapter twelve, "Place of the Tufted Jay"). Woody and Bo West, of Los Alamos, New Mexico, and I planned to take the Mazatlán–La Paz Ferry one-way to Baja and to return to Mazatlán three days later via Aero México. Our intention was to board the ferry late one afternoon, sleep on board, and be ready to explore the region south of La Paz the next morning. However, our well-planned agenda went awry right from the start.

We arrived at the Mazatlán ferry terminal at about 2:00 P.M. to learn that all overnight accommodations on board were already filled. Although we would be permitted to board, we would have to sleep in deck chairs all night. We voted against that plan and decided to try again the following day. The ferry left daily at 4:00 P.M., and we were told it would be wise to be in line by 9:00 A.M. if we expected to rent sleeping facilities. We rented a car and spent the rest of the day exploring the Mazatlán area.

By 8:30 the next morning we were back at the terminal and in a line that already was more than a hundred people long. The ticket office did not open until 11:00 A.M., but even then the line did not move. New people continued to arrive, and many of those were allowed access to the ticket office. When I asked for entry I was told I must wait in line; an armed Mexican marine stood guard. It was not until some time later that I noticed that most of the new arrivals were going first to an office on the second floor, and upon emerging from there they went directly to the ticket office where they were permitted to enter. So, at about 1:00 P.M., I decided that I would try that route. Sure enough, Juan was the man to see. He gave me a special pass to enter the ticket office below. I was immediately per-

mitted entry, and within twenty minutes had procured three ferry
tickets with tourist class bunk space, all three for 780 pesos (about
six dollars at the time). I never did figure out why so many people
were standing in line for so long. We had asked twice about the
line, and were told that everyone was required to wait in that line
for all available accommodations. Maybe so, but next time I'll know
enough to take the obvious short-cut. Six hours of waiting in the
May sunshine was a little too much for anyone who had just arrived
from the cooler east coast (as I had) or from the New Mexico highlands.

We boarded on time! Our ferry boat, the *L. M. Loreto,* was a huge
modern ship that could hold more than eighty trucks and automo-
biles in its bowels, and could accommodate 250 people in its sleeping rooms. Another hundred or more slept either sprawled out on
the deck or in chairs within a large cabin or outside in the open.
The first class *cabinas* were already filled by the time I discovered the
rites of passage, but the still available tourist class rooms that we
rented were clean and adequate.

We immediately found what we assumed was a mistake in the
way our tickets had been issued; two were stapled together, and the
single ticket was marked "Señorita West." I resolved this problem
by keeping the single ticket for myself and giving Woody and Bo
the two that were stapled together, so that they could share one room.
We then went our separate ways to search for our cabins. Mine contained four single bunks, two on each side of the room. However,
just as I was selecting a bunk, in walked a young woman of about
twenty, who seemed rather upset to find her roommate to be male
instead of female. She immediately started talking faster than I could
understand. Although I smiled and tried to explain my presence,
she must have misunderstood my extremely poor Spanish, because
off she went for help.

I decided then that the better part of valor was to find Bo and
trade tickets. By then I had realized that the tourist class rooms were
not meant to be shared with the opposite sex. But just as I picked
up my bag, the door opened again and two more young women
entered. Neither seemed surprised at my presence; in fact, they
seemed rather pleased to have a guardian such as I for the trip across
the gulf. I tried to explain that I was just leaving, that there had
been a mistake and I was about to correct my error, when the door

opened again, and in came a huge man with the first young woman in tow. He was one of the porters, if that is the right term on a ferry boat, and was no doubt there to see to it that no one was unduly hassled on his ferry boat. He could speak enough English for me to explain my situation, which he translated to the three young women. This whole process took about ten to fifteen minutes. And just as everyone seemed to understand, Bo walked in and claimed her rightful bunk. She and Woody had also discovered the error. I was relegated to another room up the hallway near the bow of the ship with three other men, two of whom snored all night while the third got up at least a dozen times to go down the hall to use the toilet. I suppose this was well-deserved punishment for my fantasies involving three beautiful dark-eyed señoritas.

Pelagics

The *Loreto* left on time, and within a half-hour we were out in the gulf and moving northwest toward La Paz. This ferry trip represented my first major crossing of open ocean in Mexico and I expected to find a variety of pelagic birds from the deck. But it was not to be. In spite of my vigil that afternoon until it was too dark to see, and again the following morning from dawn until we landed at the La Paz terminal, I recorded only six species of birds: a lone brown pelican near shore, many blue-footed and brown boobies, several magnificent frigatebirds, and, most exciting, a few sooty and black-vented shearwaters.

The shearwaters are true pelagics, oceanic species that only occur on land for the purpose of nesting. Even then, they select a few islands far off continental coasts. They nest in one- to four-foot-long burrows, which they dig in soil or vegetation. Migrants may occur off the coast in the thousands. Ralph Palmer, in describing habits of West Coast shearwaters, wrote that "100,000 is a low estimate of birds one may see in a single day during s. migration off Cal. shores" (p. 178).

Shearwaters are reasonably short-bodied birds with long, tapering wings. Their name is derived from their behavior of sweeping very low over the ocean waves, "shearing" the surface with their wing tips. They feed on fish, squid and crustaceans at sea, either from the surface or by pursuing their prey underwater. Peter Harrison, author of *Seabirds: An Identification Guide*, "once recovered several sooty shearwater corpses from crayfish pots set at over 20 fathoms (approximately 120 feet) off New Zealand" (p. 260).

Of nineteen known species of shearwaters, twelve have been reported for Mexican water. Only two — sooty and black-vented — are reasonably easy to find, coming into Mexico's Sea of Cortez in spring and summer. The sooty is well named because of its overall sooty coloration; the exception is the whitish underwing coverts. The black-vented shearwater is dark brown above and white below; the flanks and the crissum (vent) are sooty brown in color.

Boobies are also pelagic in the sense that they depend upon the sea for their sustenance. The brown booby is more likely to be found in bays than its blue-footed cousin. Both were common along the Sonoran coast, but neither was seen during the next morning near La Paz.

I found magnificent frigatebirds reasonably common along both the Sonora and Baja coastlines. For me, no other bird better represents tropical waters as does this huge creature. It looks almost prehistoric, like a modern-day archeopteryx. Its great wings span ninety inches, but the distance between its long, forked tail and gigantic, hooked bill is less than half that. Frigatebirds are the ultimate "flying machine." On an earlier trip to Los Mochis and Topolobambo, Sonora, I was amazed at the abundant frigatebirds that spent the entire afternoon and evening soaring over my seaside hotel. They remained soaring around and around above the hotel for hours on end. Because I was curious to know if they might perch overnight, before I went to bed I set my alarm to awaken me at midnight, and then reset it for 2:00 A.M. and 4:00 A.M. Each time when I was awakened, I ventured out of my room to find the same number of frigatebirds still soaring over the hotel. I am convinced they were the same birds each time, sleeping in flight.

The brown pelican is one of our coastal fishermen that is seriously threatened by the abundant use of DDT in Mexico. Although it once was a common species all along the Mexican coastlines, populations have been seriously reduced since the invention of DDT and its use as a pesticide on Mexican farmlands. Although DDT is no longer permitted to be used in the United States, and northern brown pelican populations have greatly increased since the ban, that is not the case in Mexico. The United States continues to manufacture DDT, legally, and sell it to Mexico. All wildlife within the top levels of the food chain — brown pelicans as well as peregrines, many kinds of hawks, bats and several other carnivorous mammals — continue to be affected. Also affected are the many bird species that breed in the United States and overwinter in Mexico or migrate through Mexico's farmlands.

La Paz

On arrival at the La Paz ferry terminal after the sixteen-hour crossing, we immediately took a taxi to the La Paz airport. There we made reservations for a flight back to Mazatlán in two days, rented an Avis car that we had reserved the day before, purchased some groceries before leaving town, and were soon headed south on Mexico Highway 1.

La Paz appeared to be a very pleasant city, overlooking a bay crowded with fishing boats and pleasure craft. Several sailboats were already out on the bay when we arrived. La Paz has been an important city for more than a hundred years. It became capital of the southern territory of Baja California in 1830, and is now the state capital of Baja California Sur. It was occupied by U.S. troops in 1847 and 1848, during the war with the United States. And since completion of the trans-Baja highway (Highway 1), La Paz has become a popular trading and shopping center. Its current population is 102,000.

John Steinbeck used La Paz as the setting for his book, *The Pearl*, because of the many beautiful black and pink pearls that have been found in La Paz oysters. However, the pearl fishery has completely died; locals believe that a disease in the oysters was somehow responsible. Today, the town's principal sources of revenue are tourism and commercial fishing.

As we drove south, we watched carefully for hummingbirds. We found an Allen's hummingbird at a flowering fencerow at the edge of town, and a stop at a desert arroyo forty-five minutes later produced several Costa's, but no Xantus'.

We stopped for lunch at San Bartolo, at a little roadside restaurant partially covered with bougainvilleas and smelling sweetly of citrus flowers. We had no sooner placed our order when Bo spotted a hummingbird directly outside the nearest window. And there it was! A male Xantus' was feeding at flowers of the little lime tree just outside our window. That first sighting seemed to break the spell; later we saw several more as we progressed south toward Cabo San Lucas.

The beautiful Xantus' hummingbird of Baja Sur might more properly be named the black-fronted hummingbird—more descriptive and less exotic—but it was named for its discoverer, John Xantus, a Hungarian exile, according to Edward Gruson in *Words for Birds* (p. 136). Gruson says John Xantus made his way to the United States about 1850, where he "began to live an itinerant life as a bookseller, druggist, and teacher of languages and the piano." In 1855, he enlisted in the U.S. Army, where he became acquainted with Dr. William A. Hammond, an amateur ornithologist and friend of Spencer Baird, secretary of the Smithsonian Institution. Xantus was assigned to Fort Riley, Kansas, first, then Fort Tejon, California, and then, through the influence of Baird and Hammond, from 1859 to 1861, he was appointed "tidal observer" for the U.S. Coast Survey at Cabo San Lucas. It was during this period of his life that he first collected the endemic hummingbird. Accordingly, the initial description of the new bird acknowledged its collector.

Ann Zwinger in *A Desert Country Near the Sea* writes that Xantus was unhappy when "Baird gave the type specimen of this hummingbird to George Newbold Lawrence, a leading ornithologist" to prepare the first description. However, Lawrence's description of 1862, stated: "Sent by Mr. John Xantus, whose investigations in the Ornithology of Western North America have been the means of adding many new birds to science. In compliment to him I have named it" (p. 40). In 1862, John Xantus was appointed consul in Manzanillo, Mexico. Hoever, according to Gruson, "he promptly embarrassed the State Department by recognizing a war lord in revolt. His diplomatic career came to an abrupt end. Shortly thereafter, he returned to Hungary" (p. 136).

As we progressed south, exploring the more brushy arroyos en route, we began to think about overnight accommodations which are few and far between in this area. One of the ferry passengers had suggested staying at the Hotel Palomar at the little village of Santiago, about three-quarters of the way from La Paz to Cabo San Lucas. Since it was midafternoon by the time we reached the Santiago junction, we left the main highway and drove the short distance into town. We found Santiago to be a fascinating place. The village has evolved around a marshy depression near the town square. The numerous cultivated fields and orchards are connected to this

Cabo San Lucas beach, at southern tip of Baja Peninsula, consisting of quartz sands.

water source. It was obvious that the availability of water was the all-important reason for Santiago's existence. As we circled the square, we found a little weather-beaten sign that directed us to the town's one and only hotel.

The rooms were barely adequate, but the food that evening was excellent. Some Americans we met at dinner informed us that the Palomar had once been a very special place for wealthy Americans to come in winter to hunt ducks and doves, and to get away from pressures of the outside world. U.S. President Dwight Eisenhower had been a guest there on several occasions, according to a yellowed newspaper article pasted on one wall. The classy accommodations and setting had been drastically changed in 1976, when a hurricane had destroyed the motel and grounds. We talked to owner/manager Sergio Gomez, a relative of the earlier owner, who confirmed the once important status of his hotel.

Hurricanes, locally known as *chubascos,* apparently visit southern Baja on the average of one each year. September is the usual month for hurricanes, but they can be expected any time from early summer through fall. Most originate off the Mexican or Central American coast and move northward, often crossing Baja in this area and dying out in the mountains of Sonora. More than half of the annual rainfall in southern Baja is derived from hurricanes. Downpours often result in extensive flooding and changes in the landscape. The marshy depression around which Santiago was built is the result of just such a hurricane. Across the road from Hotel Palomar was an extensive orchard of lime and orange trees and a scattering of date palms. Some sugarcane was growing along the edges and in the wetter soils. Hard brown candy, called *panoche,* is produced locally from the cane and sold in the markets. Figs, raisins, dates and sugar are the principal crops of southern Baja.

For me, the greatest attraction in Santiago was the large freshwater marsh, about the size of three football fields, seemingly out of place in the surrounding desert environment. We investigated this area late in the afternoon, after checking into the hotel, and again early the following morning. A good part of the marsh had been planted with cane, and numerous date palms circled the area. The extremely tall date palms suggested that Santiago's marsh had been present for many years, probably revitalized by each passing hurricane.

We found a total of thirty-five kinds of birds within and adjacent to the marsh. Most importantly, we found at least four pairs of Belding's yellowthroats! There also were about the same number of common yellowthroats. After watching all these birds for some time we concluded that the Belding's yellowthroats were actually defending territories. In one case I observed a male Belding's carrying nesting materials. We did not get this same feeling of territoriality from observing the common yellowthroats, and we assumed these individuals were still present as wintering birds. The field marks of the male Belding's yellowthroat were clearly distinct enough to be identified with the naked eye.

The most common birds we found there were white-winged dove, scrub jay, hooded oriole and house finch. There were a couple of surprises as well: two singing male indigo buntings, an eastern United States breeder, seemed out of place in this far western corner of Mexico, and I found four clay-colored sparrows perched in an acacia; late wintering birds, no doubt. At dusk, the air was literally filled with lesser nighthawks and mangrove swallows.

After our morning visit to the marsh, we drove west on a rough dirt road that began just behind the Santiago marsh, into the desert beyond. One purpose of exploring the desert was to find the third southern Baja endemic bird that we had wanted to see, the gray thrasher. It is Baja's only breeding thrasher, and according to Peterson and Chalif's popular *A Field Guide to Mexican Birds*, it frequents desertscrub and mesquite habitat throughout Baja Sur. It is a true denizen of the desert.

Soon after we started across the desertscape above Santiago we discovered that gray thrashers were surprisingly common. They were fairly numerous within the brushy arroyos and less so in the more open terrain. We found a nesting pair of gray thrashers utilizing one of the spiny chollas.

The Southern Tip

Later in the morning, we again headed south toward the Cape, pausing to explore a new side road we had learned about into the mountains. Although we found the new road and were able to drive up it some eight miles, it was still under construction and ended several hundred yards below the fringe of woodlands that ran high onto the slope; we could see much larger trees along the crest. We were unable to reach the uplands without an extensive hike, for which we were not prepared. The highland area of these mountains is where the San Lucas robin is known to occur. This bird has since been lumped with the common American robin and is now considered only a subspecies.

Some maps show these mountains to be the Sierra de San Lucas, but the locals regard the rugged range that extends from La Paz to Cabo de San Lucas as the Serranía del Cabo. The highest peak is the Sierra de la Victoria, just over 6,000 feet in elevation. The road we traveled was not built for comfort, but it did allow us to see the surrounding desert environment better. As we progressed higher into the mountains we found the vegetation becoming taller and thicker, and we could see it changing from an open and arid desertscape to what some desert ecologists call thornscrub or *matorral aborescente* (short-tree thicket).

This area of vegetation included a number of dominant plants,

including two of the white-barked lysilomas, at least four of the
swollen-trunked elephant trees, a couple of palo verdes, honey mesquite, several species of acacias, ironwood, and lomboi. We found
one canyon that contained a beautiful little fanpalm that I assumed
was *Washingtonia filifera.* Cacti were numerous and included *pitahaya
agria,* senita, organ pipe, cardon, and several kinds of chollas and
prickly pears.

Afternoon found us beachcombing at the southern tip of Baja,
enjoying the beautiful blue-green waters and quiet surf. The area
had obviously been discovered by others as well. Most of our route
between La Paz and the cape had been free of trash and convenience
stores, but suddenly they again appeared. Although I was impressed
with the natural beauty of the area, I was mortified by its southern
California character, which I attributed to gringo influence. We had
intended to find a place to stay overnight, and to drive the 140 miles
back to La Paz the next morning, but instead we headed north after
only a few hours along the beach. We drove the entire distance to
La Paz, and found ourselves there just in time for a late dinner.

We again followed the advice of the man on the ferry and located
the La Posada Motel, a lovely and quiet place situated along the beach
just north of downtown. It provided excellent accommodations and
food. And its proximity to the bay afforded us, the next day, with
an early morning bird hike before returning to the La Posada restaurant for a delicious breakfast of huevos rancheros. The bird of
the morning was clapper rail—a trio came charging out of a mangrove thicket in response to my spishing. They came so close that
we all had an excellent look without the aid of binoculars. It was
a fitting finale to a quick and successful visit to Baja California Sur.

9

Whales, Birds, and Abalones

Our California Pacífico flight to Isla Cedros was literally stuffed full of equipment and supplies of one kind or another. Most of the heavier pieces, parts of machinery, tools, and canned goods, were tied in or strapped along the sides. The personal stuff, like suitcases and shopping bags, including my pack, were loose and stacked one upon the other. All of the heavier freight had been sitting alongside the tiny terminal all morning. It had taken the better part of two hours to load, after the flight was scheduled to leave. Not until then were the dozen or so passengers boarded. And we, like the rest of the load, were squeezed into what few empty seats remained.

Finally, the ancient DC-3 began to taxi down the runway. At one point I wondered if we had run over some small animal that had ventured onto the dirt strip, but decided it was just the condition of the runway when most of the other passengers ignored the bumps. And then suddenly we were airborne. The plane was heavily loaded and it had taken a longer than normal time to reach airspeed. I was one of the few passengers who had secured a window seat—just in time, because my seat companion was a gentleman who was not only overweight to the point of mashing me against the wall whenever someone passed down the aisle, but who also smelled like a distillery. I discovered immediately that I was better off looking out of the window than getter further involved with the happenings inside this flying box of humanity.

The reason I had hustled ahead to acquire a window seat, on the left side of the plane, was so that I could get a good view of the region. I wanted to get a better perspective on the town of Guerrero Negro and the adjacent saltworks that we would pass over, before we started across the bay. I had carried my camera aboard, hoping to photograph the massive salt flats behind Scammon's Lagoon. But I soon realized that the plane window would make this impossible;

it was so scratched and dirty that I could barely make out anything but the most obvious features.

The plane did circle over Guerrero Negro, human population about six thousand, and then it turned west across the channel toward Cedros Island. I was able to make out the glistening white salt flats south of the town and I could also see the blue waters of Scammon's Lagoon that seemed to encircle one section. Then we were flying over Vizcaíno Bay, following the northern shore of the Vizcaíno Peninsula toward Cedros. I detected a loaded salt barge below us also en route to Cedros. Then the DC-3 touched down and we rolled to a bumpy stop. We had arrived on Isla Cedros.

The passengers deplaned immediately, and we milled around outside until all of the personal goods had been unloaded on the desert floor. There was no terminal, just the end of the runway, which was within a few dozen feet of the island's one and only road, leading to the little village of San Isidro. The local taxi drivers had not expected six additional passengers, complete with packs and equipment enough to camp for two weeks. So we had to wait for almost an hour before the two available taxis had taken the locals to their destinations first. Only then did they have sufficient room to haul us and our belongings the six miles into town.

Isla Cedros

My first impression of Cedros Island was that it was a transplanted piece of California's Death Valley, complete with desert pavement and volcanic debris. The top of Cerro de Cedros, which forms a rather magnificent high point on the southern half of the island, was surrounded by cloud and a long bank of spent cumulus clouds hung along the southern horizon. The little vegetation evident at the southeast corner of the island, near the landing strip, consisted of a few shrubs in the muddy drainages along the edge of the roadway. Two cattle egrets searched for food in a small puddle of rainwater along the road and there were a number of gulls soaring overhead. The temperature was somewhere in the mid-eighties and a light breeze out of the north made it a very pleasant day.

One of the earliest descriptions of Cedros Island was by Dr. John A. Veatch, who developed mining properties on the island in the late 1850s. He wrote, "The island is broken and rugged in the extremes. The sombre and pensive grandeur of its barren peaks attracts in a

Sea lions along rocky northeastern shore of Cedros Islands.

forcible manner the attention of passing voyagers. On a near approach to the eastern side, the naked granitic cliffs of the north,
and the broken, upheaved, and contorted slate strata of the south,
present striking and interesting features. The whole island at a little
distance presents the look as if a collection of mountain-peaks had
been compressed together and planted by Titans amid the restless
sea-waves" (Bostic, p. 23). It is a most appropriate description of
the island's topography.

Cedros Island is situated only fourteen miles off the Baja mainland, and is considered part of Baja Norte. The island is twenty-four
miles in length, north to south, and varies in width from four to
eleven miles. The total land mass consists of approximately 134 square
miles. The land surface, however, would measure considerably more,
for the terrain is a wild assemblage of ups and downs. The highest
elevation is 3,950 feet at the summit of Cerro de Cedros. Pico Gill,
the highest peak on the northern end of the island, is 3,488 feet

above sea level. The terrain between the two peaks is just as rugged. To me, the geology looked very similar to that along the California coast at San Francisco.

San Isidro is clustered around a cannery and dock, where as many as seven or eight fishing boats were present most of the time. The town's 120 or so buildings ranged from those built to last indefinitely to a few that probably required stabilizing at least yearly. Our party of biologists selected a camping site near a small spring on the south slope of Cerro de Cedros, about a mile above town. And by late afternoon of May 19, 1979, we were able to sit back and take a good look at where we were.

Salt Production and the Whales

We had an incredible view of the south end of the island and Vizcaíno Bay. The tiny dot in the bay, halfway between Cedros and the mainland, was one of the barges used to transport salt from the Guerrero Negro saltworks to the Cedros loading docks. Ocean-going vessels are not allowed to dock on the mainland, and so the processed salt is barged across the bay to Cedros Island where it is loaded. Mexico sells approximately sixteen million tons of salt abroad each year, and one-third of that is produced at the Guerrero Negro saltworks. From our position, we could see the loading station at the extreme southeastern corner of the island, quite close to the runway where we had arrived.

The Guererro Negro saltworks that we had flown over is a sprawling one-hundred-thousand-acre labyrinth of salt pans and canals. Specially designed harvesters scrape up two thousand tons of salt from the drying basins each hour. ESSA (Exportadora de Sal S.A.), the Guerrero Negro-based company, claims to produce only natural sea salt that is 99.72 percent sodium chloride, the purest available on the world market. ESSA's peak annual production is about 5.7 million tons. Japan is the world's biggest salt importer, buying about half of its annual requirements from ESSA. Smaller quantities are shipped to Canada, Central and South America, Korea and the Philippines.

ESSA's corporate logo is a spouting whale, and a most appropriate logo it is. The Guerrero Negro saltbeds form the shoreline of Laguna Ojo de Liebre, more popularly known as Scammon's Lagoon. This shallow, natural bay, which contains one of the largest undeveloped inlets on the Pacific Coast, has a saline content of four percent, compared with three percent in the open sea. It serves not only as ESSA's first saltworks concentrating basin, but also as excellent calving grounds for the gray whale. The saltier waters provide greater bouyancy to newborn calves, which must be taught to swim. And ESSA proudly declares that its activities are compatible with these gentle giants of the sea. That is one reason that the loading docks were constructed on Cedros Island rather than along the shallow waters of Scammon's or other nearby lagoons utilized by wintering whales.

Charles Melville Scammon was an American whaling captain who discovered the lagoon in 1857, and began to harvest its incredibly rich resources. Scammon became so impressed with these and other marine mammals, however, that he later turned his energies from hunting to research and in 1874 he published a book titled, *The Marine Mammals of the Northwest Coast of North America described and illustrated together with an account of the American whale-fishery.* This represents the first personal account of the whaling industry and the destruction of the great whales.

Gray whales can reach forty-five feet in length, but average only sixteen feet when they are born. Unlike other baleen whales, grays are bottom-feeders, and scoop up mouthfuls of bottom materials that, in their northern habitat, are rich in crustaceans. The water and mud are filtered out through special baleen plates. But once they reach their southern wintering grounds, the adults will not feed again until they return to their northern territories; some scientists believe that they feed throughout the year. Adults migrate six thousand miles from Alaska to the southern Pacific waters each year, the longest migration undertaken by any mammal. Newborn calves are nursed within the protected lagoons during the first two or three months of their lives. By springtime, when they are large and strong enough to travel, they head north for Alaska.

Whale-watching has become a rather popular pastime in southern Pacific waters in recent years. It has also become a profitable business for hundreds of boat owners from Monterrey to San Diego and south along the Baja Peninsula. Guerrero Negro can be considered the whale-watching capital of the world, because of the significant wintering population of grays that utilize the area. The Mexican government has designated Scammon's Lagoon and much of Vizcaíno Bay as a whale refuge. Parque Natural de la Bellena Gris is one of the first of its kind anywhere in the world.

Purpose of Our Visit

I could not help but think how incongruous it was that our team of biologists had come to study the terrestrial resources of the island, while the surrounding waters were unquestionably so much richer. And yet I had long ago discovered that desert landscapes provide unique ingredients that are even more exciting to me. The Cedros Island Project, like that on Tiburón (see chapter ten, "Tiburón"), involved surveys and monitoring of wildlife and habitat as a joint study with the Mexican government.

Those projects had evolved through an official cooperative agreement between the U.S. Fish and Wildlife Service and Fauna Silvestre, Mexico's federal wildlife agency. Participants involved scientists from both countries, but the initial team of six, of which I was a member, were all from the United States. The others were Drs. Norman Scott (leader), Tom Fritts, Bruce Bury, Cathy Blunt, and Jean Duke. This team and a second group of scientists who arrived after I departed were to study the vegetation, mammals, birds, reptiles and amphibians, and insects. I was the lone ornithologist. And we discovered early on that Cedros Island secrets, which involved flora and fauna representative of both the Californian and Sonoran provinces, were not easy to come by.

John Steinbeck wrote about this affinity in *The Log from the Sea of Cortez*. He was writing specifically about the warm water mollusks and crustaceans that he and Ed Ricketts found on their journey along the Pacific coast. Steinbeck quoted Eric Knight Jordan, the son of David Starr Jordan, who had studied the lower California region, as follows: "Two distinct faunas exist along the west coast of Lower California. The southern Californian now ranges southward from Point Conception to Cedros Island. Probably extends a little farther. The fauna of the Gulf of California ranges to the north on the west coast of the Peninsula approximately to Scammon's Lagoon." Steinbeck went on to say, "We can confirm the significance of the Cedros Island complex as a present critical horizon where the north and south fauna to some extent intermingle" (p. 181).

The plant communities that we examined on Isla Cedros were unquestionably Californian in affinity. Many more species were found that were common in southern California than in the Sonoran Desert region. Except for rare coastal strips of saltbush and frankenia, we found that a desert community prevailed from the coast to near the tops of the highest peaks. Most of this habitat was very sparse, at least partially the result of many decades of overgrazing. Goats were introduced to the island by whalers in the early 1800s, and burros arrived some years later. The most interesting thing about this habitat was that it was almost completely devoid of trees. There were no tall woody plants. The closest thing to trees were a fairly common century plant and the equally common elephant tree. This latter species is an extremely heavy, large-trunked plant that rarely was more than six feet tall, and most often grew outward rather than upward. The Mexicans refer to this strange tree as *torote blanco* (little white bull).

I identified a dozen or so kinds of shrubs, many of which were blooming in early May. The most common of these included burweed, brittlebush, jojoba, and buckwheat. In some of the cooler, moist canyons I found a few bushy sumacs.

I followed the trail above our camp on two different days to the very top of Cerro de Cedros. That was the only place where I found the "cedars" after which the island was named; the little tree is not really a cedar, but a juniper. This is an extension of California juniper, according to Jerzy Rzedowski's *Vegetación de México,* further evidence of the presence of Californian province influence. Hundreds of these bushy, stunted trees were present along the highest slopes of Cerro de Cedros.

The view from the top was most impressive. I found myself perched at the summit of a green and gray island that was surrounded by a deep blue sea below and a bright blue sky above. Wisps of fog lay in distant crevices of Pico Gill to the north. The day was so clear that I felt I could almost reach out and touch the forested ridges in the distance. I could see small patches of Bishop pines. Looking south, I could see more than just the various features on the island; I could also see across the bay into Scammon's Lagoon. Although it was too late in the season for whales, I imagined that I could have seen those creatures as well.

Cedros Island Birdlife

It was there, at the very top of the world, that I saw a blue-throated hummingbird. I heard it first, a deep hum of wings that could be nothing else but a large hummingbird: magnificent or blue-throat. It took me a few minutes to find it because it was feeding on the red flowers of a chuparosa that was slightly below me and partially hidden from view. I studied this large, slow-flying hummer for several minutes before it flew off. Although it was a female, there was no doubt. It was far out of range, there at the summit of Cerro de Cedro, but part of the natural scene, nonetheless. A blue-throated hummingbird could have been expected on the hundred or so mountain tops on the Mexican mainland, but Baja is out of its normal range. That discovery proved once again that almost anything can occur in nature. Birds are particularly prone to wander away from their more "normal" range, or to be blown off track by storms. This sighting was the first for the Baja Peninsula.

I established three transects within the desert habitat in an effort to learn about the bird population of this sparse environment. Population studies can be done in a number of ways. But I had found that the easiest and most efficient method in desert areas was by slowly walking one-mile transects, in a fairly straight line, and recording all the birds detected, by both audible and visual means, on field sheets marked off in squares representing predetermined intervals. The raw data acquired from the three routes were later converted into birds per acre.

A total of thirteen species was recorded but only eleven of these were considered to be part of the breeding bird fauna. The eleven species included red-tailed hawk, American kestrel, mourning dove, Costa's hummingbird, Say's phoebe, common raven, Bewick's and rock wrens, northern mockingbird, black-throated sparrow, and house finch. Two of these made up fifty-three percent of the population, black-throated sparrow and Bewick's wren. If the rock wren were added to this group of dominants, the three would account for sixty-three percent of the total bird population within the island's desert community.

The black-throated sparrow was the island's most abundant bird, and I found it present from the shoreline to the top of the highest peak. I estimated the population at fifty-four individuals per hundred acres. The Bewick's wren was next in abundance, at thirty-eight birds per hundred acres, followed by the rock wren (29.5), Costa's hummingbird (16.5), mourning dove (14.5), and house finch (13). The additional five species were found in lesser abundance.

What was most interesting, perhaps, was what was not present. There were no air-soaring insect-feeders, such as swallows and swifts, nor any timber-drilling or timber-searching insect-feeders, such as woodpeckers and nuthatches. The mangrove swallow and white-throated swift breed on the Baja California mainland, as do three woodpeckers: northern flicker and the Gila and ladder-backed wood-peckers. None of these birds was found to nest on Cedros Island. Although the white-throated swift nests on cliffs or under large boulders on the ground, the other missing species require trees or large cacti.

If the additional Cedros Island birds which I recorded, those that are dependent upon the sea for their livelihood, were added to the list of desert community nesters, the grand total would have been thirty-two species. I was able to survey this second group of birds during portions of two days that I spent on a fishing boat along the coast. We traveled north from San Isidro to Punta Norte, around the northern tip of the island, and south along the western side to Puerto Escondido. I added an even dozen species, including the black storm-petrel, brown pelican; the double-crested, Brandt's and pelagic cormorants; osprey, black oystercatcher, willet, marbled godwit, a large colony of western gulls, Heermann's gull, royal tern, and Cassin's auklet.

Of greatest interest to me was the black storm-petrel, a pelagic species known to nest on islands off the Pacific coast of Baja California. This is a little (only nine inches long) all-dark bird with a reasonably long, forked tail. Its flight is most distinctive; deep, vigorous, but graceful. They appear to actually walk on the water. Nests are located in burrows or among boulders. Although I observed up to eighty-five seabirds fishing together off the northern end of the island, only one came close enough for identifcation. I believe that the majority of the other birds were of this species, as well.

Cedros Island's Fishery

The fishing boat that provided our transportation was one of those docked at the cannery pier at San Isidro. Every day of the week, except on Sundays, it traveled the same route to pick up freshly caught fish, abalones, and spiny lobsters from fishermen located at strategic places along the coast. That fresh catch was then returned to San Isidro and processed there at the cannery. The Pacific sardine is the most important of the three, and Bahía Vizcaíno is considered to be one of the best spawning areas on the Pacific coast. Abalones rank second in economic importance, and spiny lobsters third.

My personal priority included abalones as first, second and third, a ranking established after the second night in camp, when we decided to hike to town for an evening of local color. After a couple cervezas in the cantina, we were directed to an adjacent restaurant where we ordered the local speciality, a plate of abalone steaks. Now I was definitely not a neophyte when it came to abalone; I had grown up in the San Francisco Bay area, and I had experienced this mouth-watering delicacy many times before. But the combination of fresh abalone, tortillas, salsa, and frijoles was enough to make me seriously consider giving up a twenty-year career in the National Park Service and becoming a San Isidro fisherman. That was just the beginning.

I ate abalones four more times during my six-day stay on Cedros. On the third day we departed San Isidro for the two-day boat trip around the island. Our first stop was about twenty miles north at the little village of Punta Norte, where four passengers were put ashore. We quickly continued north to where we looped west around the north end of the island, to turn south once again along the west coast. We finally put in at Punta Escondido, another tiny fishing village, that seemed to be dangerously perched along the very steep cliffs behind a small and surprisingly well protected bay. It was there that we took on our first cargo.

The Punta Escondido produce included eight large plastic boxes, approximately three feet by two and at least twenty-four inches deep, completely filled with abalones. There also were several gunnysacks filled with fish of one kind or another, and two huge sea trout that were dumped onto the deck. Before long we were again en route back toward San Isidro. I looked over the abalones and found at least three kinds among the load. The captain identified these as green, pink, and white. Some of the greenish abalones were as much as ten inches wide; the pinkish ones seemed thickest, and the white ones were all the smallest.

The sea was much rougher on our return, particularly along the northern end, where our fishing boat seemed to struggle. I saw none of the pelagic birds that we earlier had encountered at the northwestern corner of the island.

When we again approached Punta Norte, this time to pick up a cargo of fish and abalones, the four members of our team who had taken this trip were rowed to shore. Our plan was to camp nearby overnight, investigate this part of the island, and return the next day with the boat to San Isidro. On landing we were greeted by several gentlemen, including the village *alcalde* (mayor), who invited us to his house for dinner. We readily accepted his gracious offer, and were escorted to the largest and nicest house in town, back from the beach a hundred feet or so. I was not sure whether it had been a spur of the moment invitation or if he and his wife had discussed it beforehand, but we were welcomed with all sincerity, and she immediately set about preparing dinner for four gringos that she had never before seen.

Sitting in the corner of the main room where I could see into the kitchen, I watched as she took eight or ten abalones from a refrigerator, and began to prepare these in two distinctly different ways. Several were cut into extremely thin slices and dumped into a bowl containing a liquid that I could not identify. A second group of abalones she chopped into tiny cubes, each less than a quarter of an inch, and these she put into a preheated pan and fried just like hamburger. When that was done, she added all of the right ingredients that go into salsa, along with some additional things that I did not see, and then stirred all of this together. She then put that mixture back on the stove and cooked it some more.

In the meantime, we visited with the mayor about the island, its history, the fishing industry, and the wildlife that we already had seen and that which we still hoped to find. He was most helpful, and we all were impressed with his knowledge about the topography, ways to reach certain inaccessible parts of the island, and his willingness to be of assistance. Norm Scott and some of the others later visited a couple of those out-of-the-way areas, after I departed, based upon the directions obtained from the Punta Norte alcalde.

The most remarkable event that afternoon was dinner. I had eaten very little since early morning while I was en route to the start of an early morning transect count, and we had left port at about eleven after a lunch of a couple of granola bars. So by the time we were called to eat, after watching the food being prepared, I was more than ready. And I was not disappointed. Everything was excellent! The bowl of abalone strips was served as a salad in the form of ceviche. The second abalone dish was chili. We made burritos by roll-ing tortillas filled with that incredible abalone chili. Cold cerveza helped to round out a unique and unforgettable meal.

Since we had yet to hike into a nearby canyon to find a campsite, we left soon after dinner. We managed to find an excellent campsite not more than a mile from Punta Norte, set up camp in the dwin-dling light, and then spent a couple of hours wandering along an adjacent canyon searching for whatever might crawl, or run or fly across our path. The only animal of interest was a horned lizard that someone found partly buried in a sandy arroyo. It was kept over-night and I photographed it next day; it represented one of the en-demic species (Cedros Island horned lizard, *Phrynosoma cerroense*) known for Isla Cedros.

My early morning bird census, along the canyon bottom, pro-duced the same species that I had censused on the earlier sites. By 10:00 A.M. I had finished the transect and was exploring the coastal area that forms a broad plain at the mouth of the canyon. A light-house had been built on a rocky ledge that extended several hun-dred feet into the bay. I was able to hike along a bench above the coast for about two miles north. Abalone fishermen were already active. I observed four separate boats, each with two rubber-suited divers and an oarsman, anchored offshore a few to several hundred feet. None of these individuals was using scuba gear; they were go-ing about their work with little more than a rubber suit, a mask, and a machete.

My most memorable event of the morning was the discovery of a hundred or more sea lions along the rocky beach. I crept up to where I could watch and photograph these marvelous creatures bet-ter, and lay there on my belly for about an hour admiring their grace in the water. On land, they were awkward and lumbering. They either didn't see me or ignored me; I couldn't be sure.

By midafternoon the fishing boat returned. After a fond farewell to the mayor, we boarded the boat, along with another six cartons of fresh abalone and several sacks of fish, and headed back to San Isidro.

Two days later, following another evening of abalone steak and extras, I boarded the same DC-3 that had brought us to Cedros, and was soon airborne and heading back to Guerrero Negro and home. As we crossed Vizcaíno Bay, I thought of the gray whales that returned to this area of Mexico each winter. I decided that I must not forget to write a letter of thanks to the Mexican government for establishing the national park for the gray whales. It is important that people let these officials know of our interest in such programs. It is only through long-term commitments such as these that the significant resources which occur throughout the country will receive adequate protection.

10

Tiburón

A Seri Indian provided us transportation across the channel in the vessel he used for fishing—a long sleek, wooden boat with an outboard motor. In spite of Tiburón Island appearing to be only a short distance away, it took us a good part of an hour to negotiate the 1.2-mile passage across El Infiernillo (Little Hell) Strait. As we neared the island we could see four uniformed marines, automatic rifles in hand, watching our approach. In spite of the fact that we had informed our Seri boatman that we were expected, he took no chances and stopped well short of the beach. The Mexican marines looked very businesslike when they pointed their weapons toward us and warned us to leave. Two members of our party, Roberto Munoz and Mateo Aguayo, representatives of Fauna Silvestre, were soon recognized by the marines and we were permitted to land. Once ashore we were treated with courtesy. And several days later, before we left the island, we were treated to an excellent fish fry, with all the fresh fish we could eat, lots of fried potatoes, tortillas, excellent salsa, and tequila and lime drinks that we drank from fire-black cans. I have since cherished the memory of our farewell fish fry and the comradeship that we enjoyed on Tiburón.

Tiburón Island

Tiburón is the largest island on the Pacific coast of North America south of Canada. It is approximately 484 square miles in size, and it contains two mountain ranges that run north to south. Sierra Kunkaak forms a jagged backbone within the eastern half of the island, and contains the island's highest elevation of 1,455 feet. Sierra Menor is a somewhat lower range that makes up a second rocky backbone along the western edge of the island. Between the two ranges is a long trough known as Aqua Dulce Valley. Although the gulf side of Sierra Menor is rather precipitous, the eastern slope of Sierra

Kunkaak forms gentle bajadas, dissected by many minor and a few major drainages that terminate at El Infiernillo. Approximately twenty square miles of this eastern slope was chosen for our principal study area. The terrain includes beach, coastal dunes and flats, open desert flats, arroyos, foothills and valleys, and rocky mountain ridges.

Tiburón's vegetation, as well as that of the Sierra Seri of the Sonoran coast and eight other islands within the Sea of Cortez, had already been studied by Richard Felger and Charles Lowe. A summary of their findings, published in 1976 by the Natural History Museum of Los Angeles County, was titled *The Island and Coastal Vegetation and Flora of the Northern Part of the Gulf of California.* I found this little booklet most helpful to my understanding of the area's vegetative communities.

Starting about 1975, the U.S. Fish and Wildlife Service and Mexico's sister agency, Fauna Silvestre, developed a working agreement to undertake joint studies of wildlife and wildlife habitats in select areas. The purposes of the Tiburón project were to identify environmental disturbances and to understand better the basic roles of the major components of the ecosystem. I became involved with two phases of the cooperative agreement, conducting breeding bird population studies on both Tiburón and Cedros islands. All three trips to Tiburón were related to my involvement with this program.

There were three guard stations on the island, one at each end (La Cruz on the southern tip and Tecomate on the northwestern corner), and the one at Punto Tormento, where we landed. The only roads were between the three stations and the one that we took leading toward the center of the island, terminating at Caracol. Fauna Silvestre personnel maintained a pickup truck on the island for their various projects and had left it at the Punto Tormento station for our use. After a brief visit with the marines, we loaded our gear and set off for Caracol.

Upon arrival we found a rather spacious bunkhouse there, complete with running water, built by Fauna Silvestre for housing Mexican scientists and other visitors like us. It provided an excellent base camp from where we could hike to various places in the center of the island. It was most convenient for our purposes, and except for one overnight in the cactus forest habitat along the northeast coast, I was able to accomplish everything I wanted to do by foot from Caracol.

Tiburón Island and Caracol Research Station, base for Tiburón bird studies.

Tiburón's Birdlife

The party of scientists involved with that 1978 study included the two Fauna Silvestre biologists, Drs. Norm Scott (leader) and Tom Fritts, both employees of the Fish and Wildlife Service, and three of my colleagues: Dick Russell and Roy and Lois Johnson. Norm and Tom intended to study the mammals and reptiles. The bird censuses that I had planned required at least four transects run in each habitat, and the assistance of my three friends was essential. We established one-mile-long walking transects like those described in the previous chapter. I had surveyed the island in 1977 to find the various habitats and determine the best localities for the transects. The 1978 visit was designed to operate the transects within each of Tiburón's five habitats: littoral scrub, desert, cactus scrub, riparian, and thornscrub.

Littoral scrub habitat is that zone of vegetation influenced by the tide and salt spray. It included a line of mangroves along the coast and at numerous places where narrow fingers of tidewater reached inland for several hundred feet. It also included an area of salt scrub just above the mangroves that extended up to the arid desert environment.

We found that only seven species of birds utilized this habitat for nesting: mourning and white-winged doves, northern mockingbird, verdin, black-tailed gnatcatcher, northern cardinal and black-throated sparrow. Three of these typical desert species, the verdin, black-tailed gnatcatcher and black-throated sparrow, were equally at home in the mangroves as in the more xeric environment.

Desert habitat was the most extensive type on the island, making up approximately one-half of the study area. Vegetation there was fairly typical of the Sonoran Desert. Dominant plant species included creosote bush, palo verde, brittlebush, ocotillo, ironwood, jojoba, and elephant tree. The cactus scrub habitat was that desert environment where tree cacti—cardon, organ pipe and senita—truly dominated the scene. Saguaro cacti were present only on the ridges above the desert flats.

We found eighteen bird species breeding in the desert zone and twenty-one in the cactus scrub habitat. There were only three species nesting in the desert that we did not detect in the cactus scrub community: black-chinned hummingbird, phainopepla and brown towhee. But there were six species found within the tall cactus zone not found in the desert: great blue heron, osprey, American kestrel, Gambel's quail, northern (gilded) flicker, and mangrove swallow. The latter species was the only bird found breeding on Tiburón Island that is not also known to occur in the United States. Mangrove swallows are common in Mexico within the same general range as mangroves. This swallow looks very much like a tree swallow with a full white rump. I found ten pairs of these birds breeding within the hundred-acre cactus scrub transect, all nesting in deserted woodpecker holes in cardons.

Since the cactus forest was a considerable distance from our base camp at Caracol, and I wanted to survey this unique habitat, Mateo drove Tom Fritts and me to the area one afternoon. Mateo had already visited the area earlier to census nesting ospreys as part of a long-term, ongoing Fauna Silvestre project. We stopped at several of the

Mateo Aguayo inspects osprey nest for eggs and young on cardon cactus, Tiburón Island, Sonora.

active nests, usually perched high on a cardon cactus, and with the aid of a mirror tied to the end of a long, many-times-spliced stick we were able to peer into each nest. In most cases the two to four young ospreys were still downy but very active. Time after time we watched adults bring fresh fish to their nests from their ready supply in the adjacent waters of the gulf.

One of the active osprey nests that Mateo showed us was situated only a few feet above a nest that belonged to a pair of great blue herons. An adult of each species was sitting on the nests when we arrived. Both occupants flew off as we approached. The osprey circled the cardon several times, calling continuously. The heron flew several hundred feet away to another cardon where it sat and watched as we examined the nests. Both nests contained downy young. We then retreated to near the road and waited for the birds to return to their nests. The osprey returned almost immediately. It took several minutes longer for the heron to return. And when it did, it made three unsuccessful attempts to alight on its nest by approaching from above and passing directly over or too close to the osprey nest. Each time the osprey drove it off. However, on its fourth attempt the great blue approached its nest from below, apparently not disturbing the osprey, and was permitted to settle down. Later, having searched the literature for other examples of paired nesting between these two birds but found none, I prepared a short note on this occurrence that was published in the journal, *The Southwestern Naturalist.*

I counted a total of twenty-two cardons within the hundred-acre cactus scrub transect that possessed either active or old osprey nests. Twelve of these were being used by nesting ospreys; this seemed like an extremely high density for this large fish-eating hawk. In addition, a great horned owl nest was located in a large cavity in the side of one unused osprey nest; it contained two downy young owls. And a pair of American kestrels had appropriated another of the unused nests.

Tiburón's riparian habitat was present only within some of the wetter arroyos and washes. The tall, white-barked lysiloma tree, known locally as *palo blanco,* was the most common plant species. It looked very much like a tall, spindly acacia without spines. Other dominant plants of this habitat included several kinds of acacias, palc verde, seepwillow, sweetbush, ironwood, mesquite, desert lavender, and bursage. And at somewhat higher elevations, where these same species form heavier thickets, a thornscrub habitat occurred.

We found twenty bird species nesting within the riparian zone, and thirty-one species in the thornscrub habitat. Four of the twenty riparian birds made up forty-three percent of the total avifauna there: white-winged dove, Costa's hummingbird, black-tailed gnatcatcher and verdin. These same four species, along with ash-throated flycatcher, cactus wren, black-throated sparrow and house finch, made up more than ninety percent of the thornscrub avifauna.

A total of 105 species of birds was recorded during the six-day survey. Thirty-eight (36 percent) of these were considered to be breeding within the study area; the remaining sixty-seven species (64 percent) were either migrants or winter residents that had not yet departed. The most common bird recorded within the five habitats surveyed was the verdin. In fact, this tiny bird made up 12.6 percent of the total Tiburón Island breeding bird population. The second most abundant species was the black-tailed gnatcatcher (9.3

percent). Black-throated sparrow (third) made up 8.8 percent of the population, followed by the white-winged dove (8.4 percent), ash-throated flycatcher (7.4 percent), and Costa's hummingbird (7.1 percent). The cactus wren came in seventh at 5.9 percent. Those seven birds comprised 59.9 percent of Tiburón's total breeding bird population. None of the thirty-one additional species made up more than 4.5 percent of the totals within the five transects.

It is interesting to speculate on total bird populations for the entire island. Exact estimates of this kind are next to impossible because they would entail a thorough analysis of all vegetative communities on the island. Since time did not permit that, I arrived at rough estimates for the whole island by converting known population data to the perceived habitat units. I assumed that our twenty-square-mile study area was an adequate representation of Tiburón's full complement of plant communities. I then calculated total populations of the island's seven most common species as follows: verdin, 101,852 individuals; black-tailed gnatcatcher, 79,255; ash-throated flycatcher, 58,987; white-winged dove, 58,413; Costa's hummingbird, 54,551; and cactus wren, 47,145 individuals.

The above figures represent a lot of verdins, black-tailed gnatcatcher, white-wings, etc. They provide a different perspective on the importance of birds within an ecosystem. However, they are not very meaningful when trying to compare segments of populations. They suggest, for example, that three ospreys are equal to two verdins and one black-throated sparrow. Such comparisons are illogical. The mean weights of the three species are very different: 1,598, 6.9 and 14 grams, respectively. Ornithologists who study bird populations find that more meaningful measurements can be expressed in two biomass values. The term "standing crop biomass" is the total weight of the birdlife present at the time of the census. "Consuming biomass" is a measurement of the total energy stored as birds, or the amount of usable food that predators can utilize by consuming those birds.

Comparisons of the five measured habitats by using biomass values, then, can provide a more valuable way to access their importance, especially relating to energy flow within the ecosystem. This method of comparison makes the cactus scrub habitat far and away the most important of Tiburón's five plant communities. The standing crop biomass value was 67,037 grams per hundred acres for the cactus scrub zone, far ahead of the thornscrub habitat, with the second highest value of 16,869 grams. This was followed by the desert (12,582), riparian (8,892), and littoral scrub habitat (2,209). Consuming biomass values were similar in rank as follows: 6,333, 2,903, 2,286, 2,094, and 554 grams, respectively.

White-winged and mourning doves serve as key food sources for predators and, therefore, are good examples of the importance of biomass measurements. Tiburón's total standing crop biomass of white-winged and mourning doves amounted to 18,013 and 10,733 pounds (for the entire island of 484 square miles), respectively. Consuming biomass totals were 2,943 and 1,775 pounds.

All of the transects were run early in the mornings starting when it was barely light enough to see and ending about 10:00 or 10:30 A.M. After midmorning bird activity dropped off so much that continued surveys were of no value. Early mornings on the desert are, to me, the most peaceful and beautiful times of all. I can think of nowhere else where the combined elements of smell, sight, and other senses work so well together. I have thoroughly enjoyed my many experiences in the desert, and early mornings are the best of all.

Other Wildlife

One sense that seems to peak in the desert is a sort of kinship with other forms of life. It might be related to a curiosity, or respect for the various forms of desert wildlife that are able to make a living in such a severe environment. One example is the apparent abundance of ants that are present in deserts. And Tiburón's desertscapes were no exceptions. I was amazed by the numerous, conically shaped mounds placed in open sandy places, each with a web of cleared trails that radiated out in all directions.

One morning on the desert, as I walked slowly along my transect line carefully listening and watching for birds, I suddenly realized that I was not alone. A pair of coyotes was following me, some fifty to sixty feet away. As I continued the transect I realized that my canid companions were keeping pace with my movements. They would move when I did but stop when I stopped to record a bird or to listen or look more carefully at one place or another. The male seemed most interested. When the female wandered off as if bored with the whole affair, he stayed. He sat or lay down when I stopped for a longer than normal time. And he seemed to be getting closer

to me as I progessed along the transect. At first I ignored him completely, and that must either have frustrated him or created even
greater curiosity. Once he lay down, just like any other dog, within
twenty feet of me. Once or twice I even talked to him in a low voice.
This may have been a mistake, however, because soon afterwards
he began to lose interest in me, and suddenly he disappeared as
mysteriously as he had appeared. I regarded the entire affair as curiosity on behalf of the coyote, but it did occur to me that I might
have been the first human being that pair of coyotes had ever seen.
Maybe, until I gave myself away by talking to him, I was just another item of curiosity in the natural world of Tiburón's desert environment.

Mule deer also were present in small numbers. I found fresh tracks
each morning, but saw only two individuals during six days. Their
shyness may suggest that the island's wildlife continue to be hunted
in spite of the area being classified as an official wildlife refuge. Each
time I climbed onto the rocky ridges I watched carefully for bighorn, but found none. Desert bighorn were introduced to Tiburón
Island by Fauna Silvestre during the 1960s, and Mateo informed me
that a few still occur on the upper slopes of Sierra Kunkaak. Several
members of our party hiked into the area where bighorn had been
seen most often, but to no avail.

The desert tortoise (*Gopherus agassizii*) was also present on
Tiburón, and was one of the species listed within the U.S. Fish and
Wildlife Service agreement with Fauna Silvestre for study. Dr. Bruce
Bury of FWS and Sandalio Reyes of Fauna Silvestre studied this slow-
moving animal on Tiburón in 1978 and 1979. They located 146 individuals and estimated tortoise density at sixty-five per square
kilometer within six study sites; that's about 169 per square mile.
The tortoises dig shallow burrows in suitable places such as into
streambanks, woodrat nests, and debris. In about half of the burrows examined the investigators found two to four individuals together, suggesting greater communal habits than previously known.
The tortoises feed on a wide variety of desert vegetation, and are
most active during the warmest time of the year, especially after late
summer rainstorms.

Tiburón Island is the only known area of the Sonoran Desert that
has not been heavily grazed by domestic livestock. Only small numbers of cattle and goats lived there when the island was inhabited

by the Seris. All have since been removed. It is most important that the island continue to be protected in its natural state. On August 2, 1978, President Lopez Portillo officially declared forty-seven islands in the Sea of Cortez, including Tiburón, as wildlife refuges. The Mexican Government should be complimented for its diligent action in safeguarding this unique area. Such examples of undisturbed desert landscapes are few and far between. This single fact makes Tiburón Island well worthy of continued protection and study.

Seri Indians

The Seri Indians have been closely tied to Tiburón for all of its recorded history. They are known to have lived in the same general area for at least five hundred years, and on the island itself during the 1930s and until after World War II. Unlike the several other islands within the gulf, Tiburón possesses several springs that provide fresh water during even the driest years. But in 1965, and reconfirmed in 1978, the Mexican government established the entire island as a game preserve and hunting was prohibited. Mexican marines are stationed on Tiburón to enforce those laws.

Today, the entire Seri population of approximately five thousand souls lives on the Sonoran mainland along a sixty-five-mile strip from the village of Punta Chueca north to Desemboque. Although the Seris' native language is Hokan, used mostly among themselves, many also speak Spanish. The Seri school is located at Desemboque, largest of the Seri villages. But Punta Chueca is located at the most picturesque setting, and protected by a small natural spit that reaches out into El Infiernillo Strait for several hundred yards.

The buildings at Punta Chueca when we visited were mostly crude wood or adobe structures, although there were a few modern ones as well. The walls of several houses and animal pens were constructed with living ocotillo. I had seen ocotillo used this way elsewhere in northern Mexico. Although the ocotillo construction is not very effective in holding out storms, it looks very pretty during the rainy season when each plant is covered with green leaves. Many of the ocotillo houses included paper stuffed in the walls or plastic woven into place to help keep out cold winter winds.

Sea Turtles Two open structures had been built on the Punta Chueca beach. One was a simple, thatch-covered, twenty-foot-square ramada that provided shade for anyone wishing to sit near the beach.

A smaller pen was enclosed with chickenwire. In 1977, it was empty on my first observation, but it held two recently captured green sea turtles the next time I looked. Both had been either speared or shot in about the center of their shells. Although they were alive, it was obvious that their days were numbered. Three days later I found their guts and empty shells nearby on the beach. I assumed the meat had been utilized for soup or turtle steaks; it wasn't until the following year that I learned the rest of the story.

Sea turtles have long been part of the Seri livelihood, and probably were a popular food even before the Seris deserted their more nomadic lifestyle for one of fishing and settlements. At least two sea turtle species have been recorded within this area of the gulf, the Pacific ridley and green. Neither nests so far north, but both are known to occur there at any time of the year, even in winter. It is then that these reptiles are most susceptible to being taken by Seri fishermen. They dig into the muddy bottom of the bay when the water temperature gets below forty-five degrees Fahrenheit, and "hibernate" there with much reduced respiration rates. It is then that the Seris can often see them, partially covered with mud, resting on the bottoms of the shallower bays. These sleeping turtles are then speared, lifted into the boats and brought home. They are kept alive in pens until eaten. The Seri have long understood this local sea turtle characteristic and taken advantage of it, but marine biologists learned these facts only recently.

With the increased use of scuba gear, sea turtles wintering in the northern part of the gulf have begun to decline. Although the Mexican government has placed restrictions on the number and methods of taking sea turtles, these regulations are only as effective as the availability of enforcement personnel to implement them.

The Seri Fishing Industry One day I watched the Seri fishermen unload their day's catch on the Punta Chueca beach. There were a few mackerel, two fish species I did not recognize, and many, many sharks. One of the four boats being unloaded was so full of sharks that the fishermen had been forced to stand on the seat or sides.

Unloading the day's catch was done simply by throwing all of the fish one by one onto the sandy beach. Then the fishermen, with questionable help from several children who had arrived to help beach the boats, began to gut the fish. The innards were thrown back into the bay, and within a very few minutes the water was stained with red. The slow but steady current soon spread the bloody water out along the beach. The other fish remains eventually became scattered as well. The shark population out there soon would be feeding on its cousins. The Seri had inadvertently developed an excellent system for recirculating parts of their daily catch, a process that probably has existed for hundreds of years.

By the time the sharks were all eviscerated, it seemed the entire human population of Punta Chueca was present. Everyone there appeared to be involved in one way or another. Finally the men loaded the cleaned sharks into large washtubs which they used to haul the day's catch to a small but functioning freezer plant built a few hundred feet inland from the beach. The frozen sharks were picked up daily and trucked to a cannery in Hermosillo, I was told. But I wasn't able to learn about the final product. I knew that shark is often used for dog food. I also knew that some restaurant-served "scallops" are only specially prepared shark. Ever since then, when eating scallops, I can't help but wonder if I am really eating shark from El Infiernillo Strait.

Not all of the catch that day was frozen for transportation to Hermosillo. Everything besides sharks was taken home for personal use. But the overwhelming majority of the day's catch, shark, was taken to the freezer plant for processing. Sharks, without doubt, were a significant part of the daily lives of every one of the Seri Indians in that part of Mexico.

Seri Woodcarving Although fishing may be the Seris' oldest industry, woodcarving has recently become a business that has brought them worldwide recognition. Shark woodcarvings were especially evident on my visits with the Seris during the late 1970s. The most beautiful carving I saw was one of a thresher shark which my friend Clyde Jones bought. It was a twenty-four-inch swimming shark carved so well that you could almost imagine it ready to attack.

On my first visit to Punta Chueca, in late fall 1976, I purchased several five- to eight-inch woodcarvings for approximately two dollars each. I gave all but one of those to friends and relatives as Christmas gifts. They represented porpoises, a couple of quail, a tern, and a shark. In April, 1977, on my next visit, similar carvings had doubled in price, and by May, 1978, the woodcarvings were at least double what they had been the previous year. More recently I have found Seri woodcarvings in stores in Santa Fe, Washington, D.C., and else-

Seri Indians with fresh catch of sharks at Puerto Chueco, Sonora.

where in the United States, at prices that begin at forty-five and can run as high as a thousand dollars.

Until 1961, the only woodcarvings produced by the Seris were for utilitarian purposes, according to Bernice Johnston's little book, *the Seri Indians of Sonora Mexico*. But when José Astorga made a paperweight for a friend, he was asked to make others. The procession of figures that followed became better and better as his skill increased. Other members of the tribe picked up the art when they saw the respect and profit derived. Today, Seri woodcarvings are in great demand throughout North America. As with most other successful products, imitations have evolved: I saw several Mexicans producing "original Seri woodcarvings" on the streets of Hermosillo on my last visit.

One secret to Seri woodcarving success is the kind of wood used, ironwood. It is one of the hardest woods known, but it is a common mesquite-like tree that occurs throughout the Sonoran Desert. Suitable pieces are first trimmed to working size with machetes or large butcher knives. Further shaping and smoothing are done with a large file or rasp, although hacksaws are sometimes used. Once the piece has been well shaped and smoothed, sandpaper is used to finish the surface to the point where it can be polished. The natural reddish colors and grain of the wood help make the Seri woodcarvings especially beautiful and distinctive.

It is not surprising that the woodcarvings are representative of the natural environment that the Seris know best, the marine and terrestrial animals that occur about them. Sharks are some of the most common animals carved, being a key element of the Seri world. The Spanish word for shark is tiburón.

PART III

Interior Highlands

III

ZACATECAS
ZACATECAS ● ⌐49⌐ **SAN LUIS POTOSÍ**
SAN LUIS POTISÍ ⌐57⌐

TAMUALIPAS

Tampico

⌐15⌐ **NAYARIT**

⌐85⌐

TEPIC

AGUASCALIENTES

GULF OF MEXICO

⌐80⌐

GUANAJUATO **QUERETARO**

Puerto Vallarta

JALISCO GUADALAJARA

ʻQUERÉTARO

HIDALGO

VERA-CRUZ

Autlán de Navarro

Volcán Colima ● Cd. Guzmán

TLAXCALA ˈJalapa

Fortín de las Flores

ʻColima ⌐ ● Atenquique

MEXICO CITY
Nevado de Toluca

Chalco Puebla

Veracruz

Manzanillo **COLIMA** ⌐

CUERNAVACA

D.F.
Amecameca

Pico de
Orizaba

Córdoba

MICHOACAN

Volcanic Cordillera

Orizaba

Tierra Blanca

PUEBLA

Valle Nacional

⌐175⌐

GUERRERO ⌐95⌐

Sierra Madre Oaxaca

⌐185⌐

⌐200⌐

Sierra Madre del Sur

OAXACA

MONTE ALBÁN ▲

⌐190⌐

PACIFIC OCEAN

Acapulco

OAXACA Salina Cruz

⌐200⌐

Gulf of Tehuantepec

See map IV for El Triunfo region.

Interior Highlands

11

Volcano Country

The snow-capped summit of Popocatépetl was still almost three thousand feet above me, gleaming like a radiant jewel in the sunlight. Yet from my perch at 14,800 feet at the Las Cruces Hut on "Popo," I felt as if I was on top of the world. I had hiked only two miles above the trailhead at Tlamacas, but from that elevation I could see many of Mexico's great mountains that form an immense half-circle to the west, south and east of the Mexico City basin. Nearest was Popocatépetl's sister peak, Iztaccíhuatl, only ten miles away across the relatively narrow forested Paso de Cortez. Pico de Orizaba was eighty to ninety airline miles to the east; its summit stood out like a brilliant white star above the layer of clouds that blanketed the area in between. To the southwest was Nevado de Toluca, maybe fifty miles distant. Each of these peaks was snow-capped and they seemed to me like bright white symbols of purity in contrast to the smog-filled scene to the north.

Although there was no cloud cover toward Mexico City, I couldn't see any part of that huge sprawling metropolis. From my vantage point on Popo, the Mexico City area looked more like a foggy bottomland rather than an active and modern city of sixteen million human beings (listed at eighteen million in 1990). Greater Mexico City covers an area of over six hundred square miles and, except on a few hillside edges, is totally within a basin that is completely surrounded by mountains. The mountains literally trap the abundant pollutants from leaded gasoline, factory smokestacks, coal- and wood-burning stoves, and open fires. Mexico City is considered to be one of the most polluted cities in the world. It is said that breathing Mexico City air is like smoking two packs of cigarettes daily.

My hike on Popo came at the end of a 1981 Christmas birding trip to Mexico. My companions included Bo and Woody West from New Mexico, Ron Knaus from Louisiana, and Nape Shelton from

Washington, D.C. We already had participated in the Catemaco Christmas bird count (see chapter eighteen, "Catemaco at Christmas"), and before leaving Mexico we visited the central highlands.

I had stood there on Popo that day, at about 15,000 feet above sea level, with only a light jacket over my normal field clothes. Although early morning had been very cold, by midmorning the thin air had warmed to become very comfortable. It was exhilarating to be so high above the rest of the world. The white-capped peaks, the surrounding bright green forest, and a soaring common raven were all that mattered.

Sierra Volcánica Transversal

Most U.S. visitors are surprised to discover that five of Mexico's mountains are higher than the highest point in the continental United States, Mount Whitney (14,494 feet). Those five Mexican peaks are part of a magnificent volcanic range called the Sierra Volcánica Transversal that cuts across central Mexico from Sinaloa to central Veracruz. The highest is Pico de Orizaba, or Citlaltepetl, a Nahua Indian word meaning "Mountain of the Star." At 18,851 feet in elevation, Orizaba is the third highest mountain in all of North America. Only Alaska's Denali (formerly called Mount McKinley, 20,320 feet) and Canada's Mount Logan (19,850 feet) are higher. Orizaba is located approximately 140 miles east of Mexico City in the state of Puebla. Mountain of the Star is most appropriately named. It provides an outstanding landmark that can be visible for more than a hundred miles in all directions.

Directly south of Mexico City, on the border between the states of México and Puebla, are the twin peaks of Popocatépetl (17,781 feet) and Iztaccíhuatl (17,343 feet), Nahuatl for "Smoking Mountains" and "White Lady," respectively. Nevado de Toluca, or Xinantecatl, meaning "Naked Man," is 15,001 feet in elevation (approximately thirty-five miles southwest of Mexico City), and is the fourth highest of Mexico's grand peaks. And finally, the fifth highest is La Malinche or Malantzin (14,637 feet), seventy miles east of Mexico City. This mountain was named for Malinche, a female Mayan guide, interpreter and concubine of Spanish explorer Hernan Cortez.

Mexico's five highest volcanic peaks are part of the "ring of fire," a series of volcanic peaks along a 25,000-mile circumference around the Pacific coasts of North and South America and Asia. Mexico's belt of volcanoes, thirteen of which are considered active by volcanologists, extend from the Revillagigedo Islands—four hundred miles off the Pacific Coast, west of Puerto Vallarta—to Mount San Martín Tuxtla, which is only a few miles inland from the Gulf of Mexico near Catemaco.

New volcanoes are not unusual within this region. In 1943, Paricutin was born almost overnight. A farmer, plowing his field two hundred miles west of Mexico City, watched as a fissure opened in the ground and volcanic material poured out. The new volcano was thirty feet high the following morning, 460 feet high one week later, and had risen to a height of 1,300 feet by the time it stopped flowing. In 1952, Barcena violently emerged from San Benedicto Island, one of the Revillagigedo Islands off the coast of Colima. Volcán Colima (see chapter fourteen, "The Jalisco-Colima Circle") has been one of Mexico's most active volcanoes, having erupted eleven times since 1900. And Popo itself has recorded sixteen eruptions over the past six centuries; the most recent one was in 1935.

All five of Mexico's highest peaks serve as grand centerpieces for national parks. The special park status given these areas has enhanced their international visibility and increased attention from naturalists, mountain climbers and other recreationists, as well as providing Mexicans with a greater sense of pride. International visitors to any country concentrate on national parks because these represent the best of what exists, from both natural and cultural perspectives. Mexico's national parks provide better than average places to experience nature on its own terms, and in the national economy, tourism is second only to oil production.

Popo and Izta

The names of the twin volcanoes—Popocatépetl (pronounced "popo-ka-tep-etle") and Iztaccíhuatl (pronounced "ix-tac-see-wattle")—can hardly be spoken in the same breath. But both are extraordinary in their aesthetic appeal and the resources they possess. Both peaks have been incorporated into one comprehensive national park. The area contains extensive coniferous forest and grasslands at the base of the peaks, and a boreal forest that extends up to the upper slopes. The higher slopes above timberline are principally scree-covered, while the tops of the peaks are usually under snow and ice in winter as well as during the rainy season, from June to October.

Snow is a product of storms, and Mexico's mountain tops often possess more snow during the rainy season than they do in winter.

The best route to the twin peaks from Mexico City is Highway 190 (the toll road) to the Cuautla turnoff, just east of the toll booth, and Highway 115 to Amecameca. The total distance from the Mexico City airport is only forty-five miles. Highway 190 crosses a pass just east of the city, and from there the twin peaks of Popo and Izta usually are visible. Highway 115 descends into a broad valley before starting a moderate climb, through farmlands, to Amecameca. The village of Amecameca is situated at 8,050 feet elevation on the northern slope of the twin volcanoes. The view from the highway near Amecameca, looking back across the broad, open fertile valley, filled with hundreds of well-maintained cultivated fields, is spectacular.

The mountain scenery above Amecameca is even more spectacular and rivals any in North America. Izta is on the left and forms a massive ridge that, with just a little imagination, resembles the body of a recumbent female figure, complete with head, breast and knees. To the right is Popo, a single conical-shaped peak that reminds me of a taller Mount Hood or Rainier of the Cascade Range of the Pacific Northwest. The view of the twin peaks from Amecameca, which includes a foreground of cornfields and rock fencelines and a middle-ground of forested ridges and slopes, is just a hint of the montane environment ahead.

At least eight pine species occur within the forest that surrounds Popo and Izta, according to Critchfield and Little's *Geographic Distribution of the Pines of the World;* this 1966 publication includes distribution maps for every known pine. Several of the Mexican species are evident along the road to Tlamacas: Aztec pine occurs in rather pure stands, and can be identified by its bright green, four- to six-inch long needles, in bundles of three. Mexican white pine has bluish-green needles of a similar length but in bundles of five; they are somewhat pendulous in character. The timberline pine is Hartweg's pine, a hardy tree with short needles in bunches of five. Other pine species known for the area include Chihuahua pine; Michoacán pine; a pine known only by its scientific name (*Pinus pseudostrobus*); and Lawson pine.

In addition, an extensive area of dark green sacred fir, called *oyamel* or *abeto,* occurs on a ridge above Amecameca; it is obvious to the careful observer. This tree is closely related to the white fir of the United States, which occurs in Mexico only in northern Baja. According to Walter Pesman's *Meet Flora Mexicana,* "the specific name, *religiosa,* refers to its use for church decoration; branches often show a natural cross. Its lumber is valuable for construction purposes and for making furniture. In winter the trees are tapped for Aceite De Pola (wood oil), for medicinal, balsam and paint uses" (p. 113).

The paved road beyond Amecameca begins at the plaza and is signed for Buena Vista and Popo-Izta national park. The route runs east for about twenty miles to Tlamacas, park headquarters at 12,800 feet above sea level. Tlamacas is the center of activities for the Popocatépetl-Iztaccíhuatl national park. We found a very nice, modern stone lodge, complete with overnight accommodations and restaurant, there. Park headquarters is located across a stone plaza from the lodge, and contains a climbing office where everyone who climbs either Popo or Izta must register.

The highest portion of the Tlamacas roadway transects the boreal forest and provides easy access to this highland environment. There is a three-way junction at the Paso de Cortez, fourteen miles above Amecameca. The pass is situated halfway between Popo and Izta and named after Hernan Cortez. Cortez and his Spanish army crossed these mountains at this point on the November, 1519 march from Veracruz to Tenochtitlan, the Aztec capital; now Mexico City. The battle that ensued marked the beginning of the end of the Aztec empire.

The paved road turns to the right at the pass and continues to Tlamacas. The unimproved road that continues toward the east eventually gets to Puebla, but this route can be hazardous and should not be taken unless additional information about local conditions is obtained first. The dirt road to the left from the junction runs through extensive grasslands for about five miles to a small parking area at 12,900 feet elevation.

The parking area marks the start of the route climbers most often utilize to ascend Izta. This is a rather serious climb, however, and is often done in two or three stages. Further details of this route and others in the Izta-Popo and Orizaba areas are described in the February-March, 1978 issue of *Summit,* in an article by Herb Kincey, titled, "Climbing Mexico's Big Three Volcanoes."

Popocatépetl (17,781 feet), viewed from approximately 11,000-foot elevation. Most snow falls during the rainy season.

Birding the Boreal Forest

The most extensive habitat within Popo-Izta national park is the open pine and bunchgrass terrain between approximately 9,500 and 11,800 feet elevation. This area is dominated by Montezuma pine and an understory of coarse grasses of the genera *Festuca, Muhlenbergia* and *Arenaria*.

I first birded this habitat just off of Highway 190, along the northern edge of the park and just east of the Morelos-México state line, on the morning of December 27, 1980. I recorded thirty-nine bird species during a two-hour walk through open forest that reminded me very much of mature ponderosa pine forests in the southwestern part of the United States. The common to fairly common birds recorded included white-eared hummingbird, Strickland's woodpecker, house (brown-throated) wren, Mexican chickadee, bushtit, white-breasted and pygmy nuthatches, ruby-crowned kinglet; the black-throated green, yellow-rumped, red and olive warblers; and black-headed grosbeak. Other less numerous but interesting species were the northern pygmy-owl, pine flycatcher, gray-barred wren, russet nightingale-thrush, clay-colored robin, gray silky-flycatcher, fan-tailed and golden-crowned warblers, slate-throated redstart, and striped sparrow.

Most of the above birds were the same species that can be found in mountain forests north of the Mexican border. Five, however, were Mexican species that have not been reported for the United States — pine flycatcher, gray-barred wren, russet nightingale-thrush, fan-tailed warbler, and striped sparrow. Only one of these, the gray-barred wren, has a range that is so restrictive that it could be considered as the best avian representative of Mexico's central highlands. It is endemic to the southern portion of the Mexican plateau.

The gray-barred wren is one of the larger members of the wren family and is closely related to the cactus wren (both are of the same genus, *Campylorhynchus*) of the northern deserts. It is heavily barred on the back, while its underparts are spotted in the center and barred on the sides. The overall color of the bird is grayish, while its look-alike cousins possess more brown on their backs and tails.

There is a similar but smaller forested area, surrounded by cultivated fields, just above the Amecameca–Buena Vista junction. This area has a number of picnic tables under the tall pines, and so it is a great place to stop for lunch. I have birded here several times and although there are fewer species than in the previous area described, this is a good place to see ocellated thrasher, one of Mexico's endemics. I also recorded the buff-breasted, pine and tufted flycatchers, blue mockingbird, blue-hooded euphonia, and rufous-capped brush-finch there.

For me, the most interesting bird of the lot was the ocellated thrasher. Of ten species of *Toxostoma* thrashers in Mexico, three are endemic — Cozumel, gray and ocellated. Two of these possess obvious territorial restrictions; Cozumel thrasher is found only on Cozumel Island (see chapter twenty-one, "Island of Swallows"), and gray thrasher is limited to the desert landscape of central Baja California (see chapter eight, "South of La Paz"). The ocellated thrasher, on the other hand, is an "interior" bird "of central Mexico from Guanajuato and Hidalgo south through the state of Mexico, Pueblo and west-central Veracruz to central Oaxaca," according to the 1983 *AOU Check-list of North American Birds* (p. 572). Its habitat preference includes "oak scrub, bushy areas in arid pine-oak association and adjacent humid pine-oak forest, and in arid scrub adjoining oak woodland." The ocellated thrasher has carved its own niche within the Mexican interior.

The endemic ocellated thrasher looks very much like a curve-billed thrasher in size and shape, but unlike the curve-bill, has roundish black spots on its breast, sides and flanks. According to Irby Davis's *A Field Guide to the Birds of Mexico and Central America,* when it is "in full song" this species sounds like the curve-billed thrasher. The AOU Check-list states that the two species "appear to constitute a superspecies."

The most spectacular bird we found that day in the pine forest was the blue-hooded euphonia. The male must be one of nature's most colorful creatures, an exquisite jewel. Its crown, nape and the sides of its neck are bright blue. Its underparts are a bright cinnamon. Its back, throat, and a connecting line are purplish. And its forehead is a deep red color in the proper light. What a combination of colors! The female is less attractive; she still possesses the blue crown and red forehead, but the other colors are more subtle.

Euphonias are short-tailed members of the tanager family and rarely are more than five inches in length. They possess rather short, thick bills, and are fruit-eaters; mistletoe berries are preferred. Their nests are rather unique for tanagers; they are domed and have a side entrance. Mexico possesses four species of euphonias, and although all sport bright colors, none can compare with the blue-hooded euphonia.

Pico de Orizaba

Orizaba is considered extinct, but its perfect cone-shaped top attests to its volcanic origin. There is probably not another mountain peak in all of Latin America that can be seen from so far and from so many directions. As on Popo and Izta, snow and ice on its upper slopes is commonplace, so Orizaba stands out like a brilliant star, a mountain among mountains. I have seen the white cap of Orizaba from the Oaxaca highlands just east of Oaxaca City, more than 125 miles to the south, and it also is visible from the highway near Teziutlán beyond Jalapa.

In January, 1981, after spending several days at Catemaco, my companions and I drove north to explore Orizaba and search for two rare bird species—black-polled yellowthroat and slaty finch—that had been recorded there many years earlier. Bill Schaldach had agreed to guide us to the areas where he had once collected the two species. I had first met Bill at Catemaco during the 1980 Catemaco Christmas bird count, where I learned that he was a retired field biologist with a long history of bird research throughout Mexico. It was his directions that helped me find the Slender-billed wren (see chapter thirteen, "Quest for the Slender-billed Wren"). And when I asked him about the best locations for finding black-polled yellowthroat and slaty finch in Mexico, he told me about his experiences with those birds on Orizaba. That discussion had led to meeting Bill several days later in Fortín.

Bill and his family were living at Fortín at the time; they have since sold their property there and moved to Catemaco. Fortín de las Flores is a beautiful little town near the city of Orizaba, on Highway 150 between Mexico City and Veracruz. We found Bill at his flat across from the central plaza, and we spent several hours visiting him and his family. I was greatly impressed with his extensive knowledge of Mexico and its diverse birdlife. We left Fortín early the next morning and drove west through considerable fog for about thirty-five miles to where Highway 150 (toll road) crosses one of the major ridges on Orizaba's southwestern flank. We then left our vehicles along the highway at kilometer post 44 and hiked across country toward the distant snow-capped peak. We followed a ridge for several miles through some very patchy landscape. Abundant and extensive areas of Montezuma pine, smaller patches of jelecote pine with its long drooping needles, cultivated fields of various sizes fenced with rockpiles and huge century plants, and low scrubby areas were all intermixed. We searched each of the scrubby zones we found, because this was the kind of habitat where Bill had collected a slaty finch several years before. The dominant shrub of this habitat was charcoal shrub. The habitat looked very much like chaparral areas in the southwestern U.S. to me. Bill mentioned that it reminded him of the Argentina *páramo*—the Spanish name for an alpine meadow, usually devoid of woody plants but with short stemless plants that often produce large and showy flowers in the flowering season — where the slaty finch is common. In spite of the considerable effort we spent searching, we did not find this bird.

We did find forty-two other bird species during the day, however. Although many of those were the same as are mentioned above for Popo, we found a few others too. The most interesting of these were blue-throated hummingbird, a lone violet-green swallow, both Steller's and gray-breasted jays, bridled titmouse, hermit and Townsend's warblers, collared towhee, rufous-capped brush-finch, and black-headed siskin.

We found a few wet places along the edges of some pastureland that day, and we followed a little stream for several hundred yards in hopes of finding a good wet meadow habitat for yellowthroats, but to no avail. The area had been so heavily overgrazed that in many places sheet erosion had occurred, and deeply eroded gullies were numerous within the hilly pastureland.

I climbed to the summit of an isolated hill, situated just below the forest that formed a line of vegetation below timberline, to get a good view of the surrounding landscape. It was well worth the time and energy. The view alone, toward the snow-covered peak that formed a magnificent backdrop to the forests and fields, made the entire day worthwhile.

There at the summit of the hill I found a strange figure that had been dug into the grassy turf. The figure was approximately eight feet long, shaped a little like an extended hobbyhorse, complete with curled tail, a single line for the body, and a large head that contained a sort of topknot that curved forward. The lines of the figure had been cleanly cut into the turf two to three inches deep and three to four inches wide. Nearby was a patch of burned turf. I looked around for additional evidence of man, but found only a few scats from either goats or sheep. Nothing else. I took several photographs of this strange figure.

I have since shown the slides I took that day of the odd pattern in the turf to numerous friends, including some archeologists with field experience in Mexico, but no one seems to have an adequate explanation. One theory that has been suggested more than once is that the site was used for some type of ceremony, by sun worshipers or some other kind of religious group. I guess that explanation is as good as any; it would have been a great place for a ceremony.

We returned to Fortín de las Flores via the old road rather than retracing our route on the toll road. The older route provided us with an entirely different, close-up view of the eastern slope. We stopped once along the roadside, still quite high on the ridge, just after we crossed back into Veracruz, and spent a good part of an hour there exploring a narrow but brushy side canyon. Of the thirteen bird species recorded, one was most unusual. I identified it as a brush-finch, but it looked very different from the known and expected brush-finch species. Mexico has six species of brush-finches, all six belonging to the genus *Atlapetes,* midsized finches that prefer brush or forest edges and usually are easy to observe.

I wrote the following description in my field notebook: "Rufous cap, white supercillary, yellow throat and white below." Now that doesn't describe any of Mexico's known brush-finches, and I have wondered since then if it might have been a towhee–brush-finch hybrid, or perhaps a new species altogether. Someday I need to return to that little canyon and see if I can find another of the strange-looking brush-finches.

But there are so many wonderful new places to explore in Mexico that I will probably let that trip go until it is convenient. I would like to return to Orizaba, but next time I will approach the mountain from the north side. There is a fourteen-mile dirt road that begins at Tlachichuca, passes through the Indian village of San Miguel Zoapán (altitude there is 10,200 feet), and up the Piedra Grande road to where there are two hikers' huts at 11,400 feet elevation. According to Herb Kincey's description of the area, it is only an hour's walk beyond the huts to the foot of Jamapa Glacier. I might have a better chance of finding the black-polled yellowthroat and slaty finch in that less disturbed environment. Even if I don't find the two birds on that side of the mountain, another close-up encounter with the "Mountain of the Star" would be well worth the trip.

12

Place of the Tufted Jay

The tufted jay, unquestionably, is one of Mexico's most remarkable birds. It is a true endemic, found nowhere else. And its range in Mexico is restricted to a relatively small area of the western mountains where the three states of Sinaloa, Durango and Nayarit merge. There it is a resident of the pine and oak forests, and seems to prefer the steep barrancas (deep and narrow canyons) that occur between approximately 4,000 and 7,500 feet elevation. It is a large jay, larger than the Steller's jay of the western coniferous forests, but not as large as Mexico's brown jay.

Its color pattern is what makes it so attractive. It looks a little like the blue jay of the eastern United States, but it is more striking. Peterson and Chalif, in their *Field Guide to Mexican Birds,* wrote that it is "one of the most stunning of the jays. Note particularly its *bristly black crest* and *bicolored tail.* Crest, face, and throat black; back, wings, and basal half of tail rich blue-black; underparts, back of head, adjacent collar, and terminal half of tail white" (p. 164). The combination of its spectacular appearance and relative inaccessibility makes it a high priority species for most birders and other naturalists who like to explore the rich natural areas of Mexico.

Finding the Tufted Jay

The tufted jay was one of my most wanted Mexican birds. So one May afternoon, following a three-hour leisurely drive from Mazatlán into the Sierra Madre Occidental, I and two companions—Woody and Bo West—found ourselves perched at the edge of a steep barranca at a location where I knew we could expect to see tufted jays.

We had left our rental car along the highway and hiked along an old roadway that crossed over a forested pass to a point where we had an outstanding view of the distant ridges and canyons below. We sat in silence and admired the sweeping vista. The site had been

Forestry camp at trailhead to the Place of the tufted jay, in
Sierra Madre Occidental.

recommended by other birders who had visited the area, and Peter
Alden described the location in his book, *Finding the Birds in Western Mexico,* published by the University of Arizona Press in 1969.
The route to the barranca was well marked. It started at kilometer
post 200, beside a white stucco building with a corrugated tin roof
and with the title of the location painted on the front in large black
letters—"Campamento del Control de Prevención y Combate de In-
cendios Forestales": the local forestry camp.

We discovered that the area just behind the forestry building and
the route along the old roadway provided excellent birding. Almost
immediately we recorded band-tailed pigeon, hairy woodpecker,
masked tityra, greater pewee, pine flycatcher, Steller's jay, Mexican
chickadee, blue mockingbird, bridled titmouse, ruby-crowned kinglet, American robin, russet nightingale-thrush, several warblers (including Townsend's, red, red-faced, crescent-chested, and Wilson's),
rufous-capped brush-finch, and rufous-sided towhee.

We birded our way to the end of the roadway and the edge of

the great barranca. And as we sat there enjoying the view, we continued to watch for birds. Squeaking, using the back of my hand against my lips, attracted a Hutton's vireo and slate-throated redstart. As we were admiring the latter, which was fanning its tail and searching for insects in the overhead canopy, we realized that I also had attracted the attention of a northern pygmy-owl. This little diurnal owl of the coniferous forests sang a steady series of short-whistle notes. I imitated the call as best I could. Although it changed places several times, it never came close enough for us to see it.

It was while I was trying to draw the pygmy-owl closer that I became aware of new calls coming from several hundred feet down the barranca that could not have come from anything else but jays. Since these calls were not those of Steller's jays, which we already had seen, I was sure they were from tufted jays, the principal bird we had come to find.

I began sqeaking more loudly and emphatically. Then, far down the ravine, in the foliage of a huge oak tree, I saw the white-and-black body of a bird the size of the tufted jay. The three of us trained our binoculars on the spot, but by then the bird had moved into the canopy of another tree. However, when it again came into view there was no question about its identity. There it was! The bird of our quest, in full view and calling to others nearby in a somewhat hoarse double-noted *ro-ak*.

The tufted jays continued to call as they moved up the barranca, from tree to tree, sometimes out of sight, but always detectable by their calls or the movement of the foliage. There were at least five birds, and as they came closer we often could see two or more at a time. Finally, they came to within thirty or forty feet of where we stood. We all got excellent looks as they foraged in the oaks around us. That small troop of jays passed around us and continued down the route we had used to hike up from the highway. But later, when we hiked back to the car, in spite of searching the adjacent trees, we neither saw nor heard them.

I was never sure whether we had attracted the birds to us or just happened to be on their route of travel. They had been in sight for ten to fifteen minutes during which time they seemed unafraid and provided us with excellent viewing. They had come up the barranca through the dense vegetation to our overlook, and they then moved onward through the adjacent pine-oak forest and disappeared. We felt most fortunate to have had such an excellent and easy sighting. To have found our most-wanted species almost at the start of our quest was somewhat anticlimactic.

The Sierra Madre Occidental

Only after the excitement of the tufted jays subsided did we begin to more appreciate our remarkable surroundings more fully. I began to realize that, from this perch at the head of this particular Sierra Madre barranca, we had an excellent view of the landscape below us as well as the higher ridges to the east. Although the surrounding forest was mostly pines and oaks, we could easily see several higher stands of conifers, some of which looked considerably different than those at the overlook. I was able to identify the long-leafed pines at the overlook as Aztec pine. The scientific name of Aztec pine is *Pinus teocote,* which means "pine of the gods." It is said that only the Aztec aristocrats were permitted to use the resin of this pine for incense; today, this tree is used for producing a turpentine substitute. We also could see trees we identified as sacred fir (*Abies religiosa*) on the higher slopes. This southern fir reaches the northern edge of its range in these mountains. I have read that it is far more common on the higher slopes of the Mexican Plateau, such as on the slopes of Popocatépetl south of Mexico City, than it is in the Sierra Madre.

Other plant species I was able to identify in the immediate area of the overlook were as many as five species of oaks (Mexican oaks are generally lumped together by the locals under the term *encinos*), wax alder, the red-barked madrone, and manzanita. We could see that the vegetation within the barranca was considerably different from that around us, and so we spent the next morning exploring that area.

The barranca trail began at the overlook and ran all the way to the bottom and west toward the coast. We found several additional species of oaks (Mexico has more than 120 species), and a tall *Agave* growing among the oaks and pines—tall enough to poke its flowering stalk above the pine-oak canopy. Epiphytes (several different bromeliads and a few orchids) were common on tree trunks and branches. The barranca was a much wetter environment than the

Woodland habitat along upper slopes of a deep barranca in
Sierra Madre Occidental in western Durango.

upper slopes, supporting a whole array of different plant species and
many additional birds.

The Sierra Madre Occidental, or "Mother Mountain Range of the
West," extends over 800 miles along the western side of the Mexican
mainland. The range averages approximately 130 miles in width and
over 6,000 feet above sea level. A few of the higher peaks exceed
10,000 feet elevation. The mountains are comprised of volcanic materials that are often exposed in the deep barrancas, a few of which
may exceed 6,000 feet in depth. The barranca of the tufted jay was
just such a chasm.

The upland forest area of the Sierra Madre is part of the Duran-
gan biotic province, according to Robert Schmidt's most informa-
tive little book, *A Geographical Survey of Sinaloa.* Schmidt referred
to Lee Dice's 1943 descriptions of the biotic provinces of North
America.

Other Birdlife

We found a number of birds in the barranca that we had not recorded the previous afternoon. These included lilac-crowned parrot, white-eared hummingbird, gray-crowned woodpecker, white-striped woodcreeper, brown-capped flycatcher, green jay, brown-backed solitaire, hermit thrush, brown creeper; golden-browed, black-throated gray, Townsend's, and olive warblers; western and red-headed tanagers, black-headed siskin, and Lincoln's sparrow.

Peter Alden had reported several other birds that might be expected in the highland barrancas, which we did not find. Among those were Wagler's chachalaca (previously called rufous-bellied chachalaca), crested guan, eared trogon, bright-rumped attila, gray-collared becard, and hooded grosbeak.

We remained in the Sierra Madre highlands for four days and nights. We rented rooms at the Villa Blanca, a small hotel with very comfortable and clean rooms, and good Mexican-German food. Villa Blanca is located on Highway 40 at kilometer post 234. It is only twenty-five miles below the barranca trail and there are several good birding sites in between. Since Villa Blanca is only about forty-eight miles from Mazatlán, it is a popular destination for locals wishing to drive into the nearby mountains, and many come for brunch or dinner. We found ourselves participating in (at least from across the room) several of those evening socials. Our stay at Villa Blanca was most enjoyable.

Halfway between Villa Blanca and the barranca entrance trail were two roads built by loggers, and a third roadway that provided access to a microwave station situated at the summit of this part of the mountains. Although the logging roads were extremely dusty during dry weather, they provided us good access into the adjacent forest. These areas contained a greater variety of plants than existed along the barranca entrance route, although the dominant plant species were pretty much the same. We followed the two lower roads for a few hundred yards to where they either terminated or to where we could leave the road and work our way down the wooded slopes. Both routes provided us with a good assortment of birds.

Trogons. The most exciting bird we found was a male eared trogon, on a rather steep and densely wooded slope. We were first attracted by its call, which was not the typical double or triple call

Villa Blanca Hotel, above Mazatlán, Sinaloa, base for search for tufted jay.

notes of most trogons, but a series of separate and rather musical *co co co co co* notes that were repeated every few minutes. It took us fifteen or twenty minutes to work ourselves into a position where we could actually see the bird. Its bright red belly and white under-tail were unmistakable. It was not until then that I was sure that the call notes we were tracking were really coming from a trogon. And it was another ten minutes or so before the bird positioned itself well enough for us to see the feathered ear-coverts from which its name is derived.

Although we later saw several mountain trogons in the same general vicinity, and we found citreoline trogons lower down the mountain, this was the only eared trogon of the trip. It represented a lifer for each of us. The eared trogon is considered rare within its rather narrow range in the montane pine forests of the Sierra Madre

Occidental north of Michoacán. But since 1977 it has been recorded considerably beyond its previously known range, and has now been observed as far north as southern Arizona in the Huachuca and Chiricahua Mountains.

Trogons are gorgeous birds! They are widely distributed throughout Mexico, except in Baja, and can be found in every habitat but desert and above timberline. Six of the eight Mexican species possess a red belly; two have yellow bellies. Both the eared and mountain trogons are red-bellied birds. Besides the hard-to-see feathered "ear" of the eared trogon, it possesses three other features that are easier to use in separating the two. The tail provides the best character. That of the eared trogon is almost totally white, while that of the mountain trogon is clearly banded by three white bars against black. Secondly, the red belly of the eared trogon touches on the iridescent greenish-black of the throat and breast, while the green and red are separated by a white line on the mountain trogon. Thirdly, in males, the bill is black on the eared and yellow on the mountain trogon.

Swifts. We also found three kinds of swifts. We had seen white-throated swifts on earlier occasions within the area, and several were seen streaking overhead at this location. But the sudden appearance of two chestnut-collared swifts was much more exciting. It was one of the birds I had most wanted to find in the Sierra Madre area. The male of this species had a very distinct chestnut-colored throat when seen in good light; the female was rather drab. This bird is the only Mexican swift in which the sexes possess different color patterns. It occurs from the western Mexico highlands south through Central America to northern South America. The Sierra Madre of Sinaloa represents the northern edge of its range.

Late one afternoon we returned to the Villa Blanca about one hour before sunset. The second floor of the hotel had a stairway leading to the roof, which provided an excellent place for viewing the surrounding terrain. The view included the dozen or so ridges that seem to be lined up one after the other toward the west. As I prepared to take some landscape photographs and to wait for a potential sunset picture, I discovered numerous black swifts circling overhead. During the next hour and a half I counted seventy-two black swifts and twenty chestnut-collared swifts moving overhead in a general easterly direction. I decided that I was watching what probably was one of a daily flight of swifts returning to their roosting sites in the mountains from feeding areas in the lowlands, possibly at cultivated fields around Mazatlán. In addition to the swifts, three snowy-bellied martins passed overhead flying toward the south, and several common nighthawks circled overhead, as well. The sunset was not all I had hoped for but my visit to the roof had been a rewarding experience nonetheless.

Fruiting Madrones

Trogons primarily are fruit-eaters, rather than being insectivorous or seed-eaters like the majority of North American birds. Although we did not see many kinds of fruiting trees in the forest, one huge madrone stood out in particular. It had attracted numerous birds which we found feeding on its abundant berries. It was a truly outstanding example of madrone, a normally small species that is fairly common throughout the pine-oak zone of the Sierra Madre Occidental. The local names for madrones can be very confusing. Madrones usually are called *madrono* in Mexico, although in the Durango area they are most often called *manzanita.* However, manzanita is a common shrub that grows on these same slopes and is usually called *manzanilla* in the Durango-Sinaloa area of Mexico. Both madrone and manzanita occur northward into southwestern United States.

The madrone fruit had not yet turned red as they do later in the season, but were a leathery green color. The very large madrone, growing at the edge of a small canyon, possessed thousands of the quarter-inch drupes (berries) growing at the ends of the abundant branches. These berries were being harvested in profusion by the local avian residents.

I was first attracted to the tree by a rather nondescript bird that flew into its foliage and immediately began picking and swallowing berries as fast as it could. As I watched it, I realized that I was watching not one but a pair of Aztec thrushes. This is another species that was known only for Mexico until recently, but has now been recorded in Arizona's Huachuca and Santa Rita Mountains and the Chisos Mountains in Big Bend National Park, Texas. And on nearby branches I observed several, as many as a dozen, white-throated robins. They, too, seemed to be set upon swallowing as many of the madrone fruits as they could.

A flock of gray silky-flycatchers suddenly descended from somewhere and joined the berry-feeding frenzy. Once they appeared I realized that I had been hearing their metallic but melodic calls for some time, but the sound just didn't register until the birds were suddenly part of the scene. The gray silky-flycatcher is another fruit-eating bird of the highlands and ranges from northern Mexico to Guatemala. I have seen it often perched at the very tops of pine or fir trees, from where its very distinctive song resounds through-out the forest. Its closest relative is Panama's long-tailed silky-fly-catcher, but it is also related to the phainopepla of the American deserts. All three belong to the family Ptilogonatidae.

The lowest of the side roads, accessible at kilometer post 215, ended in less than a quarter of a mile at a little clearing that also provided an excellent view toward the west and of the surrounding slopes. It afforded a good view of the sky, and it was there that we observed a peregrine falcon that seemed to be hunting as it circled a little ravine below us for some time before disappearing to the south. We had several excellent looks at this bird and decided it was an adult tiercel (male).

Oak Woodlands

One of our four mornings in the Sierra Madre was spent exploring the drier oak woodlands approximately a thousand feet lower in eleva-tion than Villa Blanca. We drove back toward Mazatlán for about 4.5 miles to kilometer post 240 at a tiny unnamed village. We parked along the highway and walked north along a little rutted roadway that followed a small streambed that contained some rather lush riparian vegetation. Our route wove through a very arid woodland setting. Oaks were again the dominant trees, and there were several fine examples of netleaf oak, a large evergreen tree that seemed to dominate the immediate landscape. Other common trees included two or three kinds of acacia; pricklenut, a member of the cacao fam-ily; morning glory tree and kapok tree. This habitat seemed to be a transition zone between the tropical deciduous forest habitat fur-ther down the slope and the pine-oak woodland habitat that began just above.

This lower and drier area provided us with a whole new assort-ment of birds, and very few duplicates. We hadn't walked very far when we heard the repetitive mellow whistle of a ferruginous pygmy-owl. This diminutive, diurnal species is one of Mexico's most common owls. It occurs throughout the lowlands up to the coniferous forests where the similar northern pygmy-owl is often present. Birders utilize these little predators as an attractant to other birds in the vicinity whenever they occur, and we did just that.

We located the calling ferruginous pygmy-owl in a leafless oak tree growing alongside one of the evergreen netleaf oaks in the canyon bottom. For more than twenty minutes we sat nearby and watched other birds mob the pygmy-owl. The little owl finally tired of the harassment and flew up the drainage, around the next bend, and out of sight.

The most aggressive of the avian mobbers had been one of the smallest, the golden vireo. A pair of these birds had soundly scolded the pygmy-owl from the nearby oak foliage, and remained there in defiance until the owl departed. A lone sulphur-bellied flycatcher seemed to be bravest and actually flew close enough to make the owl, which is just about the same size as the flycatcher, duck its head with each pass. A blue mockingbird scolded from the oak foliage, and two or three tropical parulas flitted nervously about. They were joined by a lone rufous-capped warbler. A streak-backed oriole came by for a few moments to see what the commotion was all about. It scolded briefly but flew off down the canyon. And all the while a lone male yellow grosbeak sat in the lower branches of a nearby shrub; I was never sure that it was even aware of the presence of the ferruginous pygmy-owl.

The largest bird that was attracted to the commotion in the oak tree was the black-throated magpie jay. Several of these long-tailed corvids were observed working their way down the drainage to within a dozen or so feet from the owl before they swiftly departed back the way they had come, probably after seeing the three human observers.

Other birds we found in the immediate vicinity included both American and white-throated robins, Swainson's thrush, happy wren, three hummingbirds—white-eared, berylline and cinnamon, and an ivory-billed woodcreeper.

We walked further up the canyon to where it became more of an upland slope than a canyon bottom. At the far end we found a pair of rose-throated becards attending a nest that was hanging from a bare limb of what I believe was a hackberry tree. The rose-pink throat patch of the male was truly iridescent that day. And although I had seen this species many times before, both in the United States and Mexico, I had never seen the brillance of the throat color as it was that day.

A streak-backed oriole male was seen briefly at that same spot, but stayed only long enough for identification, not long enough for us to admire him thoroughly before he disappeared into the wooded slope above us. We attempted to find him again without success. But as we searched the slope, we were attracted to a high pitched *see see see* call nearby. It took us several minutes of searching, while the bird continued to sing its whispy song, until we finally detected the tiny bird from whence the song came, a scrub euphonia. It was a brightly colored male, in yellow and black plumage; a beautiful little bird that we might have missed before he sang his song.

Two additional birds were recorded along the canyon bottom only because we heard their calls. The cascading song of the canyon wren was unmistakable. Its presence that day in an arid oak canyon in south-central Sinaloa was reminiscent of many observations of this species in the Big Bend country of West Texas. It took us some time to find this little reddish and white songster, and when we did we found not one but two individuals foraging among the rocks and vegetation. The other familiar call was from an acorn woodpecker that we found perched on an oak snag far up the slope. It stayed on that snag for some time, and then sailed out in flycatcher fashion to capture an insect of some kind and return to its perch.

Earlier, as we had entered the canyon, we had frightened a huge flock of band-tailed pigeons (approximately sixty-five individuals) that had probably been drinking along the creekbed. We had also seen several orange-fronted parakeets moving ahead of us. As we turned around and started back, we observed a lone green parakeet fly out of a thicket of trees in a little side canyon and soar overhead toward the ridge. And further on, just before we reached the paved roadway, three black vultures flapped out of the way from where they had been perched next to a pen where fifteen to twenty goats were kept.

We returned to the Villa Blanca by noon and ate a good lunch. We rested for another hour or so, and then headed out again, up toward the higher forest to search for additional secrets of the Sierra Madre.

13

Quest for the Slender-billed Wren

Only eighty-four of Mexico's approximately one thousand kinds of birds are endemic, species that occur only within the boundaries of Mexico. Sixteen of the eighty-four species are sparrows, ten are wrens, seven are warblers; quail, parrots, hummingbirds, woodpeckers, jays and thrashers each contribute five species; and eleven other family groups have one to four representatives.

Finding these endemics within their native habitats has been a special challenge to me ever since I discovered the pleasure of birding in Mexico. And in more recent years, after my Mexican bird-list expanded to the point that I had seen most of the common species, trips have been planned around the discovery of the rarest of these endemics. Searching out the rarities also provides opportunities to find the more common Mexican species. The quest for the slender-billed wren was one of the most frustrating but rewarding of all.

Francis Sumichrast

The slender-billed wren is known to scientists as *Hylorchilus sumichrasti,* named after the man who first collected it, Swiss naturalist Francis Sumichrast. Although it is currently included in the 1983 AOU check-list and in the various Mexico field guides as slender-billed wren, a few ornithologists prefer its earlier common name, Sumichrast's wren. That nomenclature may give it a little more personality, although its founder was a rather obscure individual. However, Sumichrast appears to have been a well-rounded naturalist, having published papers on Mexican birds, mammals, and reptiles.

I discovered some information about Francis Sumichrast by researching the literature. The AOU Check-list references Sumichrast two more times: it includes a second bird species named for him, the cinnamon-tailed sparrow (*Aimophila sumichrasti*), from the Pacific slope of Oaxaca and Chiapas, and an aberrant berylline hummingbird specimen from Oaxaca that was mistakenly given specific status was also named for Sumichrast.

There is another reference to him in Pierce Brodkorb's 1943 paper, *Birds from the Gulf Lowlands of Southern Mexico*. Brodkorb wrote, "While residing in southern Mexico, the Swiss naturalist Francis Sumichrast collected some birds of the Atlantic side of the Isthmus of Tehuantepec. He recorded the occurrence of three species on the Río Coatzacoalcos, Veracruz, but did not give any specific locality. From other sources it appears to have been Minatitlán" (p. 8).

In addition, three mammals were named for Sumichrast. Dr. E. Raymond Hall's *The Mammals of North America* includes the Sumichrast vesper rat, Sumichrast harvest mouse, and Sumichrast ringtail (see chapter sixteen, "El Triunfo"). Type localities for all three were in eastern Veracruz during the 1860s. And there is another Sumichrast reference — to an 1882 paper on Mexican reptiles — in *The Snakes of Honduras* by Wilson and Meyers. I imagine that the Sumichrast wren was first collected during the later half of the 1800s.

Sumichrast's wren

The slender-billed wren has a very restricted range, and there is no evidence to suggest that its range was larger in earlier years. It is known only from south-central Mexico in the area where the states of Veracruz, Chiapas and Oaxaca meet. The area is exceedingly precipitous and not on a commonly traveled route. It is far enough off the Mexico City to Veracruz Highway to require the best part of a day's side trip to reach the proper habitat. This inaccessibility, plus the fact that this long-billed wren must be one of the world's most nondescript birds, gives it rather low priority for most naturalists.

It has most often been described as a small dusky to dark brown bird, much like a canyon wren, but without the white throat. The throat and belly actually are light brown or grayish in color; inconspicuous white specks occur on the belly. Its most obvious feature is its long bill. In *Birds of Mexico*, Blake stated that its bill is "long, slender, and almost straight." Irby Davis, in *A Field Guide to the Birds of Mexico and Central America*, says the bill is "as long as head, straight and slender."

All of the field guides agree that the bird is rare and local in occurrence and prefers dense undergrowth in humid forests. I suppose it could be considered a good example of what some birders call a "shadow" bird. This group of birds includes those species that rarely come into the bright sunlight, that prefer the dimly lighted shadows, and are less active during bright, sunny days.

Preliminary Investigations

Vague generalities were all that my preparatory research provided on where best to find this bird. Everything I read pointed to an area south of Córdoba, Veracruz, in the vicinity of Presidio, Motzorongo, and Mato Bejouco. I had written letters to four birding friends who had lots of experience in Mexico, and asked them about where they might recommend as the best place to find the slender-billed wren. They all had responded alike; none had seen it and they did not know of anyone who had. In spite of these uncertainties, I decided to explore the area south of Córdoba, along the Cuichapa to Acatlán highway, and to spend the time necessary to find this little-known wren en route back to Mexico City from a birding trip to Catemaco.

The slender-billed wren trip started with flights from various cities in the United States to Mexico City on December 16, 1980. Woody and Bo West came from New Mexico, Ron Knaus from Louisiana, and Nape Shelton and I from our nation's capital. After a short night in Mexico City, we birded our way southeast to Catemaco. There we participated in the annual Catemaco Christmas count (see chapter eighteen, "Catemaco at Christmas" for more details), explored the Santa Marta cloud forest, and searched for the many species of birds that occur in the Sierra de la Tuxlas.

On the evening before the Catemaco count, most of the participants met for dinner in the dining room of the Playa Azul Motel, where many of us were staying. It was an opportunity to learn more about the area and discuss any special birds that we should look for the next day. One of the many people there that evening was Bill Schaldach. A long-time Mexico resident and professional ornithologist, Bill had collected bird specimens throughout Mexico for several U.S. museums, including the American Museum of Natural History and Smithsonian Institution. I found him to be a fountain of knowledge about Mexican birds, their preferred habitats, and Mexican biogeography. He seems to know more about Mexican birds than anyone I have met before or have encountered since. And what's more, he had seen "Sumichrast" wrens on a "few occasions," and had even collected the species in "blocked limestone canyons" near

Presidio and Motzorongo. He described the bird as extremely secretive and preferring the dense undergrowth within mid-elevation forests. This information on its whereabouts was the best I had uncovered to date.

The Search

And so, equipped with this new lead, my companions and I left Catemaco on the morning of January 5, and drove north on Highway 180 toward Veracruz. We left Highway 180 just north of Lerdo de Tejale, after a short stop there to restore our stock of pan dulce. We traveled west on Highway 175 as far as Ciudad Aleman. There we turned north onto Highway 145 and proceeded to El Amate, where we turned northwest toward Acatlán and Cuichapa on the Córdoba highway.

The El Amate to Córdoba route is one that I would not recommend to anyone driving anything other than a suitable high-clearance vehicle. We were driving a rented sedan, loaded with five average to large people. Although the southern and northern portions of the route were paved and moderately well maintained, the middle one-third was little more than a mountain track that was either extremely rocky or terribly dusty. Needless to say, our Dart sedan was driven slowly and with a great deal of caution.

Although we realized how slow our traveling was to be, we forged ahead, intending to stop overnight at or near Omealca, where, according to Bill, we could find a hotel for the night. We could then search out suitable slender-billed wren habitat the next morning. Beyond Acatlán we found terrain along the highway that seemed to match perfectly Bill's description of the kind of environment we needed to explore. We noted several accessible canyons that we might wish to return to the following morning. Although the valleys we drove through were filled with sugarcane fields, the adjacent hillsides were clad in tropical forest. Blocked limestone outcroppings protruded from the hillsides at numerous locations.

We arrived at Omealca in the late afternoon to discover that the hotel had long ago closed; in the shade of a tree alongside a railroad track we planned our strategy. We were all very tired and dusty and would have preferred to stop for the night. I even contemplated usurping an old railroad boxcar nearby, until I noticed that it already was being used by a family with at least eight children. We decided five more people would be five too many. After some discussion, we drove onward searching for a suitable camping place. We were prepared to camp and would have preferred to do so rather than to drive on over the very rough and dusty road after dark. However the dust from dozens of trucks thick upon our vehicle and surroundings (considerable road work was underway) discouraged us from camping, and we continued at a snail's pace, creeping up one ridge and down into the next canyon, and onward. Finally, at Cuichapa was pavement, and by 8:00 P.M. we arrived at the southern edge of Córdoba. We immediately acquired rooms at the first hotel we found, an ancient one called the Imperial across the street from the railroad depot. We filled the car with gasoline, had an excellent fish dinner at a tiny nearby restaurant, and were in bed at 10:30.

Dawn found us back at Cuichapa, twelve miles south of Hotel Imperial. After a short stop at a tiny market for pan dulce, we continued driving south, backtracking over the same route we had traveled after dark the night before. The area provided marvelous scenery. The mountains seemed to rise directly out of the deep canyons, and I could not help but fantasize that each contained major populations of slender-billed wrens.

Three and a half miles south of Cuichapa we came to the little village of Xuchiles, perched on the south side of a rugged canyon containing a stream of foaming water. Blocked limestone cliffs were evident below and above the town, and it appeared that village roads might provide access to the kind of habitat we were seeking. Close up, the stream was surprisingly large, and the abundance of boulders strewn along the canyon suggested that it had a long history of turbulence following periods of heavy rainfall. Further up-canyon the steep hillsides were further clues of a young and vigorous stream, but time did not permit us to explore the headwaters. The Mexican government had declared the upper reaches of this watershed a national park, marked on our map as Parque Nacional Cañon de Río Blanco. We could see that access to this high country was possible only from the north along Highway 150.

"Canyon of the White River" was a good description of the area at Xuchiles, as well. The white limestone had been cut by millennia of streamflow, and the cliffsides along the drainage and further back along the hillsides contained a heavy growth of tropical forest.

Imperial Hotel, Córdoba, Veracruz, only an hour's drive north of slender-billed wren habitat.

Semievergreen Forest

The habitat that surrounded Xuchiles can best be described as "semi-evergreen forest," a term first used in 1955 by J. S. Beard. Jerzy Rzedowski refers to this habitat as *bosque tropical subcaducifolio* (semievergreen or seasonal forest) in his excellent 1983 book, *Vegetación de México*. It is this habitat that forms a transition between the more luxuriant rain forest and the drier tropical deciduous forest. The Veracruz semievergreen forest, which often is almost indistinguishable from true rain forest, is dominated by such trees as figs, eardrop tree, a small white-barked tree locally called *tepeguaje*, trumpet tree, and a small mulberry known only by its local name, *moradilla*.

Strangler figs were some of the most obvious trees of the area. Because of the rocky topography, their long roots seemed to embrace every imaginable object, gray woody fingers grasping the rocks like the tentacles of an octopus with captured prey. Of Mexico's seventeen species of *Ficus,* three were reported for the vicinity by Rzedowski. All of these produce edible fruits as well as a milky sap that contains a (noncommercial) type of rubber. The small but nourishing fruits are used by most of Mexico's fruit-eating wildlife.

The commonly used name for many fig species in Mexico is *amate,* a Nahuatl word meaning paper. According to Mason and Mason in *A Handbook of Mexican Roadside Flora,* "before the Spanish conquest, the Indians used fig bark to make paper. The bark was stripped from the tree, soaked in lye water, washed, boiled, and split into thin strips. These were then placed on a plank and pounded with a stone until a sheet of paper resulted" (p. 250).

The most common large forest tree at Xuchiles was the eardrop tree, locally called *orejon.* A member of the pea family, it produces a huge trunk with a wide-spreading canopy. Its common name is derived from the rather large and flat seedpods that, according to Standley's *Trees and Shrubs of Mexico,* make excellent cattle feed, "and the seeds as well as the young pods are sometimes cooked to be used for human food" (p. 391).

Tepeguaje was the common, rather thin white-barked tree scattered here and there throughout the forest. It is another member of the pea family and of the common tropical genus *Lysiloma.* These little trees do not possess spines; they have small and inconspicuous flowers, and fruit that is flat and broad. Standley reported: "The bark is astringent and is used in domestic medicine. It is sometimes chewed to harden the gums. The gum which exudes from the bark is used like gum arabic" (p. 389).

Mexico's semievergreen forest has been heavily logged throughout its range, and virgin forests are few and far between. The only natural semievergreen forest habitat left today is in areas inaccessible for logging, agriculture, and grazing.

Xuchiles

The village of Xuchiles didn't even exist on our maps, including the two Veracruz state maps we carried with us. We crossed the bridge and parked at a roadside pulloff, in front of a small, well-decorated shrine. We then walked up the road into the center of Xuchiles. Except for a small army station, located just above the shrine and in view of the bridge, Xuchiles was composed of a dozen or so houses, a few stores, a tiny railroad station, and a surprisingly large canefield.

Beyond the army station we found a cobbled roadway leading off to the west. The village *carnicería* (meat market) stood guard at the junction. Several houses lined this roadway, and further on were the green stalks of the canefield. We attracted attention at the fourth house, and a little old man (he looked to be about seventy years of age but may have been as young as fifty or fifty-five) emerged with an inquisitive look and a smile. He was both friendly and curious. After a proper greeting, I informed him that we were looking at birds and were especially interested in finding one particular species. Although my Spanish and his English were hardly compatible, he understood. I opened my Mexican field guide to plate thirty-three and pointed out the bird that we were hoping to find. Plate thirty-three contains all of Mexico's cactus wrens, the two nondescript nightingale and slender-billed wrens, and the gnatcatchers. It was obvious that he immediately recognized the slender-billed wren. And when I asked him if it occurred there, he swung his arm around and said that it was present all around in the *cañons.* His knowledge of that species, in spite of its secretive habits, seemed most evident.

After a few more comments and a *muchas gracias,* we bade him *adios* and continued up the roadway toward the beckoning hillside beyond. We turned left off the cobbled road at the first side road and walked through the cane field to where a path ran up the slope and into the forest. Coffee bushes had been planted on the hillside ridges beneath the larger trees, but the rocky ravines appeared to contain only mature, native vegetation. We birded along the path for about an hour (for less than half a mile) to a point above the stream and where the terrain seemed almost impossible to negotiate any further. We then backtracked a few yards to where we found a less obvious track that ran further up the slope, and birded along this route for another hundred yards or so.

Our first really exciting find was a small flock of emerald toucanets foraging high in the forest canopy with a flock of Montezuma and chestnut-headed oropendolas and collared aracaris. A little further on, in a small rocky clearing, we found a large party of warblers

Slender-billed wren habitat on slopes just beyond cane fields at
Xuchiles, Veracruz.

and other passerines. Included in this group were black-and-white,
black-throated green, magnolia, fan-tailed and Wilson's warblers;
both northern and tropical parulas; American redstart, masked tityra,
tufted flycatcher, brown jay, band-backed wren, wood thrush, clay-
colored robin, blue-gray gnatcatcher, yellow-throated euphonia,
yellow-winged tanager, and cedar waxwing.

We found a pair of violaceous trogons feeding in the foliage of
a fig tree and were able to watch these birds for several minutes as
they foraged in clear view. The bird's "violaceous" breast, lemon-
yellow belly, and the male's black-and-white, narrowly barred tail
were most obvious. Its tail pattern reminded me that this species
had earlier been called gartered trogon. However, the sunlight that
reflected on the male's chest provided us with a better understanding of the name now accepted for this beautiful creature. Nearby

were black-cheeked woodpeckers and an olivaceous woodcreeper searching for insects on the trunks of trees in full sight of our little party of observers. Spot-breasted wrens sang from well hidden perches among the thick undergrowth, and at least two white-bellied wrens were seen and heard as well. High above the canopy were Vaux's swift, tree and northern rough-winged swallows, turkey vulture and a short-tailed hawk.

Suddenly, almost at my feet, I heard and saw a dark brown wren-sized bird. It "skidded" past and flew to a perch near the ground on a little limestone pinnacle. It stopped there for less than three seconds, and then disappeared. A slender-billed wren! I had seen at close hand, without the need of binoculars, the bird of my quest. And I was able to follow it by sound as it progressed up the hillside. Its call has been described as a "sharp *peenck*," but I found it more like the *choak* of a very hoarse canyon wren.

We sat still and waited for its return. And in about fifteen minutes, two slender-billed wrens flew across the trail in full view, almost brushing Bo where she sat silently. In spite of our waiting for almost another hour, and hearing their distinct calls several times again, they did not put in another appearance.

Our quest for the slender-billed wren had been a success! Forgotten were the difficulties we had experienced along the previous day's route; we had discovered some exciting new habitat, and a reasonably accessible place to find another of Mexico's endemics.

14

The Jalisco-Colima Circle

The dawn chorus of birds within the humid pine-oak forest, at 9,200 feet elevation on Volcán Colima, was an incredible experience I will long remember. I lay there in my sleeping bag listening to the myriad of bird sounds around me and discovered that I was able to identify the majority of the songs. The most obvious and loudest sound, however, was that of the long-tailed wood-partridge, whose loud chachalaca-like calls seemed to echo all around me. The nearest individual was only a few yards away, although I could not see it from my position, and many others were calling between where I lay and far across the forested canyon. Their calls were a truly dominating sound.

The scattering of brown-backed solitaire songs, each like a jumbled series of fast flute-like notes, ascending in pitch and frequency, echoed around me in all directions. A slate-throated redstart was singing from the nearby pines, and almost overhead a crescent-chested warbler joined in the morning songfest. I detected the *tucka-tucka-tucka* of a mountain trogon somewhere on the slope below, and a blue mockingbird sang from a nearby thicket of vines and shrubs. A hairy woodpecker called somewhere off to the right. And as I started to climb out of my sleeping bag and prepare for the day, several gray silky-flycatchers flew up from a patch of tall lupines only a few feet away from our camp. They settled on the tops of the nearby oaks, adding their strange, metallic notes to the chorus. And so our day on the upper slopes of Volcán Colima began.

Dick Russell and I had driven up the very dusty and winding logging road the day before. We had found the Volcán de Fuego junction on Highway 110, just south of Atenquique, Jalisco, early in the morning of May 4, and slowly ascended onto the southern flank of this active volcano. We were amazed at the diversity of habitats above the cultivated fields and arid woodlands. The first change was a gradual one of increased tree size and density that produced a good example of tropical deciduous forest habitat. But that zone was little more than a narrow band, because shortly, at about 5,000 feet elevation, we entered a pine forest that looked very similar to the ponderosa pine forests of the southwestern United States. Montezuma and Aztec pines were dominant, but ocote pine (*Pinus oocarpa*) was present as well. And we found several Mexican hawthorns scattered about within the pine stands.

I was surprised at the abundance of familiar North American birds that we found during the couple of hours we spent exploring this habitat. I recorded four woodpeckers (acorn, ladder-backed and Strickland's, and northern flicker), greater pewee, dusky-capped flycatcher, Cassin's kingbird, bushtit, brown creeper, solitary and warbling vireos; the Nashville, yellow, yellow-rumped, Grace's, and MacGillivray's warblers; indigo bunting, and blue and black-headed grosbeaks. Mexican bird specialties were represented by the russet-crowned motmot, gray-barred and bar-vented wrens, both the rufous-backed and white-throated robins, russet nightingale-thrush, gray silky-flycatcher, rufous-capped warbler, collared towhee, and yellow grosbeak.

Not far beyond, at about six thousand feet elevation, the pine forest began to change to an oak-dominated habitat. We encountered a cobblestone road at 8.4 miles above the Atenquique junction that branched to the right off the main route and led to a microwave station on an adjacent ridge. Because the route was accessible and provided good open oak woodland habitat, we spent an hour or so exploring the road edge and the microwave clearing. It was a stroke of luck. Although we didn't find a lot of birds, one of those that we did record was one of my most-wanted Mexican species.

We had worked our way along the edge of the upper clearing to where we had a good view of the oak woodland. I imitated a ferruginous pygmy-owl call. Immediately a tiny bird flew out of the adjacent oak canopy into a isolated oak within the clearing. It didn't stay long, but sang a very short song that reminded me of a Hutton's vireo song. My first glance at the bird confirmed it as a vireo, but it was smaller than a Hutton's vireo and rather dull with two thin but obvious wingbars. Then it was gone, as fast as it had appeared. Dick and I looked at each other for just a second, then both exclaimed together: "That was a dwarf vireo!" We had found one of Mexico's true rarities. That sighting of such a wanted species was what Mexican birding is all about. The joy of finding a rarity in such out-of-the-way localities makes life most worthwhile.

The dwarf vireo is one of Mexico's rarest endemics. It occurs only in the southwestern mountains from Jalisco to Oaxaca. Emmet Blake included it in his 1953 *Birds of Mexico* on the basis of a single known specimen. Since then, although it is still considered rare, it has been reported from the mountains of Jalisco, Guanajuato and Querétaro to Oaxaca. The 1983 AOU Check-list reports it to winter in its breeding range and north to Sinaloa.

We continued to follow the dusty logging road upward, and discovered that the higher we drove, the more impressive our surroundings became. At around 8,000 feet elevation, we encountered a beautiful pine-oak forest draped with an abundance of mosses and epiphytes that made it look very much like cloud forest habitat. I photographed an epiphytic cactus growing on a huge oak at least one hundred feet tall. We stopped at a deserted logging camp and birded around the clearing, and again at an old road that skirted a beautiful canyon a little further on. There we decided to camp for the night. We ate a dinner from cans and munched on our ever-present pan dulce, and listened to the numerous night sounds as darkness crept in around us.

Sometime during the night I was awakened by a whip-poor-will perched on the ground less than four feet from my head, proclaiming his territory to the world. I, unfortunately, had placed my sleeping bag in the middle of his singing grounds, and not until I threw some gravel his way did he let me continue sleeping. Sometime after midnight, I was awakened again by a large owl calling some distance down the canyon. Although I was not able to identify the call for sure, the single or double *hoo* notes closely resembled the descriptions for the very rare stygian owl, a tropical species that eluded me for many years. I finally found the species in March, 1991, in Cuba.

The dawn chorus of birds lasted only until the first rays of the sun touched the higher treetops. Then the level of bird song declined by at least half. Although single wood-partridge songs were still heard occasionally, they no longer dominated the morning. The brown-backed solitaire and silky-flycatcher songs remained at about the same intensity.

I later examined the tree-like lupines, six to nine feet in height, at the edge of our campsite and discovered four active gray silky-flycatcher nests near the top of four of the plants. Further up the mountain, we found an estimated 120 individuals perched on the higher vegetation within an eight- to ten-acre area. I could not help but wonder if this highland species is a communal nester, although none of my reference books includes any suggestion that this might be the case.

We continued our drive upward on the dusty logging road, and before long we began to get some incredible views of the steaming summit of Volcán de Fuego (12,500 feet). We stopped at a pull-off at about 10,000 feet (nineteen miles from the Atenquique junction), where the road turned right and crossed an open cinder field. From there we were able to hike onto the nearby cinder cone. And as we wandered across the coal-black field, dotted with a number of Aztec and Mexican white pines and shrubs, we were showered by minute cinders from the smoking crater of Volcán de Fuego. The higher of Volcán Colima's twin cones, Volcán de Nieve (14,235 feet), was another two miles to the north. The twin peaks are separated by a long treeless ridge. We hiked up onto this ridge for almost a mile to where we found ourselves sliding backwards two or three feet with each step.

The treeline, at the edge of the cinder field, was dominated by Mexican fir. We surprised two white-tailed deer that were grazing within a little grassy area along the edge of the forest. They immediately ran across the cinder field in our general direction before disappearing around the edge of the hill, leaving us wondering why they had not retreated into the nearby forest.

It was not until we returned to our car in the shade of the tall adjacent forest that I realized that two of the nearest trees were sweet gum. This species and the abundant epiphytes growing on all of the canopy and understory trees and shrubs were good cloud forest characteristics. I searched for tree ferns, another excellent indicator of cloud forest habitat, but could not find any. The majority of the tall forest trees were oaks. Bill Schaldach called this upland area humid pine-oak forest in his 1963 paper on the birds of this region; it was a most appropriate term.

We spend several hours exploring this habitat. Again I was surprised at the large number of North American birds we recorded. Some of the common ones included band-tailed pigeon, American robin, singing golden-crowned kinglets, yellow-rumped and Wilson's warblers, Lincoln's sparrow, and black-headed grosbeak. The more exciting Mexican specialities included: Mexican chickadee; gray-breasted wood-wrens were calling insistently from each overgrown depression; we found several red warblers and were impressed with their deep red color and contrasting white cheek patches; both the rufous-capped and green-striped brush-finches, and the collared towhee. The green-striped brush-finch was the only lifer I recorded there, and I got some excellent views of this large sparrow as it searched for food in the undergrowth. The three yellow-green stripes on its black crown were most evident in good light, but difficult to discern in the shadowy undergrowth.

The three days we spent in the highlands of Volcán Colima were during a ten-day trip we were taking within southwestern Jalisco and Colima. Our visit had begun at the Guadalajara International Airport, on the afternoon of April 29, 1977, where we claimed our baggage, rented a car, and drove southwest on Highway 80 toward Autlán. We planned to drive across the Sierra de Autlán to the coast, south on Highway 110 to Tecomán, Colima, then northeast to Ciudad Colima and Ciudad Guzman, Jalisco, and finally north on Highway 33 back to Guadalajara.

The major purpose of the trip was to explore some habitats that neither of us had previously seen and find a few of the resident birds that would be new for us. Our interest in this region of Mexico had evolved from a short article on the birds of the Sierra de Autlán by Kenn Kaufman, Ted Parker, and Mark Robbins, that had appeared in the December, 1976 issue of *Mexican Birds Newsletter.* I also had acquired copies of two technical papers by W. J. Schaldach, Jr. on the Colima-Jalisco area (1963 and 1969), which had further whetted my appetite. And when I suggested a trip to Dick Russell, a long-time friend and birding companion, he enthusiastically agreed.

Sierra de Autlán

Our principal interest near Autlán were the varied habitats accessible from where Highway 80 crosses the Sierra de Autlán foothills, just 9.5 miles west of town, at a place called La Cumbre by the locals, and Puerto Los Masos on adjacent highway markers. Schaldach (1969) had described the vegetation at this point as "thick oak woodland on the ridges, intermixed locally with some pines, and heavy tropical deciduous forest in the steepsided 'barranca' (ravine) west of and below the pass" (p. 299). A trail goes up the relatively steep south slope, past a radio tower, and beyond into a humid pine-oak forest that provided a third type of habitat. We explored each of these areas for three full days.

The trail above the highway was actually an old roadway that skirts a large canyon and proceeds to climb steeply along a ridge to a point where it enters a rather impressive oak woodland. I recorded a total of seventy-four birds from along this trail; several of these were Mexican species of special interest. Four were hummers: the long-tailed hermit, berylline, violet-crowned and magnificent hummingbirds. We found a greenish elaenia along the trail above the canyon, a bird new to us both. This little flycatcher was very similar, at first glance, to an *Empidonax* flycatcher; it was about the same size and had a distinct eye-ring. It even had a posture that is more *Empidonax*-like than elaenia-like. The best characteristic, and one that was not easy to detect, was its yellow crown patch.

We found two wrens within the oak woodlands, both of which were surprisingly common. The spotted wren is a rather large wren that is similar to its northern cousin, the cactus wren, but with a white throat and spots on its breast and belly. And the Sinaloa wren, sometimes called bar-vented wren, is a smaller bird that looks a little like the Carolina wren of the United States.

One of my favorite birds of the trip was the chestnut-sided shrike-vireo; indeed it looked exactly as one would expect of a shrike-vireo mix with chestnut-colored sides. The species is almost totally restricted to oak-dominated forests at high altitudes from central Mexico to Guatemala. I watched it feeding upside down on the underside of huge oak branches high above the forest floor, a habit that is much more typical of woodpeckers and woodcreepers than for perching birds.

We also recorded several tanagers within the oak forest, including a pair of blue-hooded euphonias and the red-headed, hepatic, western, and flame-colored tanagers. Rusty sparrows were fairly common within this habitat, as well. And I found a pair of black-headed siskins feeding young in a nest about twelve feet up in an extremely thin oak in the center of the trail. It seemed like a poor location for a nest, but the three or four youngsters looked healthy and active, so the parents had evidently chosen an adequate site after all.

The barranca, the steep ravine on the north side of the highway,

contained a completely different habitat of dense tropical deciduous forest. The canopy trees of this environment may have been a
hundred feet tall, and the undergrowth contained a wide assortment
of epiphytes, thorny vines and lianas. The area contained several
birds that we found nowhere else, the most outstanding being the
rosy thrush-tanager. This species had earlier been reported for the
barranca habitat by Kaufmann, Parker, and Robbins. It took a good
deal of searching before we finally found one, a lone male, hopping
about in the bottom debris as if playing some strange game. Although very little light penetrated through the foliage onto the
ground, it seemed as if the bird stayed within the very narrow shaft
of light that did reach the canyon bottom. His rosy breast, high-
lighted by the one shaft of light, seemed to be a brighter and more
exciting color than I would have ever imagined. We were suitably
impressed.

Other Mexican birds recorded in the barranca included long-tailed
wood-partridge, blue-rumped parrotlet, fork-tailed emerald, gray-
crowned woodpecker, white-streaked woodcreeper, gray-collared becard, blue mockingbird, white-throated robin, slate-throated redstart,
fan-tailed warbler, and rufous-capped brush-finch. The most abundant of these, at least during our midafternoon visit, was the blue
mockingbird. I estimated thirty-plus individuals within the tropical deciduous forest habitat within and adjacent to the barranca.

On two evenings after dark we found eared poorwills along the
trail above the highway. This is one of Mexico's endemic species that
occurs only in western Mexico from southern Sonora south to Guerrero, and only within arid pine-oak and oak woodlands. Although
it was considered rare throughout its range, its presence at this locality had been well documented prior to our visit; Schaldach and Allan
Phillips described the bird, its range, ecology and life history in an
article that appeared in the journal *Auk* in October 1961.

We found eared poorwills calling at dusk, at 7:15 P.M., and they
continued to call until we left the area three hours later. Their song
was "a loud, clear, whistled *kyooo*," as described by Kaufmann, Parker,
and Robbins. In spite of two birds singing along the slope very near
the trail, it took us more than two hours to get close enough to one
to capture it in the beam of our flashlight. But finally we found
one sitting horizontal on a limb within a woody shrub adjacent to

the trail. We also heard a whiskered owl calling from the barranca below the highway.

On May 1, we arrived at La Cumbre at 5:00 A.M., and immediately hiked up the trail into the humid pine-oak forest habitat. Eared poorwills called along the lower part of the route until 5:35 A.M. At least three Colima warblers were singing in the canyon below the trail. The *sweeet* calls of Hutton's vireos were prominent sounds from the oaks. The canyon wren-like call of the ivory-billed woodcreeper was heard several times. And further up the ridge the dominant calls were the *ho-say Marie* of the greater pewees.

We found five hummingbirds along the upper trail, two of which were priority birds in our search. We discovered that the one lifer, the amethyst-throated hummingbird, was fairly common, but we found only one crowned woodnymph. The other three hummers seen were the white-eared, blue-throated, and magnificent, all mountain species we found fairly common at all of the highland localities we birded. We also found a lone red-headed tanager nest-building on a high oak branch.

Mammals are rarely seen in any of the numerous places I have visited in Mexico, but there are exceptions. Deer are seen occasionally. Opossums, raccoons, and smaller creatures, such as mice and rats, are often seen along the highways, and bats can almost always be found flying during the evening hours. Other mammals are unusual, to say the least. So the finding of a beautifully marked long-tailed weasel high on the upper slopes of the humid pine-oak forest was a real surprise. This weasel, which is called *comedreja* in Spanish, was marked with a black face and white mask, a beautiful cinnamon body, and long tail with a black tip. It was not at all shy, but moved along the ground from one tree trunk to another, searching for food within the various holes and under bits of bark and debris. We watched it progress along the slope below us for eight or ten minutes before it disappeared from view.

West of La Cumbre, Highway 80 drops out of the Sierra de Autlán rather steeply, providing an interesting cross section of a more arid and shorter habitat that A. Starker Leopold (1950) called tropical deciduous forest and Jerzy Rzedowski (1983) refers to as bosque tropical caducifolio. We spent a good part of a morning within this area en route toward the coast.

A description of the vegetation of this area was included within a rather extensive 1966 report on western Mexico's tropical deciduous forest by Rzedowski and R. McVaugh. They reported that the dominant plant species found along the western slopes of the Sierra de Autlán included the small white-barked lysiloma locally known as *palo de arco; Amphipterygium* spp.; naked Indian, locally called *copal* or *papelillo;* pochote; *Cyrtocarpa procera; Jatropha cordata;* lance pod or *cabo de hacha; Pseudosmodingium perniciosum;* and *Trichilia* spp. In addition, conzattia, figs, and eardrop tree are also common in places.

The Jalisco-Colima Coast

We arrived at the coastal town of Barra de Navidad during the middle of the afternoon. The heat and humidity immediately slowed our pace. After being in the cooler mountains for several days, we decided to find accommodations early, take a break, and to go out again later in the day. We drove seven miles south on Highway 200 to Cihuatlán, where we acquired a motel room for the night. And after a short rest we went out again to explore the area along the Río Cihuatlán, a river on the south side of town that also serves as the boundary line between the states of Jalisco and Colima.

Bill Schaldach, in his 1963 article, had described the habitat along the Río Cihuatlán as gallery forest, and we were eager to sample that environment. We were extremely disappointed to find only a thin line of spotty and overgrazed deciduous vegetation along a rather large but drying riverbed. The floodplain as far as we could see was little more than pastureland with an occasional farm or orchard. But in spite of the rather arid conditions there, we recorded a good number of trip birds during the two hours before dark. Two of these, the orange-breasted bunting and ruddy-breasted seedeater, were lifers. We found a citreoline trogon in a small patch of trees surprisingly close to the main highway. And we found a ferruginous pygmy-owl, perched on a small acacia, and being mobbed by a number of other birds. Included in this party were social and vermilion flycatchers, a pair of thick-billed kingbirds, and a great kiskadee.

Dawn of May 3 found us north of Barra de Navidad, along the Puerto Vallarta highway, within a very scrubby second-growth habitat that looked different than anything we had seen before. And it was well worth the side trip, because it was there that we found a male red-breasted chat. What a beautiful bird it was! And so unlike the common yellow-breasted chat of the United States. The male is spectacularly marked with bluish-gray and white, with a brilliant rosy-red breast and crissum. It stayed in view, constantly fanning its tail, for several minutes, before disappearing into the dense vegetation. The red-breasted chat is another of Mexico's endemics, occurring only along the Pacific slope, from northern Sinaloa to Chiapas.

Other Mexican birds recorded that morning included several very loud Wagler's or west Mexican chachalacas; several orange-fronted parakeets either flying overhead or feeding in some of the fruiting trees; golden-cheeked woodpeckers were common; pairs of rose-throated becards and masked tityras; a flammulated flycatcher; several very silent and apparently shy San Blas jays (another endemic to western Mexico); white-bellied wren; and grayish saltator.

By early afternoon we were driving south along the coast, past Barra de Navidad and Cihuatlán, and on to Manzanillo, Colima, the largest of the towns along the Jalisco-Colima coastline. Manzanillo, with a population of about forty-thousand people, is located between two bays that have made the area an important seaport. In recent years Manzanillo has also become a popular resort town. Although I could appreciate the peculiar topography of the area that produced the unique seaport, and the beaches were most appealing, we stopped only long enough for lunch at a little outdoor restaurant on the beach.

The Colima Hill Country

We turned east away from the coast an hour south of Manzanillo, and headed back into the hill country. The highway followed the Río Armeria for several miles, and we were impressed with the width of the channel; it undoubtedly carried a great deal more water on occasion. The dry season was very evident on this southern side of the mountains. Smoke from hundreds of set fires made visibility poor and distant views impossible. In spite of the fact that we were driving eastward into the mountains, our views were limited to less than a mile or two. This condition generally continued throughout the rest of our trip. Even when we stayed in the highlands of Volcán Colima, views were limited to the adjacent forest and mountain slopes. Long-range visibility was next to impossible.

We realized that we were experiencing a practice that has been

Lush oak-dominated forest below cinder fields surrounding Volcán Colima.

in existence for centuries. Burning of fields and grasslands, just prior to the rainy seasons, has been and continues to be a normal practice in many tropical countries. It is a practice that peoples in more temperate climates have not utilized to the same extreme. Burning has several advantages, including the reduction of the previous year's growth and to open up the ground cover for new growth. Burning also adds nutrients to the soils, and it keeps young woody plants from encroaching upon fields that have been cleared for agriculture and pastureland. Many people still utilize the cut, burn and plant concept. However, cleared *milpas* (recently cut forest areas for agriculture) are burned and planted annually until the soils can no longer produce an adequate crop. Then the old clearings are deserted and new ones are started. This ancient process was logical during earlier years of smaller human populations. But with today's limited access to new undeveloped land, and the rapid rate of soil depletion, a new system is necessary to support the ever-increasing human population.

We took a side road toward Ixtahuatlán that had recently been paved not far above the Río Armeria Valley. Although we drove only about five miles on this new road, we were able to get a much better perspective of the burned hillsides and tropical deciduous forest habitat. We also searched for a bird we knew was present in this habitat but which we had not yet found, the lesser ground-cuckoo. It is a bird of "secondary growth in arid country," according to Peterson and Chalif in *A Field Guide to Mexican Birds*. We found a pull-off along the roadway in an area that seemed appropriate. We had no sooner climbed out of the car, and had walked less than a dozen feet, when a lesser ground-cuckoo suddenly appeared in a little clearing as if on cue. We both had a short but excellent look at this medium-sized and reddish-rumped cuckoo. It was a great treat because it represented a lifer for us both. We also recorded russet-crowned motmot, white-throated magpie-jay, and, although it seemed out of place, a northern cardinal nearby.

The evening of May 3 was spent in Colima, the capital city of the state with the same name. We found the city to be a very clean and appealing one. It is situated at about 1,670 feet elevation in a large open and well-watered valley that contains considerable agriculture. The city of ninety thousand people apparently serves a large area of the state. We walked the streets, had an excellent meal in a downtown restaurant, stocked up on pan dulce, and turned in early. Our next three days were to be spent on the adjacent Volcán Colima.

15

Oaxaca

Oaxaca! There is something magical about that name. Once I traveled through the state, and explored some of its new and ancient cities and its wide range of natural habitats, I could better appreciate its special appeal. To begin with, the topography of the state is as varied as any in Mexico, extending from sea level to 11,142 feet at the summit of Cerro Zempoaltepec. Oaxaca encompasses an area of 36,371 square miles, about the size of Indiana. And its vegetation is as varied as the topography. Ten of Mexico's twelve temperate and tropical vegetation zones occur there. Oaxaca lacks only desert and chaparral.

It has been said that Oaxaca is the "most Indian" of all the states in Mexico, and any observant traveler could not help but agree. Nowhere in Mexico have I seen as great a variety of colorful Indian costumes worn as regularly as in Oaxaca. More than two dozen separate Indian groups reside within the state. Although the adjacent states of México, Veracruz and Chiapas may be better known for their various Aztec and Mayan ruins, neither has a greater number of indigenous peoples. And Oaxaca's Monte Albán, which was occupied from at least 500 B.C. through the Spanish Conquest, is considered by many as the most impressive of the abundant pre-Columbian sites in all of Latin America.

There is something else very special about Oaxaca that is difficult to describe. It may relate to the fact that a good deal of the state has not yet been discovered by tourists. It is less commercial than many. But, for me, it probably relates more to the large number of birds that can be found there. Oaxaca has a greater number of birds than any other Mexican state. Laurence Binford, curator of birds at San Francisco's Academy of Sciences, has studied Oaxaca's avifauna for more than twenty-five years. In 1980, he reported a total of 681 for the state, more than has been found in the entire countries of Guatemala or Honduras. According to Binford, about 460 of Oaxaca's 681 species are known to breed within the state's ten vegetation zones.

Zones of Vegetation

My trip to Oaxaca in January, 1975, was part of a rather extensive north to south swing through the state on Highway 190, and included a side trip into the Sierra Madre highlands. Two nonbirding friends and I had come to see the countryside, explore the principal ruins, and find as many birds as we could along our route.

Highway 190 transects three major vegetation zones between where it crosses the northern Puebla-Oaxaca border to where it descends into the Tehuantepec lowlands—arid tropical scrub, pine-oak forest and tropical deciduous forest. We found good examples of the arid tropical scrub habitat, as A. Starker Leopold called it, when we first entered Oaxaca. This same habitat was called deciduous seasonal forest by J. S. Beard in 1944, and Jerzy Rzedowski (1983) referred to it as bosque tropical caducifolio, semievergreen or seasonal forest. We passed through many miles of this habitat dominated by several large cacti, including two candelabra species, both locally called *cardon espinoso,* the smaller *órgano* cactus, and several species of prickly pears.

Some of the other common plants that Rzedowski reported for this zone of Oaxaca included several species of succulents such as yuccas, palms and agaves. Woody plant species included five or six kinds of *Bursera;* some of these produce a resin called *copal,* which is burned as incense. Copal once was important in native religious ceremonies. *Yago-lache* is the local name of a small tree which is very poisonous but the resin is used by local Indians to reduce the pain of scorpion stings. The small, white-barked lysiloma found there is the same leguminous tree species that occurs north to Sonora. The kapok tree produces fruits with long fibers that are used for stuffing pillows, mattresses and life preservers, and for insulation. Morning glory tree or *cuaunzahuatl* (Nahuatl for "mangy tree") produces large morning glory-like flowers but is leafless in winter.

We discovered a little lane off the highway not far south of the state border, running between tall cacti to a field surrounded with arid tropical scrub vegetation. The field contained corn stalks that were already two feet high, and a scarecrow that looked just like a

View east across Oaxaca Valley from Monte Albán ruins. A white-flowering kapok tree is in the foreground.

number of scarecrows I had seen in the United States. The Mexican scarecrow was just as inefficient; several painted buntings and blue grosbeaks were feeding at its feet. And a short distance further on at the edge of the field we found a solitary male orange-breasted bunting. This beautiful bird was one of the several endemic species I had hoped to find in Oaxaca. The males of the species are a strange combination of blue and yellow with a bright yellowish-green crown. Blake (1953) described the male as possessing "cerulean or turquoise-blue" head and underparts; "the wings and tail mainly dusky; lores, eye-ring, and underparts bright lemon-yellow, the breast usually tinged with orange" (p. 563). An extremely beautiful bird!

At the far corner of the field was a little thicket of tall cacti and vines. I found two more birds that are representative of Oaxaca; Boucard's wren and white-lored gnatcatcher. The wren is one of the several cactus wrens in Mexico; it looks very much like the cactus wren of the northern deserts. The gnatcatcher is similar to the black-tailed gnatcatcher; it has a black cap and very narrow, white eye-line, and considerable white along the edge of the tail. I also recorded Harris' hawk, gray-breasted woodpecker, both white-winged and Inca doves, dusky hummingbird, Nutting's flycatcher, and scrub jay. As we walked back to the car, a lesser roadrunner crossed the lane just ahead of us. This is a smaller version of the greater road-runner, the common "paisano-bird" of the northern deserts. The lesser roadrunner is found from southern Sonora in western Mexico south to Nicaragua.

Mexico's pine-oak forest zone consists of an incredibly wide variety of habitats. Almost every combination of pines and oaks occurs, from almost pure stands of various species of pines or oaks to mixed communities. Oaxaca possesses eleven species of pines, and many more species of oaks. I encountered eight pine species during my wanderings in the region. Paul Standley listed only twenty-six pine species in his classic four-volume book on the trees and shrubs of Mexico.

Michoacán pine and Chihuahua pine (ponderosa pine look-alikes) occur at low and midelevations along the hillsides northwest of Oaxaca City. Montezuma pine, sometimes called *ocote macho* in Spanish, occurs above six thousand feet elevation. This is a tall and stately tree with five-needled, drooping leaves four inches or more in length, and often grows in rather dense stands. The top branches look like large plumes due to the drooping character of the leaves. Ocote pine is similar because of its drooping plumage on top of bright green foliage. These species are often associated with Aztec pine, which has the widest distribution of any pine in Mexico. This is a three-needled pine; its needles are four to six inches in length. And Mexican white pine is common at higher elevations in the Sierra Madre. It has four- to six-inch long needles in bundles of fives; its bluish-green foliage can often be identified from some distance. Hartweg's pine is dominant at the highest elevations. And then there is Mexican weeping or jelecote pine, with its six-inch or longer needles; it too is restricted to the higher mountain slopes.

Common oaks of this zone include the widespread chestnut oak and, at somewhat higher elevations, netleaf oak. The chestnut oak is a small tree with three-inch long leaves that are "sharp-tipped, with veins ending in weak spines; upper surface smooth and shiny, lower white-downy," according to Pesman's *Meet Flora Mexicana.* Netleaf oak is a large, rounded, deciduous tree with rather "thick and stiff, wrinkled" oval leaves which possess "several small spiny teeth toward the tip; dark blue on top, tawny-hairy beneath," according to Pesman (p. 107). Other common woody plants found in the pine-oak forest include wax alder, Mexican hawthorn and Mexican elder.

Highway 190 crosses a portion of the Sierra Madre de Sur north of Oaxaca City. We found an area of arid pine-oak woodland at about six thousand feet elevation which, from all that I had read about the preferred habitat of the slaty vireo, seemed like a good place to look. The slaty vireo is one of Mexico's very local and endemic birds. Roger Tory Peterson and Edward Chalif, in *A Field Guide to Mexican Birds,* described it as "a rare, distinctly patterned vireo. *Slate-gray* with *bright olive-green* crown, wings, and tail. Chin, lower breast, belly, and under tail coverts white. Eye white" (p. 199). We left our rental car along the roadside and spent a good part of an hour exploring this habitat. But in spite of hearing a vireo-like song of a bird I could not find, and finding a number of other more common Mexican birds, we finally gave up the search and continued our drive south toward Oaxaca City.

Not long before we reached the city we dropped out of the pine-oak forest into an area that obviously has had a long history of human use. Although some of the terrain showed signs of terracing, mostly from decades of overgrazing, we could see dozens of square miles of landscape that had been worn raw. I could not help but think of similar scenes that I had either observed on site or in photographs of other severely impacted areas, from the American dust bowl, Egypt, Israel, or the Sudan. I wondered if I was looking at the major reason for the demise of the great cultures that once existed in Oaxaca.

Ciudad Oaxaca

The city of Oaxaca sits within a broad valley at about five thousand feet elevation along the western slope of the Sierra Madre de Sur. For a large city of more than 130,000 people, it was surprisingly tranquil. Oaxaca City was exactly what I would hope for in a Mexican city. We found rooms at the Oaxaca Courts, since remodeled and renamed Misión de los Angeles. We then drove to the center of town to experience the real Ciudad Oaxaca, to wander around the Plaza de Armas, and to eat at a nearby restaurant, El Patio.

The central plaza, with its huge old trees, bandstand and walkways, was all I expected. We sat at an outside café and indulged in a local cerveza while we enjoyed the evening pace of Old Mexico. After an excellent dinner, we moved to the sidewalk café at the Hotel Marquis del Valle, across from the plaza, and continued our observations of the local customs. It was there that I was approached by an Indian rug salesman.

I watched him approach from some distance. He wasn't easy to miss, because he was carrying a pile of folded textiles that was twice as high as he was tall. Somehow he wove his way through the crowd, heading straight for the sidewalk café where we were seated, stopped directly in front of our table, placed his goods on the ground, and asked in reasonably good English how much I would pay for a "beautiful Oaxacan rug?" I had no intention of buying a rug but asked if he also had serapes.

"Serapes? Si, señor," he said, and he immediately selected a second piece, as beautiful as the first, and unfolded it for my inspection. But it was another rug. I told him that I was not interested in a rug, but would consider buying a serape. He immediately responded by exclaiming that he had many serapes, and he laid out a third piece for our inspection. It, too, was a rug, but this one was really something special, with a pattern of colorful birds woven into the white background. I could not help but show my admiration for that piece of art, but I again told him that it was not a serape, and I would be interested only in a serape. We went through at least four more rugs before he admitted that all of the pieces he had to sell were rugs. Then he brought out the bird-decorated rug for a second inspection and asked me how much I would give him for that beautiful hand-woven rug.

I have never been one to drive a very hard bargain, unless I really don't care to buy. And since I had no intention of buying a rug, I decided to see just how far he was willing to go in negotiations for the bird rug. When I told him that I was running very low of money and I could not part with more than fifteen dollars, the expression on his face was worth a dozen photographs. He informed me that he was supporting his elderly mother, a wife, and five children, and that he could not possibly take less than forty dollars for this rug that he had worked so many hours to produce. He asked me to increase my price, because he knew that I liked his rug, and he would like for me to have it.

My next price of seventeen dollars produced another pained expression, and he spent another ten minutes explaining how many hours it had taken him to weave the rug and how many people were depending upon him for their very survival. Then he said that he could not possibly part with that rug for less than thirty dollars and asked me to pay his price and take it home.

I could barely stand the expression on his face when I told him that I was not really interested in a rug, only a serape, but that I deeply admired the rug because of the beautiful birds. I told him that there was no way I could go over twenty dollars, and if he couldn't accept that price, I would have to go home without his beautiful rug. He looked at me for a long time, and I wondered if he was about to shout at me, or walk away, or something else. Suddenly, he said that he would take the twenty dollars but that he would have a very difficult time explaining to his family how he had given away his most beautiful rug. He added that the only reason he was going to give in on the price was because he understood my appreciation for his hard work, and he knew that I would admire his rug forever.

By the time we parted, he with my twenty-dollar bill, and me with his gorgeous eight-by-five-foot rug, I was exhausted. We sat there over another cerveza and admired my purchase. But the Oaxacan rug salesman was correct. The bird rug has been in a prominent place in my house ever since. It has been a subject of frequent conversations, and it provides me with a wonderful memory of Oaxaca.

Oaxaca Highlands

The following morning I left the city very early alone; my friends wanted to spend the day shopping in the city. By the time it became light enough to see, I was high into the mountains where I could watch the dawn creep into the canyons far below.

Highway 175 runs north from Oaxaca across the Sierra Madre de Sur to intersect Gulf Coast Highway 180 halfway between Veracruz and Catemaco. The southern half of Highway 175 (the first 100 to 150 miles north of Oaxaca City) is one of the most spectacular routes I have ever seen. It immediately climbs very steeply up a deep canyon to an open forested plateau, then drops off again into a deep valley, and up again toward the next ridge, and on and on. The habitat in the first several valleys was arid, but good riparian habitat occurred in the bottoms. Further along, as my route continued its gradual climb upward, the valleys provided a more luxuriant growth of tropical deciduous forest. The higher ridges and plateaus that I could see were covered with coniferous forest. Several of the narrow, upland side canyons provided a barranca-like environment with dense, broadleaved vegetation. Above all of these, at the very top of the great dissected plateau, was a rather arid, mixed pine-oak forest.

There were numerous views from along the highway that would impress even the most widely traveled visitor. I was amazed by the beauty of the mountain vistas. But I was equally surprised by the evidence of humanity everywhere I looked. Although there was good natural vegetation throughout, I could see dozens of little villages, either squeezed into little valleys or perched on unlikely slopes. The residents were obviously farmers because each village, and sometimes large sections of hillsides, were terraced for crops. All of the villages bore Indian names: Guelatao, Ixtlán de Juarez, Macuiltianguis.

I stopped at the first good patch of forest, about twenty-five to thirty miles from Oaxaca City, and explored that area for about an hour. Almost immediately I encountered a small flock of dwarf jays, another of Mexico's endemics. This is a small jay with an obvious black face mask and less obvious pale bluish-white throat. I also found, in that same patch of forest, white-eared hummingbird, a male mountain trogon perched reasonably close by on a pine, greater pewee, acorn woodpecker, northern flicker, Mexican chickadee, brown-backed solitaire, solitary vireo, Townsend's warbler, and hepatic tanager. Gray silky-flycatchers were singing from a ridge just beyond, and as I returned to the car, a flock of about twenty band-tailed pigeons flew overhead.

Roadside birding also was very good, and I stopped at a number of places where pull-outs permitted. A couple of these provided good overlooks into the surrounding vegetation, including some dense shrubby areas. I was watching a happy wren, trying to entice it into better view with a few squeaks, when I noticed another little bird creeping through some weedy plants right on the roadside: a male cinnamon-bellied flower-piercer, sometimes called diglossa. What a neat little bird it was! A tiny black and deep cinnamon bird with an upturned, hooked bill — the only small Mexican species with such a characteristic. I watched it "snip" its way into the base of a small flower from which I assumed it extracted nectar. I also found a green violet-ear and magnificent hummingbird at this same site; they were feeding at a pink-flowering shrub that I believe was senna, called in Spanish *retama*.

Another of the available pull-outs was located at the bottom of a rather deep barranca that contained a good habitat of broadleaf vegetation and a trail that followed the bottom for several hundred yards. There I found a fruiting tree that I identified as a hackberry, that was full of feeding birds. I sat at a comfortable distance away and watched what took place. Within less than an hour I had added a couple of dozen birds to my trip list. Mexican specialities seen there included spot-crowned woodcreeper, tufted flycatcher, several rufous-backed robins, a pair of Aztec thrushes, ruddy-capped nightingale-thrush, crescent-chested and red warblers, chestnut-capped brush-finch, and collared towhee.

On one of the upper plateaus was an area that reminded me very much of the high arid landscape of Las Vegas, New Mexico. Patches of grass, low-growing prickly pears and scrub oaks dominated this habitat. And sure enough, the birds there could just as well have been in southern Arizona or New Mexico; common raven, eastern bluebird, red-faced warbler; the vesper, lark and chipping sparrows; and lesser goldfinch.

The tallest and densest stands of coniferous forest were not at the highest elevations but along the middle slopes and benches. I identified at least four species of conifers there: Montezuma, Mexican white and Aztec pine, and sacred fir. Some of the area had been logged in the past, and a few of the old logging roads provided access into the forest. In one place I found three species of jays; the Steller's, gray-breasted and unicolored. It seemed incongruous to find all three of these jays utilizing one habitat. I couldn't help but wonder about the interrelationships of the two closely related species of *Aphelocoma* jays, gray-breasted and unicolored. Do they interbreed in that area? Other Mexican species recorded there included ruddy woodcreeper, gray-barred wren, russet nightingale-thrush, golden-browed warbler, and rufous-capped brush-finch.

I drove to Valle Nacional that day, a small town on the Gulf side of the range, before returning to Oaxaca well after dark. It had been a thoroughly enjoyable day in the mountains. I had found a total of eighty-four species of birds and had seen some magnificent country, the beauty of which continued to amaze me.

Monte Albán

The following day was set aside to visit Monte Albán. Dawn found us wandering along the entrance road, which passed through a rather arid landscape. Only a few of the shrubs and trees possessed leaves, but one of the leafless trees had large white, trumpet-shaped flowers near the top. This was the silk cotton tree, or *cabellas de ángel* (angel hair). It is a fairly common species of the tropical deciduous forest zone in the Oaxaca region. We also enjoyed good views of the Oaxaca valley, fifteen hundred feet below us.

Although we didn't find a great variety of birds along the Monte Albán entrance road, we did discover a Oaxaca sparrow among the scrubby vegetation. This little sparrow is a Mexican endemic restricted to northwest and central Oaxaca where it is considered rare and local in occurrence. It was rather dull in appearance. Edwards (1972) described it best: "Top of head dark reddish brown; upperparts mostly light reddish brown; back has blackish brown streaks; wings and tail tinged with gray; sides of head mostly light grayish brown except darker thin line through eye, and nearly white malar streak; submalar streak black; underparts mostly pale gray; tail longer than that of other *Aimophila* sparrows; bill black" (p. 266).

The ruins of Monte Albán, Spanish for "White Mountains," are located on a fifty-five acre terraced plateau overlooking the Oaxaca valley. The immense hilltop ruins once were the cultural center of a city that encompassed an area of over fifteen square miles. Archeologists tell us that the ruins were inhabited for more than twenty-five hundred years and served a succession of different peoples. Five distinct periods have been identified.

Although the area was inhabited from as early as 4000 B.C., construction of the city did not begin until approximately 500 B.C. The earliest sculptures depict distorted figures and others with facial features resembling the jaguar that represent Olmec traits. Monte Albán reached its cultural peak during this period, with a sophisticated society possessing a calendar, a writing system, and highly developed pottery. The second phase began at about the start of the Christian era and lasted for about three hundred years. The change was probably due to conquest by the Mayans who contributed an observatory and a change in ceramic style. They also constructed a drainage system to channel and store water.

Mayan ascendancy was followed by a third period, when Zapotec characteristics dominated, that lasted until about 700 A.D. This era was characterized by a tripartite social division of priests, clerks, and laborers. Phase four (700 to about 1000 A.D.) involved a hiatus in construction with a gradual decay of the structures; other cities, such as Mitla and Yagul, were developed then. Also during this period, the Mixtecs invaded from the northwest and conquered many of the Zapotec cities. From then on, in spite of additional occupation after 1586 when the Aztecs established a military base here, Monte Albán was used more for a burial place for the Zapotecs and later Mixtecs than as a city. More than 150 tombs from this later period have been uncovered.

The city reached its maximum size between A.D. 500 and 600, when it housed as many as thirty thousand people and served as the focal point for a population in excess of sixty thousand living within the valley of Oaxaca. The Monte Albán hillside is carved into over two thousand terraces that were used for both agriculture and housing. The single greatest problem with the city on the hill was that all water had to be carried up steep stairs from the valley, or from dammed up side canyons, to supply the governing elite that lived there.

The Monte Albán site has been mostly restored to display the numerous stepped platforms and varied structures that are arranged on a north-south axis with two huge platforms at either end of an enormous sunken plaza. The platforms contained arrangements of pyramid-temples, palaces, patios and tombs. Structures along the edge of the great plaza include a ballcourt, without stone rings, and a pyramid with an internal staircase that is protected on both sides of the entrance by hieroglyphics of serpents and a man with a great headdress. Most of the buildings were plastered, and some were probably painted and elaborated by current stucco figures.

Stelae (stone carvings) and hieroglyphs occur throughout the ruins, tantalizing the imagination. One interpretation identifies a headdress as an ancient space helmet, suggesting that the site was visited by extraterrestrials. One of the best preserved of the Monte Albán stelae, located on the south platform, shows a jaguar wearing the

Monte Albán ruins, near city of Oaxaca, focal point for more
than sixty thousand people around A.D. 500–600.

headdress of the rain god, Cocijo. The stelae at the "Platform of
the Dancers" seem to depict stylized dancers engaged in a kind of
ecstatic ritual; interpreters of the "writings" suggest that the figures,
which all appear lifeless, nude, and sexually mutilated, represent
dead and tortured enemies. Another idea advanced is that they represent the ill and deformed, and that the structure was an early hos-
pital. Some of Monte Albán's stelae are considered the oldest known
written texts in the New World.

Today, the Monte Albán complex of stark stone structures perches
on its hilltop overlooking a more modern city and associated farmlands. Yet they powerfully evoke a sense of history and the mystery
of human existence; contemplation comes easily in the early dawn
overlooking the valley of Oaxaca.

16

El Triunfo

The resplendent quetzal is often thought of as the world's most beautiful bird. But more importantly, it represents the last living association with ancient Mexico. The quetzal was venerated as a religious symbol by the ancient Aztecs. In fact, Quetzalcoatl was the Aztecs' principal god. Both the Aztecs and the Mayans made headdresses and capes from tailfeathers of the resplendent quetzal; their use was reserved for ceremonial dress by the high priests and rulers. When Hernan Cortez arrived in the New World he was presented with a cape of quetzal feathers by the Aztec ruler Montezuma, who mistakenly believed that Cortez was the returning god, Quetzalcoatl. Cortez had arrived in the same manner and in the same year that Aztec legends said Quetzalcoatl would return from the sea to rule his people. And finally, centuries later, the colors selected for the Mexican flag are those of this beautiful bird. Yet, despite all the significance placed upon this unique and gorgeous creature throughout the country's varied past, the resplendent quetzal today is very close to extinction in Mexico.

There is only one place left in the entire country where one can be reasonably sure of finding the resplendent quetzal — a wild and remote section of the Sierra Madre de Chiapas known as El Triunfo. There, within El Triunfo's highland cloud forest, the resplendent quetzal continues to survive under special protection given the area by the state of Chiapas and the Mexican government. A fifty-thousand-acre tract of virgin forest has been set aside as a special nature preserve to sustain the last remnant population of Mexico's ancient and most notable bird.

Logistics

El Triunfo is not an easy place to reach. The logistics in visiting this relatively obscure and wild valley are monumental. But the natural treasures still to be found at El Triunfo and vicinity are so enticing that a visit to this Shangri-la is a must for anyone wishing to experience Mexico's more remote places and see some of its rarest wild creatures. El Triunfo had been on my agenda for several years. So, when Victor Emanuel Nature Tours offered an expedition there in March and April, 1985, I decided my time had come.

The trip began at Tapachula, a small but busy city in the extreme southwestern corner of Mexico. Twelve of us had flown to Tapachula via Mexico City. We loaded our gear, boarded two Volkswagen microbusses, and drove north on Highway 200 toward Tonalá. At Mapastepec, 70 miles north of Tapachula, we turned off the paved highway onto a gravel road that ran east toward the mountains. In about one hour, which included a brief and successful stop to find the giant wren, we reached the little village of Colonial Guadalupe. We stopped there to visit with Señor Rodrigo Arqueta L. to confirm earlier arrangements Victor had made for assistance. We would need the help of Señor Arqueta's wranglers to reach our destination. We then continued an additional eight miles to the end of the road where four arieros and pack stock awaited us. From there we began a twenty-five-mile trail that would take us to El Triunfo.

Along the Trail to El Triunfo

The first afternoon's hike was confined to the lowlands where temperatures were in the nineties. The trail gradually ascended the western slopes of the Sierra de Chiapas, and temperatures dropped with elevation. On that first afternoon, the four-mile trek along the Río Novillero, in and out of the tropical deciduous and tropical evergreen forest habitats, taxed our strength and endurance. We all were glad to reach Paval, our camping destination for the night. The site was located in a clearing just above the clear waters of the Río Novillero and at the head of a large, steep and wooded canyon.

Paval provided us with our first good opportunity to search for wildlife and to examine the varied plantlife. The habitat around the clearing contained a wide variety of vegetation that seemed to be a mixture of evergreen and deciduous forest habitats. I later found a good description of the area in Jerzy Rzedowski's 1983 publication, *Vegetacion de Mexico*. Rzedowski referred to this environment as bosque tropical subcaducifolio. By using Rzedowski's description, along with Paul Standley's classic book, *Trees and Shrubs of Mexico*,

I was able to identify quite a few of Paval's more obvious trees and shrubs from notes and drawings I had made in the field.

One of the more common species we had encountered along our route was a fairly short tree with numerous clusters of purple flowers and large ovalate leaves. Our arieros called it *primavera*, Spanish for spring. It is also known as trumpet tree or *Tabebuia rosea.* Eardrop tree and apes earring were two of the common canopy trees, both members of the pea family. They possess typical mimosa-like foliage and produce seedpods that are utilized by both wildlife and humans. Another tall canopy tree present within the forest was balm tree, *balsamo* in Spanish. It is known for the balsam liquid that is derived from the trunk and utilized for medicines and perfume. According to Standley, the balsam collection process includes the physical beating of a band of bark around the trunk until it is thoroughly crushed. Cuts are then made in the bruised bark, and as the sap begins to seep out it is set on fire. This is soon extinguished and left for fifteen days until the balsam begins to run. It is then collected on pieces of cotton that are placed in the cuts, then squeezed into jars of boiling water and collected off the top when it floats to the surface. Standley doesn't say whether the trees survive this treatment.

Another tree of this habitat that produces a useful resin is the sausage tree, locally called *coapinol.* The fragrant amber-like resin is very gummy and is chewed or used as incense in churches. The sausage name comes from the seeds which are large and dark brown in color. Another prominent tree is the tall, thin gumbo limbo, easily identified by its smooth, reddish trunk, often with peeling bark. This is the same species of gumbo limbo that occurs in Florida and the West Indies.

We took a couple of hours the next morning (and an even longer time on our return trip) to bird the clearing and surrounding forest. I had heard three nightbirds during the night; the pauraque, mottled owl and striped cuckoo. I had not been able to identify the cuckoo calls although the bird had been active very near my tent throughout the night, and continued its melancholy two- or four-note whistle call during the first couple hours after dawn. Because of its parasitic nature, laying its eggs in other birds' nests, it rarely shows itself, perhaps because of the likelihood of being mobbed by other birds. We all had an excellent look at this cuckoo, but only after taping the call and playing it back to entice the bird into the open.

I also found Prevost's ground-sparrow nearby, a tody motmot and long-tailed manakin on the dry hillside above camp, and an emerald-chinned hummingbird feeding on some red *Salvia* bushes along the trail. And someone discovered a family of plain chachalacas (until recently considered a separate species and called white-bellied chachalaca) feeding in fruiting trees on the hillside north of camp.

Some of the other Mexican birds found at Paval included several raptors—the broad-winged, gray, and short-tailed hawks and bat falcon—that put in their appearance as soon as the day was warm enough to produce thermals. A crested guan was spotted at a considerable distance without the aid of binoculars by one of our sharp-eyed arieros. The squirrel cuckoo and lesser ground-cuckoo were also found there, and I recorded a pheasant cuckoo about one mile above camp. Orange-fronted parakeets were abundant and a lone pair of yellow-naped parrots were seen flying overhead as well. Two species of motmots, the blue-crowned and turquoise-browed, were found along the edge of the compound. Hummingbirds recorded included violet sabrewing, cinnamon, and berylline hummers. A number of of flycatchers were seen: paltry tyrannulet, yellow-bellied elaenia, common tody-flycatcher, eye-ringed flatbill, and the royal, boat-billed, social, brown-capped and sulphur-bellied flycatchers; a yellow-olive flycatcher was constructing a round pendant nest of black moss. A pair of scrub euphonias had built their nest in a gourd left hanging on a post on the edge of the clearing. A pair of yellow-winged tanagers were nest-building on an adjacent tree.

We covered considerably more ground the next day, our first full day on the trail. Our route began to climb steeply out of the canyon almost immediately, and within a couple hours we began to switch-back through evergreen forest where oaks seemed to increase with elevation. By midday, oaks and associated broadleaf trees dominated the slopes. Some twelve miles above Paval we reached our second campsite, at Cañada Honda. It was there, just as we approached our camp, that we discovered a small flock of azure-rumped tanagers, one of the most important of the many birds we had hoped to find.

Although it sometimes is called Cabanis's tanager, azure-rumped is a much more descriptive name for this lovely species. Even that name, however, does not do it justice. Its head, back and rump are a deep greenish-blue color in good light. Its wings are blackish but show bluish color along the edge of each feather. The front of the bird is blue-gray on the throat, gradually fading to a much lighter color, almost white, on the belly and crissum. Careful observations disclosed distinct black spots on its chest.

The azure-rumped tanager may be one of the rarest birds in the world, primarily because of its very restricted range—only in the southern portion of the Sierra Madre de Chiapas of Mexico and adjacent Guatemala. We were extremely fortunate in finding this bird both en route up the mountain and again in the same general area on our return trip, nine days later.

A few of the other outstanding birds recorded at Cañada Honda and in nearby oak-dominated habitat included the fulvous owl (after dark), white-faced quail-dove, and emerald toucanet; rufous sabrewing feeding at heliconia flowers (this large hummer is the principal pollinator of this plant, replacing the more common long-tailed hermit of Mexico's eastern tropical forests); emerald-chinned hummingbird, gray-collared becard, Nutting's flycatcher, orange-billed nightingale-thrush, rufous-and-white wren, red-legged honey-creeper, brown-capped vireo, slate-throated redstart, and white-winged tanager.

Also near Cañada Honda, feeding high in the treetops over the trail, we encountered a troop of spider monkeys. There were at least twenty individuals, both males and females and a number of infants and youngsters. They raised a great ruckus once they realized that we had discovered their presence; they had been very quiet before then. Several members of our party had already walked on by and missed this rare opportunity to see wild monkeys in their natural environment. I watched as they made their way, swinging and scrambling from tree to tree, up the slope and out of sight. But it was an extra special three or four minutes that I will long remember.

Cañada Honda marked the western edge of the El Triunfo nature preserve. But we saw no evidence whatsoever that we were entering a protected area. I was later told that all the posted signs had been destroyed by poachers and others who hoped to claim more and more of the area for coffee plantations. We had started to see planted coffee bushes at Paval, and we encountered seventy Guatemalans who were en route across the mountains to Finca Prusia, a well-known coffee plantation several miles below El Triunfo to the east. There were no indications that the land was under protected status anywhere on the western slope. We found numerous places on the drier hillsides where fires had been started, some of which had burned several dozen acres of vegetation. Our arieros informed us that the fires were set by the Guatamalans who were unhappy about the preserve.

We left Cañada Honda by 8:00 A.M. on our third day, and continued to climb upward through the evergreen forest. Then suddenly, at about 5,500 feet elevation, pines and cypress replaced oaks and other broadleaf trees. It took us approximately three hours to pass through this very distinct belt of conifers. Then, just as suddenly, we were out of the conifers and walking through a forest of huge trees loaded with an amazing assortment of bromeliads and other epiphytes. We had reached the cloud forest habitat of the Sierra Madre de Chiapas.

We crossed a pass at about noon, and then began a rather gradual descent through the mesic forest into an obvious valley. Mist and clouds greeted us there, and we learned that we were experiencing a very late *norte*. The storm created a surrealistic scene that restricted our visibility to less than a few yards. A little more than an hour later we walked out into an open valley. We had arrived at El Triunfo!

Our party of eager but wet souls was led to a tin-roofed structure, El Triunfo's research station, where we were allowed to spend the night. After "setting up camp" in our overnight dorm, I ventured out again to experience the real cloud forest face to face. But I soon discovered that the driving rain had forced even the wildlife to seek shelter. By late afternoon I was ready for a meal of freeze-dried food and forced to remain indoors to anticipate the coming dawn.

El Triunfo Preserve

What a dawn it was! There was not a cloud in the sky. I watched the sunlight begin to creep down the hillside, enthralled that I had really arrived at the El Triunfo Shangri-la of my dreams. As I stood there pondering that reality, a male resplendent quetzal in full breeding plumage suddenly shot out from a treetop not more than a hundred yards away. His appearance provided several of us with an unbelievable view of dazzling green, red and white in a display flight that I had previously only read about. It was an experience that more than compensated for the difficulties encountered in negotiating first the Mexico City airport and then the long trek to El Triunfo. And during the early morning, as we established our new camp, we were able to watch at least three separate male quetzals display just above the clearing.

The tiny village of El Triunfo was located at 6,070 feet elevation and surrounded by higher ridges, some of which exceeded 9,000 feet. The clearing provided us with several Mexican birds of interest. A number of gray silky-flycatchers cavorted about several of the surrounding treetops. The shy blue-and-white mockingbird was mostly evident by its song, but it provided me with several excellent looks. A pair of flame-colored tanagers were feeding at bromeliads. Yellow grosbeaks were most numerous and their clear robin-like songs dominated the morning sounds. The abundant sparrow of the clearing was the rufous-collared sparrow, a close relative to the familiar white-throat and white-crowned sparrows of the United States.

El Triunfo's cloud forest is one of the largest and most spectacular left in Mexico. The term "cloud forest" was utilized by Leopold in his 1950 description of Mexico's vegetation zones. J. S. Beard (1955) referred to this habitat as either montane broadleaf forest or (for the shorter ridge-top version) elfin woodland. Jerzy Rzedowski called it *bosque mesofilo de montana.*

Cloud forest habitat usually is found between 5,000 and 7,500 feet elevation. It is maintained by moisture-laden air currents that rise from the humid tropical lowlands to form clouds and rain in the upland. Annual precipitation in this zone may range from 40 to 118 inches. It produces a climate that is usually cool and moist but not subject to freezing. The results are a multilayered forest with an abundance of both temperate and tropical flora and fauna. Although the total area in Mexico occupied by cloud forest is small — less than one-half of one percent of the total land mass — the number of endemics and other unique flora and fauna to be found within this habitat is exceptional.

Typical cloud forest trees may reach 95 to 130 feet in height, and a few of the largest ones may have a diameter at breast height of seven feet. Some of the more prominent canopy trees at El Triunfo included apes earring, also present at this upland elevation, hand-flower tree, which has blossoms with extended stamens that resemble five fingers; and cigarbox tree, *cedro* in Spanish — its reddish brown wood has great strength, is fragrant and easily worked, and is used to make cigar boxes. Several of the cloud forest trees are closely related to temperate zone species that occur within the United

States. A few of those genera include *Prunus* (plums), *Rhamnus* (buckthorns), *Liquidamber* (sweet gum), *Eugenia* (myrtles), and *Quercus* (oaks).

Although the canopy trees of the cloud forest can be spectacular, it is the understory, composed of medium and small trees, that makes up the bulk of the forest and sets the area apart from most other habitats. Tree ferns, of the genus *Cyathea,* are among the most obvious forms and may reach thirty feet in height. Numerous trees and shrubs of the Maleastoma family occur throughout, all identified by their unique lance-shaped leaves that possess three central ribs rather than a single one. One of these is the tropical blueberry, a short tree that produces small sweet, blue berries sometimes sold in local markets.

The ground cover of the cloud forest can be almost as spectacular as the overstory. *Selaginella,* associated with several kinds of ferns, can form large patches. *Piper,* locally called *cordoncillo* (Spanish for "small braid"), is also common. Two fairly common red-flowered shrubs that were blooming in late March included loose-flowered lobelia and wax mallow or giant fire dart.

The trees and shrubs of the El Triunfo cloud forest almost without exception were festooned with an outstanding assortment of epiphytes, plants that grow on another for physical support but not as a source of nutrients. Bromeliads of varying sizes, from little ones that look like ball moss to giant, fleshy plants high in the treetops, were abundant, as were a wide assortment of mosses, lichens, and ferns. Also abundant were a wide variety of *Philodendron*-type vines that could be found from the ground to the tops of the highest trees. It was like a gigantic greenhouse. I soon realized that cloud forest habitat contained an amazing number of tree and shrub species that are able to produce flowers and fruit at the same time. I found and photographed more than twenty examples of plants bearing both flowers and fruits.

Approximately 50,000 acres (20,000 hectares) of the El Triunfo cloud forest was established as a Santuario de Fauna y Flora del Gobierno on May 20, 1972. The preserve was placed under the special protection of the state of Chiapas, and under the general overview of Dr. Alvarez del Toro, of Tuxtla Gutierrez. It was Professor del Toro who had played the key role in establishment of the preserve. In 1984, however, the preserve was transferred to the federal government, and is now under the protection of SEDUE, the Secretariat for Urban and Ecological Affairs. The head guard at El Triunfo, Ishmail Galves G., was retained. And it was Ishmail who met us upon our arrival and gave a great deal of his time and energy to making sure that our visit was not only one of observations and photography (not collecting), but also to assure our success in finding the horned guan, the rarest of the many birds protected within El Triunfo cloud forest.

When Robert Andrle did his study, "The Horned Guan in Mexico and Guatemala," in 1965 on the animal's biology and status (published in *The Condor* in March–April, 1967), he found greatly reduced populations at twenty-four localities examined. Andrle summarized his findings as follows: "The Horned Guan's survival has been assured up to the present time only by the difficulty of access to its habitat and remoteness from human populations, conditions which have been altered in various parts of its range by new settlements, increasing deforestation, and more hunting pressure. To ensure the species' future preservation, legal protection must be afforded and enforced, and adequately controlled refuges established" (p. 107). By 1972, El Triunfo preserve became a reality.

According to Ishmail, the Mexican population of horned guans had then declined to about fourteen pairs. Four or five of these occurred on the El Triunfo preserve, but even this population had declined during the previous several years. They were very difficult to find, and had it not been for Ishmail's expertise in detecting and finding the bird within the forest, we might have missed one of the world's most magnificent birds.

Horned guans are larger than turkey-size, but are almost totally arboreal in their habits, coming to the ground only occasionally for dust-bathing or foraging. The vast majority of their time is spent feeding and resting in the upper half of the forest strata, where fruit is readily available. The bird possesses glossy green-black plumage on its back, head, tail and belly, but a finely streaked white breast. Adults have a broad white bar across the underside of the tail, and a red throat patch that can easily be missed. But the most unusual character is the surprisingly large vermilion-colored spike or horn, or casque, that occurs on the crown, just above the eye. This feature seems to dominate the head so much that the bright yellow bill goes unnoticed.

In spite of the bird's size and relatively unwary behavior, seeing it was no easy task. It took Ishmail's trained ears to detect the bird's very deep and soft mooing-like calls. Once a horned guan was pinpointed, it was still difficult to work quietly into a position (usually several hundred feet from the trail and up or down extremely steep slopes and through thickets of very dense vegetation) from which we could actually see the bird in the equally dense foliage of the feeding tree. During the course of three days in which we diligently searched the El Triunfo forest, every member of our party had good looks at this incredible relict species.

We found a wide assortment of birds during our full five-day stay at El Triunfo. Many of these were important for me and the other birders who were actively trying to find and observe all of Mexico's unique avifauna. Although the El Triunfo trip did not produce an exceptionally long list of birds, it did produce a list of exceptional quality. Mexico's Sierra Madre de Chiapas is home to as many as three dozen bird species that either do not occur anywhere else in Mexico or are extremely rare elsewhere and can best be seen there. Of the 186 species of birds I recorded within the sierra, from the time we left the paved road until we returned to it at Mapastepec, twenty-six were new Mexico sightings for me.

Specialities of the El Triunfo Preserve included two guans, the horned and the highland guan, sometimes called black penelopina or black chachalaca. The white-faced quail-dove was surprisingly common about the forest edges, and I found chicks, just out of the nest on Easter morning. Barred parakeets were seen flying over in closed, fast-flying flocks, and I found four individuals feeding in a tall tree on top of a ridge on our first morning of searching for the horned guan. A blue-tailed hummingbird was found feeding on flowers of shrubs growing very near our camp on two afternoons during our stay. The tiny wine-throated hummingbird, sometimes considered to be conspecific with the bumblebee hummingbird, was seen a number of times along the edges of the forest; one male was found defending a group of flowering shrubs nearby. Every one of our party was able to see it well. All of us also had great looks at the resplendent quetzal. One of the toughest birds to see well was the very secretive blue-throated motmot. It took a good deal of work, including recording of its calls to entice it closer, before we had successful views of this highland speciality. And I discovered a tawny-throated leaftosser in a secluded and sheltered area in the canyon bottom, and watched it forage, like a towhee, on the forest floor.

We found small numbers of black-throated jays near our camp and within the forest; I also recorded unicolored jays on the trail toward Finca Prusia. Rufous-browed wrens were fairly common throughout the forest, and although it was heard numerous times, I had only two good observations of this very buffy-colored house-wren. There were three thrushes of special interest at El Triunfo, the mountain and black robins and spotted nightingale-thrush. Both robins were seen at the clearing, and their songs were dominant within the forest throughout the day. The spotted nightingale-thrush was another matter. Although it was present on the ground and in the lower vegetation throughout the forest, it was very difficult to see well. This is a beautiful thrush with a black head and olive-brown back, white front and belly tinged with yellow and spotted on the breast, and with bright orange legs and bill. None of the illustrations in the field guides do it justice. Two special sparrows were found at El Triunfo, yellow-throated brush-finch and white-eared ground-sparrow. Both are colorful and unique birds that reach the northern edge of their ranges within the Chiapas highlands.

Additional bird species recorded at El Triunfo included: band-tailed pigeon, white-tipped dove, singing quail, mottled and fulvous owls, violet sabrewing, green-throated mountain-gem, magnificent hummingbird, mountain trogon, emerald toucanet, hairy and golden-olive woodpeckers, both the spotted and spot-crowned woodcreepers, scaly-throated and ruddy foliage-gleaners, scaled antpitta, white-throated spadebill, tufted flycatcher, yellowish flycatcher, rose-throated becard, gray-breasted wood-wren, brown-backed solitaire, ruddy-capped nightingale-thrush, slate-throated redstart, golden-browed warbler, blue-crowned chlorophonia, blue-hooded euphonia, common bush-tanager, cinnamon-bellied flower-piercer, chestnut-capped brush-finch, and hooded grosbeak.

Some of the North American birds found at El Triunfo, either as wintering or as migrating species, included zone-tailed hawk, Vaux's swift, western wood-pewee, Hammond's flycatcher, Swainson's thrush, cedar waxwing, solitary vireo; the Tennessee, Nashville, Townsend's black-throated green, black-and-white, worm-eating, MacGillivray's and Wilson's (most numerous) warblers; northern waterthrush, Lincoln's sparrow, and rose-breasted grosbeak.

Each night, soon after dark, we could hear the strange bark-like calls of a creature we were told was a *cacomistle*. One night I detected two different pairs of these nocturnal mammals reasonably close to camp. When I first asked about the calls, they were identified as ringtail calls. But I had lived with ringtails in the Southwest for years, and had never heard them make such calls. On my last morning at Triunfo, however, I found an adult "ringtail" feeding on fruit in low trees just above camp. Although it had the same physical features as the northern ringtail (*Bassariscus astutus*), it was considerably larger. It was not until I returned home and checked Dr. E. Raymond Hall's *The Mammals of North America,* that I realized that the El Triunfo ringtail is a separate species altogether, *Bassariscus sumichrasti* (see chapter thirteen, "Quest for the Slender-billed Wren" for details about Francis Sumichrast). It is 31 to 40 inches in length, compared to the northern ringtail, which is 24 to 32 inches in length. The mystery was solved.

We left El Triunfo on Easter morning after a couple of hours of birding the clearing and nearby forest. I left that highland valley with a great deal of emotion. It had been a fascinating and exciting several days in probably the most remote place I have ever visited. Exploring its canyons and slopes provided me with more than just another wilderness experience: I was left with a personal commitment to trying to do something more to help protect this fragile ecosystem from further exploitation. I felt urgency about helping convince others of the importance of El Triunfo as one of the last places of its kind on earth. And I can only hope that El Triunfo is able to live up to its own name, "The Triumph." Being there was indeed a triumphant experience for me and my friends, and led us to hope that Mexico will continue to keep El Triunfo intact for all of mankind. There are no substitutes left.

PART IV

Tropical Mexico

Tropical Mexico

17

Jungle

Some of my earliest boyhood fantasies were set in equatorial forests, usually in the African Congo or South America's Amazonia. Although some of those daydreams were Frank Buck "bring 'em back alive" stuff, most were of exploring the unexplored and or the discovery of a rare or unique jungle cat or bird of prey. Although those fantasies were dormant for many years, they were renewed when I finally had the opportunity to visit tropical forests in Mexico, Panama and Africa. My interest and enthusiasm for the jungle had not diminished. I discovered the equatorial forests of my early fantasies were just as exciting in later life, although the tropical forests themselves are today only remnants of what they were during my boyhood.

Tropical forests, sadly, are considered the world's fastest declining natural systems. This is in spite of the fact that those ecosystems contain a greater array of plants and animals than any other place on the face of our planet. We are losing fifty acres of this spectacular habitat every minute, according to the *Global 2000 Report to the President,* a report developed by the U.S. Council on Environmental Quality. A companion report on *The World's Tropical Forests,* prepared in 1980 by the U.S. Interagency Task Force on Tropical Forests, states: "Estimates indicate that closed tropical forests have already been reduced by human activities by more than 40 percent. And the best available projections indicate, that, unless governments individually and collectively take action, by the end of the first quarter of the next century the world's closed tropical forests will be nothing but scattered remnants . . ." (p. 15).

What Is a Jungle?

The term "jungle" has been used to describe everything from dense, dark, and humid forests to the more chaotic environments in cities and workplaces. Here it is used to mean the tropical rain forests that occur only within a broad belt along the equator, rarely extending beyond the Tropic of Cancer in the north or the Tropic of Capricorn in the south. These forests require a minimum of seasonal variation where temperatures and humidity remain high and relatively constant, and annual rainfall exceeds that utilized by the vegetation. Any additional precipitation runs off or is impounded. The Choco rain forest of Colombia, South America, is one of the wettest places on earth; annual rainfall there exceeds 235 inches.

Consideration of jungles must also address their multistoried character. Rain forests are usually described as five-tiered systems that include a ground-floor herb layer (although usually sparse), a shrub layer, understory, canopy, and emergent layer. The emergent vegetation consists of a few of the tallest trees that rise above the rest of the forest canopy.

One of the earliest definitions of tropical rain forest habitat was that of Alfred Russell Wallace (codiscoverer with Charles Darwin of natural selection), who in 1878 wrote that "instead of the endless repetitions of the one form of (tree) trunk, such as are to be seen in our pine, or oak, or beechwoods, the eye wanders from one tree to another and rarely detects two of the same species" (p. 241). Although Wallace's description was related only to the vegetation, it is safe to say that one of the most important characteristics of rain forests is that the number of species, of almost every type of life form, is far greater there than in any other forest community.

Robert MacArthur provides numerous comparisons of species richness (numbers of species) in tropical and temperate environments in his classic book, *Geographic Ecology*. Some of his best examples relate to insects and breeding land birds. A total of 545 insect species were collected in a wet lowland tropical forest in two thousand sweeps of a net; the same number of sweeps in a mixed Massachusetts forest yielded between 360 and 410 species for various months. In a study of ant distribution in the southern hemisphere, only two species were found at Tierra del Fuego at the southern tip of South America; 103 species were found at Buenos Aires, Argentina; and 222 species were recorded at São Paulo, Brazil.

The distribution pattern of breeding land birds in the western hemisphere is also revealing. The gradient in numbers in comparable sized areas increases toward the tropics between Alaska and Panama. A total of 49 species nest on Alaska's north slope, 128 spe-

Typical jungle growth, with taller emergent trees, near Palenque, Chiapas.

cies nest in Canada's British Columbia, 150 are found in Oregon, 270 in southwestern Mexico, 412 in the Oaxaca-Chiapas region of Mexico, and 600 species nest in a comparable sized area in Panama. Kricher pointed out that "breeding bird diversity increased almost twenty-five times from Greenland in the arctic to Colombia on the equator" (p. 123).

Plantlife

Anyone who has had the good fortune to step into a tropical rain forest (see chapter nineteen, "Palenque") cannot help but be impressed with the abundance and diversity of plant species. Most striking is the great abundance of trees because of their dominating trunks and great masses of foliage. A rough estimate of 200 tree species per hectare (2.5 acres) is often used for lowland rain forests in the western hemisphere. But that number can be considerably larger in other tropical regions. A total of 375 tree species was identified from about 2,750 individual trees in one twenty-three-hectare (57.5-acre) sample area in Malaya. In contrast to this, a maximum of thirty-five tree species has been recorded in one hectare at Great Smoky Mountains National Park, an area considered to be the best remaining example of North America's eastern temperate forest.

Rain forest tree identity is not a simple matter, however. The leaves, branching systems, and crown forms of different trees are often so much alike that many require flowers or fruits for identification. This is particularly true for mature trees. Young leaves may be considerably larger than the older leaves which are more likely to be exposed to more sunlight and rain in the canopy. The older leaves are not only smaller, but most have smooth and shiny surfaces, and possess "drip tips" that aid in water runoff. Examine the leaves of the common weeping fig, an Asian species widely grown in the United States as an ornamental plant in homes, offices and shopping malls. Drip tips are important in the tropics because wet leaves are more susceptible to being covered by lichens, liverworts, algae and mosses that can reduce photosynthesis.

P. W. Richards found that even though unrelated rain forest trees may look alike superficially, they differ in a number of less obvious characteristics, such as "usual mature height (which determines the place of the tree in the forest structure), the growth rate, life span, shade tolerance, reproductive strategy, type of dispersal mechanism, phenology of leafing, flowering, and fruiting" (p. 152). Various species have different and staggered flowering and fruiting seasons so that there is no time of year when nectar, fruit, and seeds are not available.

Tropical rain forests therefore contain a much greater variation of habitats than can be found within the temperate forests. Although stratification certainly exists, and rain forest fauna select for preferred habitats, layering is more a function of succession or dynamic changes under way within the forest than of certain flora in a stable condition. Irregularity is the rule.

Some tropical ecologists give great credit to tree-fall gaps in the forest for habitat diversity. Gary Hartshorn found that seventy-five percent of the trees in his Costa Rican study plot were dependent upon tree falls. A falling giant can create a sizable area where increased light and temperatures can start new plant growth that may not otherwise be possible. Many plants are colonists that can't tolerate deep shade but can compete if given a chance in brighter places. Those species must start their growth almost immediately if they are to get ahead of the numerous grasses, ferns and vines, many of which can chemically inhibit the germination of some seeds. Hartshorn's studies suggested that the rain forest actually replaces itself this way every 80 to 135 years. Another study, by Egbert Leigh, Jr., revealed that tree fall rates generally exceeded one percent a year for all sizes of trees. Adrian Forsyth and Kenneth Miyata discussed this issue in their excellent book, *Tropical Nature,* and concluded that "it seems more appropriate to view virgin tropical forest as a patchy, constantly changing mosiac generated in large part by unpredictable tree falls" (p. 36).

I never cease to be amazed at the number of plant species I recognize at the edges of the tropical forests. It is reminiscent of a huge greenhouse containing some of the world's most popular house plants. Some of Mexico's best examples include bird's nest ferns, *Peperomia, Begonia,* purple heart, prayer plant, dumbcane, *Philodendron,* and *Syngonium.* Various philodendrons grow sixty to seventy feet high or more along the trunks of many tree giants. But once inside the forest the soft-stalked plants with broad leaves occur only at light gaps.

Some of the ground layer plants along the forest borders possess huge leaves and are often mistaken for philodendrons. Ceriman, sometimes called perforated philodendron, gunnera, and anthurium, are the best examples. It is not uncommon to see native people using these giant leaves as umbrellas during sudden downpours. Many of these plants have been cultivated and produce very showy indoor ornamentals in temperate zones.

Faunal Diversity

Forest openings or borders also are excellent places to find a good variety of other life forms, especially insects, birds and reptiles. A good many of these animals frequent the openings because of the availability of specific flowering plants that may not occur elsewhere, while others are there to prey upon those animals present as grazers or pollinators.

The theory that forest openings and resultant changes help to

Elephant ear, common at wet areas in the jungle. Locals use the huge leaves for umbrellas during rainstorms.

create high species diversity is in direct contrast to an older belief that high species diversity in jungles exists because that environment represents some of the oldest and most stable natural communities on earth. The argument was that greater age and stability allowed for wider specialization. Although the jury may still be out on those theories, one of the more widely accepted causes of high species diversity is related to "geographic isolationism." This idea relates to the great abundance of complete systems in jungles that fully support a large set of species. The American tropics produce species at a far greater rate than the temperate and arctic regions because there is less need to seek more favorable habitats. Sedentariness reduces interchange within population, increasing isolation and the stability of subpopulations. Tropical populations are less likely (there is less need) to cross barriers like rivers and low mountains than are temperate populations.

Another significant factor in species diversity is the longer grow-ing season for plants and small animals, which allows for many more generations each year; this in turn exposes more individuals to the effects of natural selection. The wider variety of resources permit greater specialization, and the more specialized the species, the less they compete. Reduced competition requires less energy, enhances larger populations, and increases resistance to extinction. Competi-tion, however, results in greater species divergence or specialization, and the interactions between the species become more complemen-tary rather than competitive.

Leafcutting Ants. The invertebrate populations — insects, milli-pedes, centipedes, spiders, and lower life forms that live on the forest floor is remarkably high. Some of the best known of these creatures are ants, and the leafcutting ants (*Atta* spp.) are the most obvious. They live in colonies of several million individuals that construct nests that may be ten to twenty feet in diameter and up to two feet high. These nests are well-marked because of the numerous trails that radiate out for as much as a hundred yards in all directions.

Leafcutters occur throughout the tropics, and a few reach the United States. The Texas leafcutter ant (*Atta texana*, a species closely related to the tropical forms) is fairly common in eastern Texas and, according to E. O. Wilson (1971), there is one species that occurs as far north as New Jersey's pine barrens. My first observation of leaf-cutting ants was in a small city park in Tepic, Nayarit, where I watched hundreds of individuals carrying their booty down a tree trunk, along the edge of a paved path, to their nest underneath a section of the same path.

Leafcutting ants most often are detected along their trails where thousands of individuals can be found going and coming about their business of bringing pieces of freshly cut green leaves to their nest. Some pieces of leaves are so much larger than the transporter that the trails look like miniature rivers crowded with tiny green sailboats. The large worker ants are usually accompanied by small workers whose job is to guard the defenseless carriers against parasitic flies which lay their eggs on the necks of the leaf-carriers.

All of the leaves are gathered from the upper canopy and in such a way so that no one tree suffers from "overgrazing." The leaves are cut by workers on site and carried down the trunk and along the cleared trails to the underground chambers of their nest. The leaf-cutters do not consume the leaves themselves, but feed only on tiny fungi that they "grow" within their underground chambers with pulp derived from the chewed-up leaves and their own excrement. These ants and their fungi are dependent upon one another. Their underground gardens are tended with care.

Birdlife. No group of jungle animals is as obvious as are the birds, and there are a number of avian families that are synonymous with tropical forests. Parrots, guans, toucans, trogons, motmots, and ant-birds are some of the best known. However, almost every North American bird family has additional tropical representatives, and many of those are truly spectacular.

For me, tropical hummingbirds have long been a special interest. They pose a considerable challenge in identification because of their tiny size and (usually) momentary encounters. They may be rather drab in appearance, such as the little and long-tailed hermits, or offer bright flashes of color, such as the white-necked jacobin, purple-crowned fairy, and fork-tailed emerald. Of Mexico's fifty-two known hummingbirds, fifteen frequent the tropical forests. Those species possess special characteristics for feeding on the nectar of flowers of the tropical vegetation. Examples include extremely long bills for reaching deep into tubular flowers, decurved bills designed for feeding on heliconia blossoms, and shorter bills for smaller flowers.

Hummingbirds frequent every layer from the forest canopy, where a few may specialize on flowering bromeliads, to the herb and shrub layers. On one Palenque trip I was surprised to find the abundant and loud squeaks in the forest came not from a party of birds at an army ant column but from five territorial little hermits. Each bird—presumably all were males—sat on a low perch calling in an attempt to attract females. These courtship areas are called leks, places where several males gather to display. Apparently, the accumulated noises of several displaying males help to attract the females. And the tiny males were adamant! Their tails were pumped up and down with each squeak.

Another bird group that contains many more tropical than temperate zone representatives is the family of tanagers. Mexico has twenty-two tanager species (compared with only five for the United States) and many of these are rain forest residents. I have been particularly partial to the little euphonias. These brightly colored tanagers feed primarily on mistletoe berries and many nest within rain forest bromeliads.

The scarlet-rumped and crimson-collared tanagers, species often seen together, are two of the most beautiful of all the tropical forest residents. They are both forest edge or gap birds, and usually are reasonably common (see chapter nineteen, "Palenque"). On each Mexico trip, when I see my first scarlet-rumped tanager I marvel all over again at its contrasting velvety black and deep scarlet colors.

Then there are the woodpeckers and their look-alike cousins, the woodcreepers. Six woodpeckers — black-cheeked, smoky-brown, golden-olive, chestnut-colored, lineated and pale-billed — are humid forest residents, while eight woodcreepers — tawny-winged, ruddy, olivaceous, wedge-billed, strong-billed, barred, ivory-billed and streak-headed — occur within Mexico's rain forest habitat. I admit a partiality for the woodcreepers. They are an active and bright (although always brown to deep rust in color) family of birds, and because of their preferences for the shadows are exquisite representatives of Mexico's tropical forests. My favorite is the tiny wedge-billed woodcreeper that can easily be overlooked in the forest. Like many other forest birds, it will freeze when you first enter the forest; if you wait quietly for a few minutes, it will resume normal activities. Its dainty appearance and wedge-like bill (used to pry out insects under bark) are unique for this fascinating family of tropical birds.

Forest Canopy

One of the most distinctive features of the rain forest is its dense canopy that exists between thirty and 150 feet above the forest floor. Except at openings, the habitat forms a closed system of intertwining limbs and vines, providing arboreal pathways that are every bit as important as those on the ground. The varied habitats within the canopy support a vast assortment of arboreal wildlife, including an incredible variety of insects and other invertebrates, as well as salamanders, amphibians and reptiles, birds and mammals, all able to meet their requirements without leaving the canopy. In a study of mammal density and biomass in the rain forest on Barro Colorado Island, Panama, John Eisenberg found seventy percent of the mammal population within the canopy; twenty-five percent on the ground, and five percent utilized both habitats equally.

Another conspicuous rain forest feature is the tremendous assortment of epiphytes, which can occur on every part of the trees and
shrubs. Epiphytes include lichens, mosses, liverworts and ferns, as
well as orchids, bromeliads, and arboreal cacti. Although these plants
grow on other plants, they are not parasitic. They must depend upon
the nutrients obtained from soil that occurs on their hosts and dis-
solved minerals found in rainwater. Vines, by contrast, must have
their roots in the ground. Some other plants, even trees like strangler
figs, may begin life as epiphytes by sprouting from seeds lodged in
tree crevices, but send out aerial roots to the gound. Once a toehold
is obtained they can grow much faster, and can then develop into
massive trees that may eventually envelope and destroy their hosts.

Epiphytes may be so numerous on some tree limbs and trunks
that their hosts are almost totally hidden, and these gardens of epiphytes themselves provide habitat that can support a rich assortment
of wildlife. Bromeliads grow in such a way so that they can collect and
hold considerable amounts of rainwater and thus serve as homes for
insects, salamanders, tree frogs and birds. These canopy habitats are
a world of their own. And many wildlife species that reside there are
considered rare because they are almost never seen. For example, the
huge but beautiful metallic-blue morpho butterflies may be common in the canopy, but are only occasionally seen at ground level.

Nutrients

An obvious question arising is what benefit does the host tree receive
from supporting the various epiphytes? A 1985 article on Colom-
bian rain forests by Nalini Nadkarni suggests that canopy rooting,
in the form of threadlike filaments, is able to store nutrients from
the organic matter held and utilized by the epiphytes and transfer
these nutrients to the host tree. The result is a mutually beneficial
association.

The availability of adequate nutrients, enough to support the
massive forms of rain forest vegetation, is of particular interest because the giant trees are not able to obtain the bulk of their nutrients from the soils, as do their temperate cousins. The ground cover
in tropical forests is usually only a thin veneer of decaying matter,
and soils here do not possess the deep and rich humus that can be
expected in temperate forests. Although litter falling out of the
tropical forest canopy is considerable, and continues throughout

Milpa cut into tropical forest. Locals use these small patches for growing beans, squash, and other foods.

the year (amounts are estimated to be at least twice as much as in the rich deciduous forests of the eastern United States), the abundant fungi make short work of the fallen materials.

The dense rain forest canopy filters out extremely high percentages of both sunlight and precipitation, preventing these from reaching the forest floor. Less than two percent of the sunlight that falls on the treetops also falls on the understory. A 1973 report on the stratification of tropical forests by Alan P. Smith suggests that sun flecks, tiny unfiltered spots of sunlight, provide forty-five to seventy percent of the total light reaching the forest floor. The lack of direct sunlight and minimum air movement help to perpetuate the constantly moist and warm environment perfect for fungi. These abundant saprophytes — plants that receive their nourishment from dead and decaying plants and animals — are the main decomposers in the forest.

Tropical vegetation has adapted to the thin layers of litter by establishing a vast web of tiny rootlets and attached strands of fungi, just below the ground surface, that are able to trap the necessary nutrients before they become lost. This interwoven mycorrhizal mat can readily be seen by brushing aside the thin top layer of litter. This system, combined with the abundance of ground-dwelling termites and myriad of other insects that help to break down the larger woody pieces, produce an almost litter-free forest floor.

Rain forest trees are able to obtain nutrients in yet another less obvious way. Many possess hollow trunks that serve as homes or temporary shelters for animals that drop masses of nutrient-rich materials inside the tree. This readily available material is limited for use to the host tree only.

Thus, although tropical rain forests do contain exceptionally high concentrations of nutrients, the vast majority of these are tied up in the trees themselves. Few are available in the soils, which are nutrient-poor. This is why, when tropical forests are cut and burned, although grasses and shrubs may respond to the new open conditions immediately, the soils are not able to support long-term grazing or agriculture. And once the few remaining nutrients are used up, even the semiproductive grasslands are likely to disappear. The chance that a mature rain forest will ever recover in our lifetime is remote. Loss of these natural systems, complete with their great species diversity, is a disaster from which the world may never recover.

18

Catemaco at Christmas

Sunrise from the foothills of the Sierra de Tuxtla was an unforgettable sight. As I reached the crest of the hill, I was able to trace the low ridge that separates the zinc-blue Laguna Sontecomapan from the ashen Gulf of Mexico beyond. Around me mist was rising from the wet grasslands, and the few remaining rain forest tree-giants looked like grotesque ruins from another world. Gradually, the eastern horizon was turning from gray to gold to red, and the increasing glow across the Gulf was a prediction of a new and exciting day.

The last of the pauraque songs had echoed from a small patch of nearby forest as I had struggled up the steep grass-covered hillside. Just as I assumed that song had ended the nighttime sounds, I heard the repetitive call notes of the crepuscular ferruginous pygmy-owl from below, somewhere near the roadway where I had started my walk thirty minutes earlier.

I stood there in awe and watched the first rays of the morning creep toward me from the adjacent highlands. As the bright red ball in the east started to separate from the earth's clinging horizon, I heart parrots calling from their roosts in a patch of forest south of me. As I strained my eyes to catch a glimpse of those noisy birds, I was attracted to the squawks of other parrots in flight, silhouetted against the bright skyline. I could make out the stocky shapes of *Amazona,* but it took some time before I could clearly see their red foreheads and yellow cheeks to identify them as red-lored parrots. Also on the skyline were white lines of cattle egrets, on their way to feeding sites nearby. I counted thirty in one flock, and discovered three smaller flocks even closer that totaled about fifty-five birds. Two individuals that trailed the last group were the larger and more graceful great egrets. Then suddenly a falcon crossed my field of vision. It took me another second or two to locate that medium-sized raptor, larger than an American kestrel and not as long-tailed as the aplomado falcon. It was a peregrine, one of the swiftest and most powerful of raptors, probably hunting the lower wetlands for an early morning meal. It was the only peregrine detected on that count day.

So my day began that early morning at Catemaco. It was the start of a thirteen-hour day in which I counted every bird I could find within one designated area, one of twenty-one sectors within a fifteen-mile-diameter circle. I recorded 110 species within my rather small count area. The full complement of fifty-two counters recorded a total of 21,351 birds of 292 species during that one twenty-four-hour period on New Year's Eve, 1974. We had gathered at Catemaco to take part in the second Catemaco Christmas bird count, a census that resulted in the highest number of birds ever recorded anywhere on a Christmas bird count.

The year before at Catemaco I had been one of only twenty-seven counters who had recorded 11,665 individual birds of 248 species. Our goal that second year was to find three hundred or more species, which would have been a landmark high for Christmas bird counts. Since the inception of these annual counts, which began as one count with twenty-seven participants in 1900 and expanded to 1,478 separate counts with 35,200 participants by 1984 (throughout the United States and adjacent countries as far south as Venezuela), they have been an important part of thousands of birders' Christmastime activities. But the magic three hundred had never been reached. We believed that the Catemaco area provided the necessary habitat diversity and accessibility, and that it could be done with adequate counters and a little luck. In spite of eight consecutive Christmas counts at Catemaco, however, from 1973 through 1981, the goal of three hundred was not reached. The highest number of birds found on a Catemaco count (295) was recorded by twenty-seven counters in 1978.

Count totals can include only birds recorded within the count circle during one twenty-four hour period (midnight to midnight) during the Christmas holidays, from about December 20 through January 5. Birds seen a few days before or after the count day are also reported, but not as part of the official count. Most of those birds are detected by counters exploring their count areas before the count, or just afterwards when people are trying to relocate birds seen on the count day. For example, at Catemaco in 1974, ten additional birds were found during the count period but not on the count day. And in 1978, thirty-one additional species were recorded.

Count results and area descriptions, as well as the names of all the counters, are published annually by the National Audubon Society in cooperation with the U.S. Fish and Wildlife Service, in one volume of *American Birds*. The tremendous database accumulated since 1900, especially for those sites where counts began early in the century, reveals some fascinating trends in bird populations. Most importantly, this information provides indications of which species have increased or decreased over the years. More often than not the changes can be related directly to habitat changes within or adjacent to the count circles.

Catemaco

The possibility of locating an exceptionally large number of birds within a relatively small area was the initial purpose of an organized count at Catemaco. Even so, it wasn't easy to entice dozens of birders to gather together approximately eighteen hundred miles south of the Texas-Mexico border to count birds at a time when most people are at home celebrating the Christmas holidays with family and friends. It took someone with a lot of enthusiam and charisma, and confidence in the area. That individual was none other than Victor Emanuel, an avid birder and Mexico enthusiast. It was Victor who first identified the potential at Catemaco and organized the first and all other counts in the 1970s and 1980s. In more recent years, Victor has established the highly successful tour business Victor Emanuel Nature Tours (VENT) offering tours throughout the world; all of his tours to Mexico provide outstanding opportunities to see and enjoy birds and their natural habitats. See chapter sixteen, "El Triunfo," for an example of one VENT tour.

The Catemaco area had tremendous potential because of the exceptional diversity of available habitats. The best description of the count area was that published with the 1974 Catemaco count report: "center about 7-½ miles N of the town of Catemaco, elevation sea level to 5500 ft; habitat coverage: lowland rain forest 35%, lowland fields and scrub 20%, remnant cloud forest 12%, lake and urban 10%, tropical upland scrub and pasture 8%, elfin cloud forest 5%, mangrove-lined lagoons 4%, oak-rain forest ecotone 4%, gulf and beach 2%.—Dec. 31; 4:30 a.m. to 8:30 p.m. Clear. Temp.

55 degrees F. Wind variable, 0-8 m.p.h. Fifty-two observers in 21 parties, total party-hours, 255 (211 on foot, 38 by car, 6 by boat); total party-miles, 280 (181 on foot, 89 by car, 10 by boat)" (National Audubon Society, p. 546).

Catemaco Count—1974

Extensive amounts of rain forest had been cut and burned within the Catemaco region. Some of that clearing had been done just before the 1974 Christmas count. Smoldering logs were found in one part of the count circle. But in spite of this mass destruction, most of it initiated through get-rich-quick schemes of the fast food industry in the United States, some portions of the original rain forest remained. The count area contained scattered patches of forest in the lowlands and larger areas of forest on the upper slopes of Sierra de Tuxtla. Cloud forest habitat was present only on the highest peaks.

My count area along the lower slopes of Cerro Viga included a patch of rain forest about five acres in size, with a small stream — narrow enough to get across by stepping on one or two rocks — that flowed through it, and a crisscrossing of cattle trails. Although the impact of cattle was beginning to create trampling and erosion, the trails provided me with easy access into the heart of the forest. I first birded the more open places outside the forest and along the stream; it was there I found a male violet sabrewing. It was feeding on some bright red flowers at about head-height, and I was able to get close enough to take a couple photographs of this large, metallic-violet-colored hummer.

I was surprised at the great variety of birds encountered inside the forest canopy. This isolated patch of rain forest apparently had attracted many species of birds and other wildlife that had been displaced when the adjacent forest had been cut, and I was the beneficiary of their short-term residency. I was most surprised to find an abundance of North American warblers. Magnolia warblers were most numerous, but orange-crowns, Nashvilles, and Wilson's were also abundant. In addition I recorded a few black-and-white, yellow-rumped, and hooded warblers; American redstarts and yellow-breasted chats; and lone worm-eating, yellow and Kentucky warblers, and an ovenbird. I had found a Lucy's warbler and northern water-thrush earlier along the stream. Some of the other wintering U.S. birds found in this patch of forest included several least flycatchers, blue-gray gnatcatchers, gray catbirds, wood thrushes and white-eyed vireos, and lone warbling vireo and summer tanager.

The most common bird in that patch of forest was the brown jay. There were at least forty-five of these large corvids, including several yellow-billed youngsters. Almost as common was the boat-billed flycatcher. Both of these birds can be loud and obnoxious, and adding several band-backed and spot-breasted wrens and yellow-winged tanagers to that chorus produced a very noisy patch of forest.

Below the slope on the east side of the road was a large swampy area where I spent most of the afternoon; the greatest activity occurred late in the day. At first glance the area appeared to be little more than very moist grassland, but I had learned differently the year before when I tried to cross it to locate some shorebirds that I had seen settle in on the opposite side. I had walked only about 120 feet when suddenly I found myself sinking into the mushy turf. I was above my boots in mud, and I had a difficult time making my way back to solid ground. Having learned my lesson once, I spent the afternoon wandering back and forth along a mile of roadway recording birds by listening and watching.

The most abundant bird there was the gray-crowned yellowthroat, but I also found several white-collared seedeaters and blue-black grassquits. It was a good place to find wintering buntings, and I recorded both indigo and painted buntings. Out of the corner of my eye I detected a large duck-like bird, arriving and settling onto an open branch of a shrub across the swampy area about four hundred yards away. I immediately suspected that it was a Muscovy duck, and a few seconds later confirmed this through my spotting scope. As the evening shadows began to stretch out toward the east, bird activity picked up. Several cattle egrets began to move across the horizon, probably some of those that I had recorded earlier. There, too, were a little blue heron and two tricolored herons. Behind those was a pair of brown-hooded parrots. A lone common snipe suddenly erupted from the swamp and darted away like an elusive target.

As darkness began to settle into the lowlands, just when it was almost impossible to see across the swamp, a large brownish-streaked bird, with a long bill and legs, suddenly flew up and away: a limpkin. Apparently it had been there all along, feeding in the tall grass within one hundred or so feet from where I was standing, although I had not seen it. The limpkin was bird 109 for the day. I folded up the scope, put it in the back seat of the car, and climbed in. As I turned the lights on for the drive back to town, not more than a hundred yards away, sitting on a fencepost right next to the road, was a common potoo. Number 110 for the day represented a fitting climax for a day that had started with a pauraque, another member of the caprimulgidae family.

Catemaco Count — 1973

Over the years, the most productive section of the Catemaco count circle has been a large tract of undisturbed rain forest beyond the marsh, about eighteen miles north of Catemaco. The buildings of the Los Tuxtlas biology field station, which is operated by the Instituto de Biología of the Universidad Nacional Autónoma de México, mark the spot. Birding can be excellent along the roadway, for perhaps a half-mile in each direction, as well as on the grounds of the *estación biologica* itself. Institute scientists have installed an excellent three-quarter-mile nature trail (called the Darwin Trail) around a miniature canyon on the coastal side of the road. Many of the trees and shrubs are marked. Permission to take this trail is required.

The major path to the upland forest begins in front of the headquarters building. This trail leads far beyond the estación grounds through some beautiful country and eventually onto the summit of volcán San Martín Tuxtla. In 1973, Jim Tucker and I were assigned to census this forest. It was a remarkable day in the field. Although I recorded one bird fewer than I did the following year, many of the birds that first year were new for me.

Our day started again at dawn, in the opening at the station, where almost immediately we found a double-toothed kite. It apparently had been perched there overnight, and we watched as it disappeared toward the coast. Then we were attracted to the loud *keeowe* call of a circling black hawk-eagle, and we found five keel-billed toucans sitting on trees around the station as if waiting to be counted. A pair of blue-crowned chlorophonias were busy feeding on a bromeliad-festooned tree to one side of the clearing. And it took us several minutes to locate a rufous mourner, a reddish robin-sized bird that was sitting at the edge of the clearing singing its loud and suggestive wolf-whistle song.

Just across the road from the estación was a fruiting fig tree that was attracting large numbers of birds. We recorded more than a dozen

Muddy trail near Sierra de Tuxtla Research Station. Hikers include three locals and two birders, Ron Knaus and Nancy Strikling.

species there. The previous afternoon, when several of us had visited the area while scouting our count sectors, we had stood around and watched the comings and goings at this tree, a huge specimen that dominated the canopy. In two hours I had recorded eighteen species of birds utilizing that one tree. Of those, the bird of the day was a male lovely cotinga. This catbird-sized bird was undoubtedly one of the most beautiful birds I have ever seen. It is overall bright cobalt-blue, except for patches of deep, rich purple on its throat and chest; its wings and tail are black edged with purple. Its Spanish name is *azulejo real,* meaning "little royal blue." Although I have

seen this bird several times since, the observation of that first lovely
cotinga, feeding in the sunshine in the top of that tropical fig, has
remained a special memory.

Jim and I spent the better part of the 1973 count day exploring
the mountain trail. The first couple of miles were rather steep and
muddy, and I was surprised by the amount of use the trail received.
It served as a main thoroughfare between a small Indian village located
near the top of the first main ridge and the roadway. Bus service
was available from there to Catemaco or north to Montepio. Among
the people encountered, the men usually were dressed in immacu-
late white shirts; the women were in colorful dresses and many carried baskets or bundles on their heads. Several of the men apparently were taking fruit or chickens (a pig in one case) to market,
and were loaded down with their produce. Very few of these folks
wore shoes or sandals, and they had the widest feet I had ever seen.
These people are some of the few remaining Popoluca Indians, who
still speak the ancient Nahua language.

Trailside birding was spectacular that day. Citreoline, collared and
violaceous trogon calls were heard constantly. I watched a blue-
crowned motmot, the largest of the Mexican motmots, as it sat quietly
on a tree branch, moving its strange racket-shaped tail from side
to side like a slow clock pendulum. I counted a total of twenty-five
black-throated shrike-tanagers during the day, and I found my first
plain xenops there as well. The scientific name, *Xenops minutus*
for this bird is most appropriate; it is tiny, about the size of a small
sparrow. It is buffy in color, although the tail and wings are reddish
in suitable light, and rather nondescript except for two very distinct
characteristics: a white mustachial strip and a rather large upturned
bill. The plain xenops is a tropical forest bird that prefers edges and
usually is seen climbing about in vines and other hanging vegetation.

I birded a small clearing along the trail about one mile above
the estación, where there was a lot of bird activity along the edge.
I must have spent close to forty-five minutes within that clearing
before I spotted a lone howler monkey in a tall fig tree watching
me. It was stretched out along a big limb about seventy feet above
the ground, pretty well hidden from my view. The incident made
me wonder how often I had been watched by other jungle animals
as I went about my business. Howlers were fairly common at Catemaco. They could be heard almost every evening and morning, their

booming calls resounding through the forest for a mile or more.

Beyond the Indian village the trail gradually drops down along a forested slope to a small but sparkling blue lake. That lake was one of the most surprising and welcome sights of the day. It was like a bright jewel imbedded in the green slopes of the Sierra de Tuxtla. I stopped to photograph the lake from a place where I could include both the lake and the upper forested slopes. There was one lone fisherman on the lake, standing in a dugout canoe. I watched him as he cast his throw net and pulled it back in, netting one to three pan-sized fish from each cast. It was there, while I was watching the fisherman, that I spotted the white hawks, soaring along the upper slopes beyond the lake. Those three pure white raptors, slowly circling above the contrasting blue lake and green rain forest, were one more of the beautiful memories I have from that day.

Catemaco Count — 1975

On the third Catemaco count, on January 2, 1975, I volunteered to cover the town and lakeshore. Although the freshwater lake, rural environments, fencerows, and secondary patches of forest that my wife, Betty, and I censused were not as exciting as the primary forest, we found a greater number of bird species (113). We recorded ten kinds of wading birds; eight kinds of waterfowl, including 285 lesser scaup; seven gulls and terns; eight raptors; and eighteen warblers. The bird of the day was a lone mangrove cuckoo that we found along the edge of the lake just beyond the Motel Playa Azul. It turned out to be a count "exclusive," the only one reported.

The town of Catemaco is situated at 1,215 feet elevation on the northern shore of Laguna de Catemaco, a freshwater lake about ten miles long surrounded by the foothills of Sierra de Tuxtla. The lake is considered by many to be the most beautiful lake in Mexico. The human population of Catemaco in 1975 was about twenty-five thousand, but the town serviced a much larger population of farmers, fishermen and the like that lived nearby. Catemaco had become popular as a tourist attraction, and was busiest during the winter holidays. It provided several good accommodations and restaurants. The church of the Virgin del Carmen dominated the east side of the central plaza, and there was an excellent restaurant in the Catemaco Hotel on the north side of the plaza. On the opposite corner was the Hotel Berthangel. I had stayed at the Berthangel on three differ-

Lake Catemaco, situated south of Sierra de Tuxtla and at base of
Santa Marta highlands. The town of Catemaco is visible on right
edge of lake (Left edge of picture).

ent occasions, when the Motel Playa Azul (my favorite place to stay)
was filled; two of those visits had included New Year's Eve. If being
part of the local celebration is desired, Hotel Berthangel is a great
place to stay; it is not recommended as a place to get some needed
sleep after a long day in the field.

Catemaco is located in the southern part of the state of Veracruz,
just off of Highway 180, the main highway along the Gulf of Mexico
between the cities of Veracruz and Villahermosa. Although a paved
road goes into town, the various features beyond are accessible only
by poorly maintained dirt roads, and these at times are barely pass-
able. One of these roads makes almost a complete circle of the lake,
passing through the villages of Coyame and Tebanca. Just before
Tebanca, a side road branches to the east and leads into the Santa

Marta highlands to the village of Bastonal. This route is steep and difficult to negotiate, particularly during rainy weather. In 1981, I found that small patches of cloud forest habitat still existed along the upper slopes. I recorded five hard-to-find birds in that area during two days of exploring; purplish-backed quail-dove, emerald toucanet, scaly-throated foliage-gleaner, black robin, and plain-breasted brush-finch (this bird has recently been lumped with the chestnut-capped brush-finch).

The graveled road north of the Coyame junction goes beyond the field station to Montepio, a tiny fishing village on the coast and at the mouth of the Río Máquino, approximately thirty miles distance from Catemaco. The village of Sontecomapan, the swamp and the field station are all along this route. The Christmas count circle extends north only to the station and the adjacent forest, and southeast only part way around Lake Catemaco to Coyame.

Catemaco Count — 1981

My count sector on December 30, 1981, included an area from the Coyame village and roadway north to and including the village of Sontecomapan. The area also included a pretty little nursery and the village of Dos Amates, about halfway to Sontecomapan. Our party of five started at dawn along the heavily eroded track near Dos Amate with a calling pauraque. We ended the day in an isolated little valley near Coyame where I found a laughing falcon perched at the very top of a solitary fig tree overlooking a grassy pasture that contained numerous singing white-collared seedeaters. It was one of the few times that I had heard a laughing falcon, which is a fairly common raptor of the tropical lowland forests and borders. It has a strange but musical call that resembles a human laugh. A fairly large hawk, about the size of a redtail, it can usually be identified at a considerable distance because of its rather upright stance and black facemask. On closer inspection, the bird is a very buffy color from the front and, although the back of the head is buffy, from the back the bird looks much like most other hawks, except for a hard to see buffy collar. Its tail is well marked with black and buffy bars. This species has a reputation as a predator on snakes.

A total of thirty-four counters found only 188 birds on the 1981 count, far below any of the previous counts. The reason for this low number is uncertain, although a review of the missing species sug-

Early morning on Sontecomapan Lagoon, with fishermen in foreground and Sierra de Tuxtla in background.

gests that the extensive clearing of the Catemaco forests had begun to take its toll on wintering forest bird populations. There were several species missing from the 1981 count for the first time. Among those were seven raptors — sharp-shinned, Cooper's and gray hawks, great black-hawks, ornate hawk-eagle, barred forest-falcon, and bat falcon; the plain-breasted, ruddy and blue ground-doves; ruddy quail-dove, brown-hooded and yellow-headed parrots; three woodcreepers (tawny-winged, wedge-billed and barred), buff-throated foliage-gleaner, plain xenops, black-faced antshrike, red-capped manakin; the royal, yellow-olive and ochre-bellied flycatchers; and six warblers, the Tennessee, yellow-throated, and Kentucky warblers, ovenbird, and American and slate-throated redstarts.

It is estimated that approximately two-thirds of the birds that breed in North American forests overwinter in tropical forests from Mexico to South America. A study was conducted by Dr. John Rappole of the University of Georgia, just below the *estación biologica* to determine the effects of tropical deforestation on migrants. The results were not encouraging: "In 1973, the study site was a six-hectare area of relatively undisturbed rain forest. In 1980, only one hectare of rain forest was left. The rest of the site now consists of a hodge-podge of pasture, cornfields, and second growth. Our studies indicated that as a result of this clearing there was a 40 percent reduction in the total population of forest migrants" (Deis, 1981, p. 9).

The Catemaco Christmas bird counts provided good incentive for a number of birders to spend their Christmas holidays in a fascinating part of Mexico. It was not only great fun, but helped to quantify bird populations and identify problems facing them in that swiftly changing portion of Mexico.

19

Palenque

Palenque is a name that stirs the heart of any New World archeologist. It is likely to have the same effect upon any naturalist in Mexico for quite a different reason: this outstanding Mayan ruins site is set in one of the most accessible rain forest habitats remaining in Mexico. The five-tiered forest forms an impressive backdrop for the Palenque ruins, as dramatic today as it must have been when Mayan priests sacrified humans to pay homage to their gods.

The Ruins

Palenque is considered by many people to have the most beautiful of all the Mayan ruins. Their placement within the green womb of the forest and the great curtain of tall trees provides for a truly outstanding scene with a sense of remoteness unlike that at most other Mayan ruins. One can understand how it was possible for Palenque to go unnoticed by the conquering Spaniards for more than two hundred years.

Archeologists J. Eric S. Thompson, Charles Gallencamp and others wrote that Palenque was first settled about 300 B.C., but did not reach its peak for another six hundred years. Then, until the end of the seventh century, it became the Mayan pacesetter as a religious and political center. This was the "classic period" for Palenque when the pyramids, aqueduct, and numerous other structures were built, many of which represent the finest known examples of Mayan culture. That period of growth and development probably reached a peak about 700 A.D., then gradually declined until the site was deserted in the late ninth century. The reason for this abandonment is not entirely clear, although most archeologists speculate that it was directly related to a collapse of Palenque's agricultural system. A general revolt at the same time against the harsh rule of the priestly caste also acted to destroy the social structure and government.

The Palenque ruins cover an area of only fifteen square miles, but this area contains an estimated five hundred ruins. Only thirty-four of these have been opened for study and visitation, the largest being the Temple of Inscriptions. It was there, but not until 1952, that Mexican archeologist Alberto Ruz discovered an inner chamber containing the tomb of a priest or ruler called Pacal the Great, who ruled from 615 to 683. Ruz wrote of his first sighting into the tomb: "My first impression was that of a mosaic of green, red, and white. Then it resolved itself into details—green jade ornaments, red painted teeth and bones, and fragments of a mask. I was gazing at the death face of him for whom all this stupendous work—the crypt, the sculpture, the stairway, the great pyramid with its crowning temple—had been built. . . . This then, was a sarcophagus, the first ever found in a Maya pyramid" (Gallencamp, p. 95).

That discovery changed all earlier theories that the Mayan pyramids were little more than the bases for temples that were constructed on top, not built as burial sites. The crypt contained six standing and three seated stucco priests, larger than life-size, on guard. The sarcophagus was ten feet long and seven feet wide and with a five-ton lid, covered with numerous heiroglyphs. But the tomb contained another feature that had not previously been discovered in Mexico, a small tube leading from the tomb up through the entire structure to very near the floor of the temple building. Many archeologists believe that this tube, called a "psychoduct," was like the *sipapu* of Hopi kivas, to allow communications between the priests and the underground spirits.

The largest and most complex of Palenque's structures is called "The Palace." This structure of at least twenty-five rooms rests on an artifical platform that is 228 feet long and 180 feet wide. Several of the lower rooms were used for steam baths, complete with drains in the floors which led to an underground aqueduct. Other rooms were used for bathrooms that were connected to a separate septic tank. The Palace tower contains the astronomical symbol of Venus, the star, on the third level, suggesting that this could have been an astrological observatory. Some of the earliest descriptions of this and other Palenque sites are included in a fascinating book written by John Lloyd Stephens and containing numerous illustrations by Frederick Catherwood, titled *Incidents of Travel in Central America, Chiapas, and Yucatan.* Many of the artifacts recovered from the tomb, including the jade death mask, are on display at the National Museum of Anthropology in Mexico City's Chapultepec Park.

The Palenque Forest

Just behind these fascinating ruins is an equally fascinating world of tropical rain forest, complete with all of the unique flora and fauna that occur in these natural settings. This forest was studied by Dr. Faustino Miranda, who called it "los bosque de *Tabebuia guayacan*" in his classic 1952 book, *La Vegetación de Chiapas*. The plant genus *Tabebuia* is a confusing one; it is often called *Cybistax* in older publications. The point is that Miranda considered this plant so dominant at Palenque that he used its name in describing the entire forest. Standley described this plant as a shrub or tree that may be sixty-five feet tall and "one of the most showy and most beautiful of American trees and an extensive stand of them is a sight long to be remembered" (p. 1321). Its blossoms range from white to deep purple-pink. The local name for this tree is *maculiz prieto,* (*blackish hardwood*).

Miranda listed several additional trees that he found common in the Palenque rain forest, among them *Brosimum alicastrum,* a fairly common tropical tree that Walter Pesman (1962) calls bread-nut tree because of nutritious fruits "halfway between maize and beans." *Beroullia flammea* is a tree that may be 130 feet tall and produces bright red flowers and long brown fruits. Its wood is soft and spongy, and the tree is sometimes locally called *palo calabaza.* I have found no common name for this species. *Pithecellobium leucocalyx* is the local form of apes earring, one of the numerous members of the pea family. The common name is derived from the reddish, twisted seed pods. The best way to identify this tall tree is by the strange foliage that consists of two pairs of twin leaflets that grow on short, thin stalks along with a pair of small spines. *Quercus skinneri* is one of the few large oaks that occur in this habitat. And *Sweetenia macrophylla* is Mexico's mahogany tree, locally called *caoba.* Although the true mahogany tree, source of top quality wood for mahogany furniture, is a West Indian plant, this tree is an excellent substitute. Its hard and heavy, red wood is also used for furniture, as well as for canoes and numerous other purposes. This tree has rather large, glossy, opposite, compound leaves, and a thick trunk with dark gray, splotchy bark. It can be one of the tallest of the rain forest trees.

This portion of Mexico's southern Gulf coastal plains has relatively high temperatures and humid conditions throughout the year; occasional northerly winds provide for cooler periods from October to March. The period July through October is hurricane season when occasional storms form in the Gulf. These usually cause intensive rainfall that sometimes floods the coastal plains. The annual rainfall of 60 to 120 inches for this area is the highest recorded in Mexico.

Palenque's Birdlife

I have visited Palenque only during the dry season, from December through April, and have had beautiful clear days on all four trips. A typical day usually starts at dawn along the entrance road. It is only three miles from the very pretty and preferred Chan-Kah Hotel to the Palenque ruins parking area. The roadside provides some excellent forest border habitat and I can think of no better place to find two of Mexico's most striking birds, the scarlet-rumped and crimson-collared tanagers. The male scarlet-rumped is one of my favorite Mexican birds—totally jet black, except for the vivid red lower back and rump, and red eye. The color pattern of the crimson-collared tanager is black, crimson, black, crimson and black; the black is a beautiful glossy one, and the crimson is deep and intense. The exception to these bright colors is its rather large silverish bill. The Spanish name for this colorful species is *tongonito real,* "little royal tanager." Both of these tanagers are gorgeous and unmistakable birds.

Early in the mornings, before the ruins are full of tourists, birding in the open Palenque compound and along the edges can be excellent. Wandering about the grounds, it would not be unusual to find blue-crowned motmot, both the citreoline and violaceous trogons, two of the large-billed tropical birds—chestnut-collared aracari and keel-billed toucan, yellow-bellied elaenia, royal flycatcher, three euphonias (scrub, yellow-throated and olive-backed), masked tanager, yellow-tailed oriole, and both the chestnut-headed and Montezuma oropendolas. Once on the morning of Christmas Eve, from a perch atop the Temple of Inscriptions, I recorded six outstanding raptors. The double-toothed kite and bicolored hawk were seen along the edge of the forest. Gray, short-tailed and white hawks and bat falcon were observed flying directly over the ruins.

I recorded another raptor—aplomado falcon—later that same day in a most unusual setting, at the plaza in "downtown" Palenque.

Although this long-tailed, bird-falcon occurs all along the Gulf coastal plain as far north as Texas, and during the six years I lived at Big Bend National Park I had checked out more than a dozen reported aplomado falcon reports, I had never before seen this bird. And so, when our party of birders—Jim and Cilla tucker, Arnold Small, Benton Basham, my wife Betty and I—arrived at Palenque and heard that an adult aplomado had been seen every evening for several days at the town plaza, we took advantage of the situation.

We learned that the bird waited until late dusk, just when the village street lights were turned on, to fly down one side of the street, make a loop around the lighted square, and go back down the opposite side of the same street and away. Apparently, it found easy meals of numerous cicadas around the lights at that time of evening. We arrived at the plaza in plenty of time, and situated ourselves on the stone steps of the huge church, watching the street in front of us. Sure enough, almost like magic, the minute the lights went on we saw the falcon. I must admit that at first I had doubted the whole story, but we watched the bird fly toward us along one side of the street, capturing and eating several insects on the wing. When it circled the plaza it passed almost directly overhead. Then it headed back down the street and disappeared into the darkening sky. It was one of the easiest lifers I can remember, but I decided to count it anyway.

Ambiance

Entering the Palenque rain forest is simply a matter of walking behind the ruins, and in a few yards stepping from one world into a completely new one. It is like passing from one bright, sunlighted setting into a dimly lit room. It takes a few moments to adjust to the new surroundings. At first glance, the forest is like a huge greenhouse—greenery everywhere, a world completely dominated by the abundant trees, shrubs, herbs, and vines, almost without interruption. There are a few places in the canopy where some light is able to enter, and these few shafts of sunlight seem a little like spotlights that highlight extra green spots in the foliage. In the rare instances when those spotlights reach the forest floor, they create a scene reminiscent of some luxuriant setting from W. H. Hudson's *Green Mansions.* I have secretly searched the area for Rima, the beautiful jungle girl.

The first impression of the dimly lighted, green world lasts only as long as it takes for the other senses to adjust to the new environment. The next impression is related to the sounds of the forest, which can be just as impressive. It usually takes a few minutes for the birds and other forest residents to adjust to your presence; some of the more mobile and seclusive species may leave or hide. Before long, however, unless one made too much commotion when entering, most of the animals continue where they left off. Then, as they commence singing and foraging, a completely new level of awareness comes into play: an awareness that the rain forest fauna is as rich as the flora. Bird songs and calls, echoing and reverberating, seem to come from everywhere. I have entered the Palenque rain forest, gone only a dozen steps or so, and stood in one place for approximately three hours, continuing to find different birds, reptiles, amphibians, and insects all the while.

Many of the bird songs come from the forest canopy, which may be 120 or more feet high. Although these canopy birds usually are extremely active as they move about from place to place, feeding on the abundant supply of fruit, seeds, nectar and insects, they are often difficult to see. I have found that one of the best ways of observing tropical forest birds is by staying put and letting them come to me. This works especially well when a fruiting tree is available, and since the rain forest contains numerous trees that may be fruiting and flowering at the same time, this is not difficult. It also works well when a bird party is encountered. Since these groupings can include two or three dozen species, I have been able to record a good variety of birds by standing still and observing the various members of the party as they pass by. And on a few occasions I have discovered a band of army ants, and have been able to maneuver myself into a position to watch the bird activities that take place along the edges of this moving flood of insects.

Army Ant Experience

Army ants—those in Mexico are scientifically known as *Eciton burchelli*—are some of the most interesting creatures of the tropical forests. Their presence affects every other living thing. The colony follows a nomadic life-style, moving about only during the daytime, from one overnight bivouac site to another. These sites may include a variety of protected places from hollow logs to overhangs. An army of ants may number up to twenty million individuals, and so this mass of little black ants, moving at about one foot per minute, represents a formidable influence upon the environment.

Every morning the army leaves the bivouac site, led by the largest soldiers, in search of food. Captured prey is passed back along the column for use by the smaller workers and large winged males that service the lone queen. The largest soldiers, often three times the size of the smaller workers, are concentrated along the outer edges of the colony. These soldier ants possess extremely heavy, sickle-shaped jaws. Amazon Indians utilize these large-jawed ants for "stitching" wounds. Once the ants are enticed to bite across a wound, which holds the edges close together, the rest of the ant's body is twisted away to leave the head serving as a natural clamp.

The army ant colony captures or consumes almost every edible creature in its path. And this mass movement, which can form a hundred-foot-wide-front, can create considerable havoc among the wildlife that is encountered. I have watched army ants move across the forest floor, over logs and vegetation, often crawling onto small trees or into holes and burrows. Wherever they go there is a flurry of activity at the front. Because of the slow speed of the army, the majority of the mobile animals are able to escape from the ants. But when they move and take flight they expose themselves to other predators that take advantage of their predicament. And there are several additional sets of wildlife, primarily birds and larger insects, that have learned to follow the ant colonies to use the flushing effect of the ant soldiers. There are several tropical birds that seem to forage either exclusively or very heavily upon the insects that can be captured with the aid of army ants. Antbirds of the family Formicariidae apparently have evolved in direct reliance on army ants.

One of my most exciting birding experiences at Palenque occurred at an army ant swarm that I encountered very near the ruins. I was initially attracted to the site, from a distance of twenty to thirty yards, by the continuous twittering and chattering of an obvious bird party that seemed to remain in one place longer than normal. As I carefully moved forward, trying not to disturb the various species, I began to see considerable bird movement within the lower vegetation and near the ground. Early on I had identified the distinct calls of the two fairly common ant-tanagers, the sharp chattering of the red-crowned and the slower, "grinding" double notes of the red-throated ant-tanager. And I had detected another strange chattering call that I began to zero in on. Then from about fifty feet I saw a black-throated shrike-tanager. It had just captured a large green katydid, which I watched it swallow whole. Then just behind it, dashing here and there among a tangle of vines, was a tiny black bird with one white wing bar below a series of tiny white dots. Although I had never seen it before, I immediately was able to identify it as a dot-winged antwren.

It was not until then, when I saw the antwren, that I began to realize that I had found army ants. The abundant birds, many of which I had not yet seen or identified, were there in response to the available prey being dislodged by the ants. Since I did not want to disturb the birds, I searched the ground through my binoculars to find ants. It took me several minutes to locate any, but when I did I discovered that one finger of the colony was quite close. Several thousand ants were within thirty feet of me to my left. I apparently had moved onto the scene from the side and had somehow missed some bird activity closer to where I now stood. As that realization took hold, I began to detect several additional birds all along the army ant front, which seemed to extend for another seventy or eighty feet ahead of me.

I tried to stand perfectly still, moving only enough to watch for birds and maneuver my binoculars into place. I found three species of woodpeckers from that spot. A male black-cheeked woodpecker was perched on the trunk of a little tree just inches away from several hundred ants. I think that it captured some of the ants that came too close. A chestnut-collared and a lineated woodpecker were higher in the nearby trees; they seemed oblivious to the action below. On the other hand, woodcreepers were taking full advantage of the ants. They not only were capturing insects that they seemed to find on various tree trunks and branches, but I watched all three species— olivaceous, spot-crowned and streak-headed—fly out from perches and catch insects on the wing, very flycatcher-like behavior. I heard the loud descending whistle of an ivory-billed woodcreeper nearby, as well, but it did not appear to be part of the anting party.

The bird of the day was a male great antshrike, a large (eight inches) black-and-white, crested bird with a striking red eye. It apparently had been perched very close to me but I did not see it until it flew away and across the army ant mass to another perch. It stopped there, just long enough to capture a huge green insect of some kind, tear this apart with its shrike-like bill and swallow the three or four pieces, and then flew off to where I could not see it. In spite of remaining with the army ants for another two hours or so, I did not see this bird again.

Another very special bird I saw that day was a scaled antpitta. I discovered it quite by accident, as I was watching one forward finger of the army ant colony that had moved onto a little rise of ground directly ahead of me. The bird was standing right at the top of the rise and I first saw only its silhouette, which in itself is difficult to mistake for any other bird. It turned then and hopped a few inches toward me into better light. I could see the very rich brown underparts, gray head, and the gray-green back. Although I have seen this antbird a few times since, that first sighting represents one of those wonderful images that comes back to me time and again.

Some of the additional birds I found at the army ant swarm that day included squirrel cuckoo, blue-crowned motmot; the royal, sulphur-rumped and ochre-bellied flycatchers; and white-breasted wood-wren. Several wintering North American birds—including gray catbird, wood thrush, ovenbird; worm-eating, magnolia, and hooded warblers—were taking advantage of the easy meals. And I saw golden-browed and fan-tailed warblers; the blue-gray, gray-headed and yellow-winged tanagers; lesser greenlet, green shrike-vireo, and black-headed saltator.

Other Sites

There is a trail that starts from one side of the Palenque parking lot and runs through some very tall, dense forest, then skirts the edges of some fields and crosses a number of little streams. The trail leads for many miles into the adjacent countryside. I have found the forest and streamsides along that trail very good for birding. That forest habitat has produced for me several hard-to-find species like ruddy quail-dove, ruddy foliage-gleaner, white-necked puffbird, cinnamon becard, ochre-bellied flycatcher, both the speckled and rufous mourners, rufous piha, thrushlike manakin, lovely cotinga, and red-legged honeycreeper.

Just beyond the forest, where there are thickets of bamboo, is the only place I have consistently seen the white-collared manakin. Most often this little, short-tailed bird can first be detected by its unique habit of wing-snapping, a sound that can be heard for some distance. Wing-snapping is part of the manakin courtship dance, which it performs near the ground. Emmet Blake, in *Birds of Mexico,* described this dance as follows: "The male jumps back and forth between two twigs, the dancer usually landing facing its previous perch, and each jump initiated by a loud 'snap' of the wings" (p. 331).

Palenque's Future

It is extremely sad to discover that so much of Palenque's surrounding rain forest is disappearing. As the mature forest is lost, so is the rich fauna dependent upon it. A few years ago, the road between Palenque and Bonampak, another of the more recently discovered Mayan sites, was little more than a dirt track. That road is now paved, and so another of Mexico's wild areas is open to all comers. The result will undoubtedly be increasing development and deline of the tropical lowland rain forest.

On more than one evening, after dark, friends and I had driven the old track southeast from Palenque. We drove that route because it provided us with a better insight into the virgin rain forest after dark. We drove slowly, rarely faster than five or ten miles an hour; there were places where even that was too fast. The dirt track was a good place to find spot-tailed and tawny-collared nightjars. Their bright eyes reflected for a hundred feet or so, and we could then slowly creep closer for better views through our binoculars.

One night, high in the adjacent forest canopy, our spotlight reflected eyeshine. We set up a spotting scope and, with the little light generated by the car battery, were able to identify a tree sloth—a large, greenish-colored animal hanging upside down in the highest part of the canopy. We were most fortunate to have spotted it and watched it for some time as it stripped leaves from branches and placed each bunch into its very small mouth. I was amazed at its extremely slow but graceful movements, almost as though it was living in a world of slow motion. I learned later that we had found a three-toed sloth, and that this area of Mexico represented the northern edge of its range. Sloths rarely come down from their high perches where they feed exclusively on the leaves of a few tropical trees. Their peglike teeth grow continuously because they have no protective enamel cover. Their greenish color comes from algae that grows in their hair. And a species of moth lays its eggs in the hair; the re-

Rain forest habitat near Palenque, cut to provide pasturage for cattle, which supply beef for the fast-food industry.

sultant caterpillars feed on the algae. This is just one example of the jungle interrelationships linking all of Palenque's creatures. In the long term, they all depend upon others for their continued existence.

Today, only remnants of this once vast jungle can be found within the Palenque vicinity. Thousands of acres of Mexico's forested landscapes have been cleared during the last twenty years or so to provide grazing lands to support the fast-food industry of the United States and other first world countries. Much of the coastal lowlands of Veracruz, Chiapas and Campeche have been changed from exceedingly diverse natural systems that are found in rain forests, to a depauperate system of pasture habitat.

For now, considerable benefits are being derived from the new industry, although little of the profit will ever end up in Mexico.

The big bucks will be made in the United States, and Mexico will end up with barren landscapes and eroded faith in the free market. All the while, very few visitors to Mexico understand or care about what is happening to the changing landscapes. The grazing cattle and open grasslands create a pastoral scene that is most pleasant to the eye. But underneath the green, artificial facade is a disaster about to erupt.

I suppose that my memories of the natural landscape before it was cut and turned into pasturage should be enough. But it is not. It is time for thinking people to acknowledge the ravaged landscape for what it is and begin to take a stand. Humanity should no longer permit such desecration. The remaining rain forests must be given the same protection the government affords the ruins. An enlarged preserve will provide even greater economic benefits for years to come. Ecotourism must be recognized as an important factor in Mexico's long-term prosperity.

20

The Yucatán

I counted at least sixty black and yellow or gold orioles of five different kinds in the tree. Altamira, orange, orchard, hooded, and yellow-backed orioles were all feeding on the tree's small and inconspicuous greenish-brown flowers. Individuals and groups of three or four orioles came and went during the thirty or forty minutes that we watched the flowering kapok tree. We also identified at least four kinds of hummers there. Cinnamon hummingbird was most common, but wedge-tailed sabrewing, green-breasted mango and buff-bellied hummingbird were feeding at the flowers, too. Other birds that we recorded in the same tree included both golden-olive and red-vented woodpeckers, tropical kingbird, social and boat-billed flycatchers, blue-gray gnatcatcher, clay-colored robin, rufous-browed peppershrike, four species of warblers (Tennessee, black-and-white, yellow-throated, and black-throated green), and several yellow-winged tanagers. It was like an avian smorgasbord.

The flowering tree was a kapok, locally called *pochote*. But what made these bird sightings so extra special was that they took place just outside our cottage within the beautiful grounds of Hacienda Chichén at Chichén Itza. Except for the abundant flowers, the branches of the tree were mostly bare, providing a great opportunity to see the birds in the open. There were several other trees within the compound. Plumleaf figs were some of the largest and leafiest trees I had ever seen, but no other trees possessed such sweet flowers as did our very own *pochote*.

Our party of four had arrived in the Yucatán capital city of Mérida the night before, on January 15, 1978. Dick Russell, a long-time friend, and I had met at Houston and flown Aero México together to Merida. There we met Bo and Woody West, who had come from Los Alamos, New Mexico, to join us for our tour of the Yucatán. By the time we met at the airport, rented a vehicle and found our hotel (the Hacienda Inn, where I had made reservations), it was late at night. So after an excellent breakfast the next morning, we had set out to explore a route eastward across the northern end of the Yucatán Peninsula toward Cancún.

Chichén Itza

Chichén Itza, seventy-five miles from Mérida, is without doubt one of the world's finest archeological complexes. The name is a Mayan term that means, "Mouth of the Well of the Itza," and *itza* means "water wizards," according to Ronald Wright in his 1989 book, *Time among the Maya*. Although a good deal of the previously accepted history of Chichén is now being reconstructed based upon recent findings and updated analysis, one thing is sure. It is one of the largest and best restored of approximately fifty thousand registered Mayan sites on the Yucatán Peninsula. And the Hacienda Chichén is located on the grounds of the complex within a beautiful setting of handsome trees and gorgeous flowers and shrubs. The central building is a 360-year-old hacienda that was built by the Spaniards and later used as headquarters by Carnegie Institute archeologists. The ruins form an incredible backdrop to the historic hacienda, and the numerous trails that run from one site to another provide excellent routes to observe the natural vegetation and abundant birdlife.

Archeologists tell us that the Chichén area has been occupied continuously since at least 1000 B.C. The earliest Maya-speaking inhabitants were farmers (corn was the dominant produce) who lived in straw or wooden huts. Major changes in the area's art, science and social structure took place about 250 A.D., probably resulting from an influx of new peoples from the south, believed to have been the Puuc-Maya. This period produced a fairly distinct culture that flourished until the late 600s. Archeologists Morley and Brainerd speculated that a gradual decline occurred as the priests gained greater power because of the perceived necessity of ceremonies and sacrifices for the production of crops. For whatever reason, this period was followed by a time of quiescence.

Beginning about 900, a period of phenomenal growth occurred at Chichén. The change in culture may have been a natural one created by increased contacts with other cultures to the south. However, most archeologists believe that the change was caused by the arrival of the more advanced Toltecs, led by their man-god Kukul-

The flatness of the Yucatán Peninsula, readily apparent in view of Temple of the Warriors at Chichén Itza.

can (Quetzalcoatl in the Nahua language). The Toltecs had come from Tula, their capital city northwest of Mexico City, via Veracruz. From the tenth through the twelfth centuries, at about the same time of the Norse voyages to Vinland, Chichén became the great government center of the Mayan world. It was then when the vast majority of the magnificent features were built. Michael Coe wrote that "not only was there a synthesis of styles at Chichen Itzá, but also a hybridization of Toltec and Mayan religion and society. Jaguar and Eagle knights rub elbows with men in traditional Maya costume and Mexican astral deities coexist with Maya gods. The older Maya order had been overthrown, but it is obvious that many of the native princes and priests were incorporated into the new power structure" (p. 142).

However, about 1250, for no apparent reason the Toltecs deserted

Chichén and moved a hundred miles to the west where they built the completely new but walled city of Mayapan. This city of twelve thousand people became almost a replica of Chichén Itza, but with somewhat smaller structures. Although the religious importance of Chichén continued, its population declined. There is good evidence that Mayan pilgrims continued to visit the site until the Spanish conquest. Mayapan fell to Mexican mercenaries by the mid-1400s.

The physical remains of Chichén Itza are scattered throughout a three-square mile area that contains hundreds of restored buildings and ruins. The largest and most imposing structure is El Castillo (The Castle). This is a four-sided seventy-eight-foot high pyramid that was constructed for the worship of Kukulcan. The structure has a flight of ninety-one steps on each side. Ninety-one times four equals 364; these plus the upper platform represent the 365 days of the year. Inside this structure is an earlier temple that contains a red painted chac mool (a jaguar-like figurine) set with seventy-three pieces of jade. Toltec features were "simplified and square-shaped compared to the curvilinear elaboration of the Maya work," according to Morley and Brainerd. The ruins of Chichén are an exquisite blend of both cultures.

Another of the impressive structures is the Caracol Observatory, a forty-eight-foot-high circular tower built upon three great platforms. The tower contains a circular interior staircase that has given it the name *caracol,* meaning snail in Spanish. The tower has slits and holes in the upper part which were utilized to align the stars, sun and moon for study. The Mayans were able to calculate the cyclic motion of the earth, and their calendar was more exact than any other the world has known. Two hundred years before the birth of Christ, they developed a calender that lost only two hours every 481 years. The modern Gregorian calendar loses twenty-four hours every four years. The Mayans were the first people to understand the abstract concept of zero, and computed a figure of 365.2420 days for every year. Our modern time measuring techniques tell us that the solar year actually spans 365.2411 days.

Chichén's great ballcourt, the largest and finest in all Mesoamerica, has been restored to the point that one can easily imagine the fierce games that were played there. Losers were sacrificed! Relief panels at the base of the walls depict losers being prepared for their death. The court consists of two parallel walls 272 feet long and separated by a playing field 199 feet wide. A stone ring, depicting a serpent, is situated twenty-three feet above the ground at each end. The purpose of the game was to control a hard rubber ball, using only the athlete's elbows, hips and knees, and to pass the ball through the ring. The game was part of a religous rite, and the ball was symbolic of the sun; it was not permitted to touch the ground.

The sacred well (*cenote,* from the Maya *dz'omot*), is situated at the end of the three-hundred-yard "sacred causeway," which begins at the Platform of Venus, a ceremonial dance platform. The cenote is a natural circular sinkhole two hundred feet across and filled with water to approximately sixty-five feet below the rim. The water has been measured at forty feet deep and there are another ten feet of mud below that. Archeological studies suggest that Chichen's cenote was used to sacrifice humans as well as valuable objects to the gods, particularly to the rain god, Chac, especially during periods of drought. Underwater explorations have discovered fifty human skeletons, many precious stones, and another four thousand pieces of odds and ends of everyday Mayan life. The bottom of the well provided archeologists with a rich midden of materials that helped them piece together much of the Chichén Itza puzzle.

Water has always been a scarce commodity in the Yucatán. And the sacred well was undoubtedly the reason that Chichen Itza was located there. Almost all of the Yucatán Peninsula is made of limestone. Rainfall runs off immediately, seeping into underground channels and lakes. Water, therefore, before pumps came into being, was available only where caves occurred or where the surface layers had caved in to form natural sinkholes. Chichén's sacred cenote was one example.

Flora and Fauna

The view from atop El Castillo was a most impressive one. Not only did we get a better understanding of the magnitude and layout of the ruins, but it provided us with our first perspective of Yucatán's terrain and vegetation. It appeared that all fifteen thousand square miles of the state of Yucatán were perfectly flat; maps show a line of low hills called the Puuc Hills, sometimes called the Sierrita de Ticul, in the southernmost part of the peninsula.

Actually, Yucatán's vegetation is more varied than its terrain. The tip of the peninsula contains either low dunes and salt flats or mangroves and a coastal scrub environment. Just inland from this coastal zone is a band of thorn forest habitat that forms a fifty-mile strip across the entire peninsula. Further inland is a much broader band of tropical deciduous forest. Chichén Itza is located within this zone. Further south and west is tropical evergreen forest, and rain forest habitat makes up the southeastern quadrant of the Yucatán. This description is based upon A. Starker Leopold's 1950 paper, "Vegetation Zones of Mexico." However, since then much of the forest has been cleared for grazing and other purposes. Today, the best examples of Yucatán's natural habitats are those that are protected in the numerous archeological zones.

Yucatán's tropical deciduous forest is a short-tree forest that loses its foliage during the dry period of the year. This is the vegetation zone which Rzedowski called bosque tropical subcaducifolio, semi-evergreen or seasonal forest. It requires twenty-four to sixty inches of rainfall annually, and most of that occurs in summer. A 1977 Mexican government (Secretaría de Agricultura y Recursos Hidráulicos) assessment of this habitat reported that the dominant tree species included fish poison tree (locally called *habin*) a small tree that develops long and thick, flanged seedpods; when the toxic seeds are thrown into streams, they poison the fish. *Ya-axnix* is the local name of a common species of *Vitex* (related to the exotic chaste-tree of the United States) that, according to a study by Miranda in 1958, is another of the dominant trees of Yucatán's tropical deciduous forest. Gumbo limbo (locally called *chacah*), because of its peeling reddish bark, is one of the most obvious trees of this habitat. The local bird-of-paradise, or *kitamache,* is a small member of the pea family with showy, bright red flowers. Lance pod or *balche* resembles a locust tree with its varicolored, peaflower-shaped blossoms; the fruit of this species is lance-shaped, and the name *balche* is derived from the fermented drink made from the bark. And the thin, white-barked tree is the local *Lysiloma,* locally called *tzalam.* The common shrub of this zone is yellow trumpet.

Las Coloradas

We drove east from Chichén for twenty-six miles to Valladolid, the second largest town in the state of Yucatán, where we turned north toward the coast. We stopped after thirty-two miles in Tizimín and, after acquiring rooms for the night, continued toward the coast and

Las Coloradas. The vast coastal lagoons are home to the greater fla-
mingo. It was too late in the day to reach the coast before dark,
however, so we birded along the roadway which passed through the
strip of thorn forest habitat, some of which had been cleared. The
result was a rather bizarre savannah-like environment. We turned
around after dark about halfway to the coast. As the automobile
lights reached into an open field, we picked up bright red eyeshine.
It turned out to be a Yucatán endemic, the Yucatán poorwill. We
all had an excellent look at it sitting on a fencepost, and we saw
several more en route back to Tizimín.

Dawn of January 17 found us in the coastal scrub habitat north
of Río Lagartos at Las Coloradas. It was there that we found a family
of Yucatán wrens, another of Yucatán's endemics. This species is very
much like the cactus wren of the northern deserts. The coastal scrub
formed an extremely dense, low vegetation dominated by sisal, a
palmetto, morning glory tree, *Pseudophoenix sargentii* (a date palm-
like plant), trompillo, and sea grape.

We followed the roadway east over white sandy dunes for several
miles to where it ended at the tiny resort of Chiquila; the main feature there is a small sulphur spring, rare on the Yucatán. Almost
immediately we located the flamingos, more than a thousand of them,
several hundred yards to the south across the shallow lagoon. Those
long-legged birds were standing together in an area of only a few
hundred yards; they created a pinkish glow across the shimmering
flats. A dozen or so birds in flight, necks outstretched, formed a
long aerial line off to the right. Their peculiar gobble-honking calls
resounded across the flats. Although this bird can be found at other
locations along the northern coast, such as near Celestún, it apparently nests only in the vicinity of Las Coloradas.

En route back to Valladolid and Highway 180 we found a side
road only three miles south of Río Lagartos, which entered an area
of thorn forest that seemed relatively undisturbed. We left our vehicle on the side road and spent a couple of hours exploring this
habitat. The morning was already very warm, and we found few birds.
However, two of these made our stop there worth the effort: hook-
billed and double-toothed kites. Both birds were seen from close
range. The hook-billed kite had been expected, although I could
not help but be impressed with its lumbering flight. But the double-
toothed kite seemed out of place; it is more a bird of the heavier

forests than of the thorn forest habitat. As we walked back to the car, we "herded" eight black-throated (or Yucatán) bobwhite, another of the area's specialities, ahead of us.

Cancún

By 3:30 that afternoon we reached the state border of Yucatán and Quintana Roo. And by 5:00 P.M. we had secured rooms in a hotel in Ciudad Cancún. Since there was still considerable time left before dark we drove back toward Mérida twenty-seven miles (to near kilometer post 288) to find the "chicle trail," a place we planned to explore the next morning. A month earlier I had corresponded with Barbara de Montes, a birder living in Cancún, who had sent me the directions to several good places to visit in the area. One of Barbara's recommended sites was the chicle trail. We found the trail and walked along this track until dark. We added only one species to our list; red-throated ant-tanager was trip bird number 162.

We returned to this same site early the following morning, and found the area well worth the return visit. The chicle trail was so named because it had been cut into the forest by latex gatherers (*chicleros*) due to the abundance of chicle trees growing there. The native chicle tree, called *ya* or *palo maria,* is one of the area's most important plants. It furnishes very durable wood, fruit (*sapodilla*) that is considered one of the best in Latin America, and latex which after processing is mixed with sugar, glucose syrup and a flavoring for making chewing gum.

The latex gathering process is rather complex. The tall grayish trunks are first cleared of loose bark to about thirty feet high. Then slanted incisions are cut into a herringbone pattern and the tree is allowed to drain for twenty-four hours. The thick, gooey substance seeps downward from one cut to the next and collects in a leather pouch attached below the lowest cut. The material is boiled with water to remove any impurities, and then poured into wooden molds lined with leaves. The hardened blocks can then be stored and transported to market. Each tree can be tapped only three times during its lifetime and must recover for four years betweeen tappings.

We recorded sixty-eight bird species along the chicle trail during the morning. Four birds were particularly important because they represented not just new trip birds but lifers, as well. The first of these was the tropical pewee. We found several rose-throated tanagers, a

The Chicle Trail, cut through the forest near Cancún to provide access for chicleros.

bird that is known in Mexico only from the Yucatán Peninsula. We observed a pair of white-throated spadebills in courtship. And just before we turned around to head back, five blue ground-doves were discovered perched together on a branch of a gumbo limbo tree.

The next day, January 19, we met Barbara de Montes, and spent the day exploring some of her favorite haunts in the Cancún region. These areas included a water purification site, where she showed us several kinds of orchids and other epiphytes she had studied. We added crested guan and citreoline trogon to our trip list there. At the old airport, just south of town, we added keel-billed toucan, white-bellied emerald, Caribbean elaenia and Yucatán vireo; the latter two were Yucatán specialities.

A third area visited was south of town near Puerto Morelos, where we followed an old narrow-gauge track, once used for logging, into the forest. We walked for about two miles but saw few new birds.

However, we will long remember this site as the "place of dirty water." When we first arrived, a half-dozen children were playing near where we parked the car. We talked with them briefly and told them we were looking at birds and would return shortly. The children immediately informed us that they would watch our car for us. Three hours later, when we returned to claim our car, they were still on guard. What's more, they had decided to wash our car. But the only available water was a mud puddle nearby. The car had needed washing before, but afterwards it was an urgent necessity. I had to use water from my canteen to clean the windshield before I could see the road well enough to drive back to Cancún.

The resort city of Cancún is a planned tourist city located on Cancún Island and connected to the mainland and Puerto Juárez by a causeway. A twelve-mile-long boulevard runs the length of the L-shaped island past dozens of hotels, restaurants, shops and other tourist attractions. Modern Cancún was built during the 1970s, and is one of several special complexes developed by the Mexican government for the purpose of increasing the tourist industry.

We left Barbara at her home and then drove south almost a hundred miles to Playa del Carmen, located on the mainland just across the channel from Cozumel Island. We arrived at dusk, acquired a room on the second floor of the Hotel Molca, located at the ferry pier, and enjoyed a huge fish dinner washed down with a Tecate *y limon.*

We spent the next day on Cozumel Island, a beautiful and contrasting environment. Cozumel has many fancy resorts that cater to various sporting and recreation activities, but the east side of the island offers wildlands that are rarely visited. A loop road circles the southern end. The fact that two bird species occur on Cozumel and cannot be found elsewhere enticed us to spend the day there (see chapter twenty-one, "Island of Swallows").

Cobá

Thirty-six miles south of Playa del Carmen is Tulum. This Mayan site, dating from about 700 A.D. to the arrival of the Spaniards, has a unique setting on a cliff overlooking the Caribbean. Tulum features a nineteen-foot thick wall that circled the city. We stopped there only long enough to walk through the site, then turned northwest toward our destination for the next couple days, Cobá.

The twenty-six-mile approach road and accommodations were brand new. Villas Arqueologicas, complete with tennis courts, had been open only a few days. It was so new in fact that our party of four was the first to stay in the large double room assigned us. Every meal we ate there was excellent. The Villas Arqueologicas was one of five Mexican hotels leased and operated by Club Mediterrané, a French corporation.

Cobá, pronounced with the accent on the last letter, is a Mayan word meaning "wind-ruffled water." It undoubtedly is one of Mexico's largest and most unusual archeological sites, located on a surprisingly large freshwater lake, Lago Cobá. Cobá covers twenty square miles within the heart of Yucatán's rain forest habitat. Cobá forms the hub of a system of ceremonial roads, called *sacbeob* (Mayan for "white roads"), that radiated out to sixteen other Mayan cities. The longest of these roads extended for a hundred kilometers (about sixty-two miles) in an almost perfectly straight line to Yaxuna, southwest of Chichén Itza. The roads were constructed of limestone blocks placed over a gravel base that elevated the roadbed by at least two feet, and averaged thirty-two feet in width; some portions were eighty feet wide.

The central area of Cobá includes more than six thousand structures; only a few have been excavated and studied. The largest of these, called El Castillo, stands 138 feet tall and measures 180 by 200 feet at the base; it is the largest Indian structure on the entire Yucatán Peninsula. It has 120 steps leading up six terraces to the highest platform, from which the view is truly spectacular. That view provides a perspective unique for the Yucatán, because the entire area is dotted with small freshwater lakes. The numerous structures poking above the very dense and bright green forest, combined with the sparkling blue dots of water, give the area a special character.

To date thirty-two stelae (stone pedestals covered with hieroglyphics) have been uncovered among the ruins. Archeologists report that stelae were designed to commemorate special events in Mayan lives, and often include specific dates of events. The stone slabs have been dated from 623 to 800 A.D., but Cobá was active well into the middle of the fifteenth century.

Of all the Mayan sites I have been fortunate to visit and explore, my favorite is Cobá. The reason for this is partly related to its mystery. The story of Cobá's human history is still very little known, and the excavations and research were actively under way wherever we went. Cobá's appeal also related to its natural setting within the rain forest, and the presence of the numerous freshwater lakes.

Undisturbed rain forest habitat is the most diverse vegetation type in the world, but almost all of the remaining rain forest found in the Yucatán is second growth. Although the character of this secondary environment is greatly inferior in species richness to what was once present, it still possesses many of the key plant species and a good representation of fauna. The most obvious tree species were chicle and bread-nut tree. The latter species has six-inch-long evergreen leaves that feel leathery to the touch. The gray to reddish trunks often form large buttresses at their bases. And the plum-like fruit are edible, tasting a little like spicy potatoes. They can be eaten raw, but more importantly can be ground into meal and used for making bread and tortillas. Other tree species found at Cobá included mahogany, gumbo limbo, papelillo, kapok tree, cigarbox tree, and pimienta.

We recorded ninety-four species of birds during our two-day exploration of Cobá. The numerous lakes provided a habitat that is unusual in the Yucatán, and so we added several species that preferred that habitat. Most surprising of these was a pair of black skimmers that cruised back and forth on Laguna de Cobá all day on January 21, seeming out of place on fresh water. We also found a solitary boat-billed heron perched in the tules along the edge of Laguna de Cobá. We heard both sora and ruddy crake along the shoreline as well. The crake was very vocal at dawn and dusk, and its very distinct whinneying call was easy to identify.

Mangrove vireo was surprisingly common within the forest edges near the lakes. This bird on first sight looks like a large white-eyed vireo, but it has a yellow eye-line rather than spectacles, and a white eye; its song is very different too. I watched a pair chasing one another in a brushy area just behind the Villas Arqueologicas. Also in the immediate area was an eye-ringed flatbill. It first appeared to be a large *Empidonax,* but its bill is very broad and, although this is not readily seen, incredibly flat. This must be the world's greenest flycatcher.

Southern Yucatán

We left Cobá at midafternoon on January 22, and drove to Carrillo Puerto, about ninety-five miles south, to spend the night. The next day we drove on to Chetumal, the capital city of Quintana Roo and the entry city to Belize. Much of the landscape we drove through had been cleared for grazing, but the area close to Chetumal was mostly wetlands. We stopped at an area called Laguna Milagros and walked along that waterway for a couple of hours.

The bird of the day was the slate-headed tody-flycatcher. We heard it calling for at least seven or eight minutes before we finally discovered it sitting near the top of a low tangle of brush only fifty or sixty feet away. The voice was totally different than that of any bird I had previously heard. The struggle to locate it was maddening, since I knew it was a species I had never seen. When it finally shifted its position, although ever so slightly, we were able to pick it out and watch it for several minutes. This tody-flycatcher being a new bird for me, I made pertinent notes as follows: "Yell. crissum, brown-gray on top, very short tail, lg. bill, yellowish line in ft. of eye, two short wing bars."

Chetumal, a city of approximately ninety-thousand people, is situated at the southernmost point on the east coast of the Yucatán at the mouth of the Río Hondo; across the river is the country of Belize, formerly British Honduras. The city is located on far and away the finest bay on the Yucatán. The bay is protected by a peninsula that extends south from the outer coastline and by the barrier island of Ambergris Cay—owned by Belize—part of a huge coral reef. The area was once the center of Mayan boat-building. The first Spaniards to arrive here were shipwrecked and enslaved by the Mayans, later to be freed by Cortez and serve as interpreters. One of the captives married a Mayan princess and fought against the Spaniards for many years.

We spent January 24 exploring the southern portion of the Yucatán, which we could reach from Highway 186. This is the east-west route that transects the lower peninsula, across a hilly karst zone, from Chetumal to Escárcega, Campeche, approximately 160 miles. We spent several hours at Kohunlich, a little-known but impressive Mayan ruin less than forty miles west of Chetumal. This isolated site is well maintained and provides a good example of the later Mayan period. It was occupied from the last years before the Christian era until the thirteenth century, and its heyday was approximately 400 to 700 A.D.

The most distinctive structure at Kohunlich is the Pyramid of the

Masks. Its staircase is flanked by eight different five-foot-tall stucco masks which represent the Mayan sun god and are very reminiscent of the Toltec stone heads. The upper part of the pyramid contains four tomb chambers at different levels. The ball court, which has been completely restored, is 110 feet long but contains no rings.

The Kohunlich ruins cover an area of less than a square mile, but a portion was built on a low hill that provides excellent views of the surrounding landscape. Also, the Mayans had constructed numerous ditches and little lagoons for holding rainwater; these structures, today, provide for a wider variety of habitats than would normally exist. The forest is all second growth but includes a surprising abundance of Cohune palms. This palm looks a little like a date palm, but has a fruit that resembles a small coconut. It is grown commercially throughout the region for the oil that is derived from the fruit. The product is utilized for soap, candles, and machine oil.

The combination of the hilly character of the area and the several lagoons and ditches provided an exceptionally good habitat for a diverse flora and fauna. Five of the fifty-eight species of birds we recorded at Kohunlich were found nowhere else during our Yucatán tour: gray-headed kite, crane hawk, gray-necked wood-rail, vermiculated screech-owl, and greenish elaenia. Of these, the screech-owl was most unexpected, primarily because it was calling during the middle of the morning. It was perched on a small tree along a path that crossed the hill, and I walked right by it trying to track down its insistent calls. It was not until after I had walked back and forth twice that I finally detected the bird. Joe Marshall's description of the song, included in Peterson and Chalif's *A Field Guide to Mexican Birds,* fit perfectly: "a long trill on 1 pitch, like a spadefoot toad, starting softly, gradually swelling, then it cuts off abruptly" (p. 83). I had just about decided that I was hearing a spadefoot toad instead of a screech-owl. I was much relieved when I found the bird.

Remnant of Rain Forest

Night found us back in Chetumal, but we were out by dawn the next morning en route north. We had asked several people along the way about where we might yet find some virgin forest; all of the forest we had visited in the lower Yucatán had been second growth at best. Most of it had been changed to a savannah-like habitat by clear-cutting and subsequent grazing. We finally had met a gentleman at Kohunlich (I believe he was in charge of the archeological work under way there) who seemed to understand our question and know the country sufficiently well to answer it. He suggested an area along Highway 293 west of El Cardenas and just below Valle Hermosa. We decided to check out the place since it was along one of the routes we could take on our return trip to Mérida.

We did find some seemingly undisturbed rain forest there, but even as we explored the area, which consisted of less than two or three square miles, we heard chain saws in use in all directions. Probably we were the last outsiders to see that tiny remnant of tropical rain forest.

We located a pull-off and trail at kilometer post 16, had a brief lunch, and then entered the forest. Almost immediately we discovered an ornate hawk-eagle, perched in a huge bread-nut tree. It seemed to think it was well hidden and sat there until we all had an excellent look at this beautiful raptor. A pair of masked tityras and a white-lored gnatcatcher were found in the same tree. And we could hear blue ground-doves calling nearby; they were surprisingly abundant within those woods. We added dusky antbird, rufous piha, sulphur-rumped flycatcher, long-billed gnatwren, and red-crowned ant-tanager to our growing Yucatán list. Those humid forest species will be lost once the rain forest is replaced by pasture and cattle.

Uxmal

We arrived at Uxmal well after dark, but were able to find rooms and meals at the Hotel Hacienda Uxmal. This rather classic hacienda compared favorably with Hacienda Chichén, but nothing so modern and classy as Villas Arqueologicas on Lago Cobá. Uxmal is far enough north to be back within the drier tropical deciduous forest habitat, and we found few avian surprises the next day. We added only lesser roadrunner, pauraque, and blue-crowned motmot to our trip list. Of the sixty-eight species recorded there, we found a surprisingly high percentage (47 percent) were wintering North American birds, more than at any other location we had visited.

The Uxmal ruins represent the best preserved of all the pure Mayan cities in Mexico. Morley and Brainerd stated that "the most beautiful Puuc-style buildings in Yucatan are to be found at Uxmal. In this region the Mexican influence, so strongly noticed at Chichén

Uxmal's Pyramid of the Magician, five distinct temples, one upon the other. The upper temple is 125 feet above the ground level.

Itza, is almost non-existent" (p. 293). The city had been constructed from 500 to 1000 A.D. and more or less abandoned at the height of its development. Its heydey was at the same time that Charlemagne was crowned. Unlike most other Yucatán settlements, which were built around a cenote (water source), Uxmal utilized cisterns (*chultunes* in Mayan) to collect rainwater; some of these are still in use today.

The Pyramid of the Magician is 125 feet high, is oval rather than rectangular in shape, and, to me, is the single most impressive structure on the Yucatán. It is really five different temples in one, and contains five openings along the face of the pyramid that lead to the five segments. Pyramid of the Magicians was built over a three-hundred-year period. The base is Temple Number One, the oldest, and dated at 569 A.D. It was ornately decorated with masks of the rain god Chac. Temple Two had a pillared inner chamber that was constructed high above ground level, and can be reached by a stair-well that lies under the present exterior staircase. Temple Three was built onto the rear of Temple Two but was later covered over. Temple Four sits on top of the oval base and can be entered through the jaws of a stylized mask. And Temple Five is a rectangular structure at the very top of the pyramid. It can be reached by 150 steps that are flanked by masks which depict the rain god.

The entire site of Uxmal includes only fifteen to twenty ruins, often connected to or superimposed upon each other, all within a relatively small area of less than half a square mile. The Mayan style of architecture is best represented by the platforms, false roof combs and corner decorations, and a corbel arch. Since Uxmal is only forty miles south of Mérida, it is one of the most visited Mayan ruins in the world.

Celestún

We returned to Mérida the following day and, without stopping, continued through town and west to Celestun, a tiny fishing village on the west coast. We had decided to visit one additional habitat to find another of Mexico's endemic birds, the Mexican sheartail of the coastal scrub. This is a tiny bronze-green hummer with a long curved bill and long forked tail. The male possesses a red gorget and a tail unlike that of any other hummingbird; it has black outer feathers with a kind of scalloped, cinnamon-colored inner lining. We found only two males during a several-hour search.

The coastal environment at Celestún was quite different from the coastal scrub along the north and east edges of the peninsula. Lagoon marshes and swamps occur along a narrow coastal strip, just inland of which is thorn forest habitat that is quite savannah-like in character. One tree we had not seen earlier, but which was very evident and numerous near Celestún, was yellowsilk shelltree, lo-cally called *chuum* or *cosito*. It is a small, white-barked tree that, in early spring, bears large, bright yellow flowers on leafless branches. We also found an odd evergreen tree-shrub with lots of stiff, sharp leaves: jacquinia, called "sick," by the locals. A mimosa was fairly numerous, sisal agave was scattered throughout, and we found several of the same plant species we had recorded along the northern coast at Las Coloradas.

Vehicles being used by fishermen at Celestún to haul their catch to the cannery.

There was only one place to stay overnight in Celestún, an old and run-down motel along the main street. I later ranked it as the poorest accommodation I had experienced in Mexico (an army cot on a cement slab); but it was at least a place to sleep. The picture-memory I have of downtown Celestún is of the balcony of a store across the street from the hotel where two young boys held up a huge boa constrictor to show us. The snake must have been twelve feet long, and they could barely hold it up high enough to show it off. They wanted to sell that dead snake to us. We tried to express disdain for killing of such a beautiful reptile, but I doubt if they got the message.

Located near the tip of a long and narrow peninsula that extends south along the coast, Celestún is principally a fishing village. The highway crosses the channel as it enters the town, and here we saw the twenty or so fishing boats beached. We watched as the day's catch was unloaded from five boats, long open wooden vessels with out-board motors, onto several trucks. The fish are then taken into town to a cannery. Two of the trucks were Model Ts, about 1920 models, and seemed to be in better working order than the newer pickups.

We returned to Mérida later that afternoon, January 27, and stayed again at the Hacienda Inn. We enjoyed another excellent seafood dinner at a downtown restaurant, where we went over our bird notes and reminisced about our Yucatán adventures. I had recorded a total of 263 bird species, of which twenty-four were lifers. We had driven 2,564 kilometers (approximately 1,538 miles) in a Hertz rental car that had cost ninety-six dollars. My round-trip plane fare of $382 had been my greatest expense. Adding all of my expenditures to-gether, including the cost of fuel, the numerous good and bad rooms, and the various meals and other food, I had spent a total of about $750. That was only $31.25 for each life bird, not a bad cost for such an enjoyable excursion.

21

Island of Swallows

Cozumel in the state of Quintana Roo is the best known of Mexico's many islands, and represents many things to different people. It has a world-class reputation for beautiful and crystal clear waters, with visibility to depths of 150 to 200 feet. Cozumel has become a beacon to divers from all around the world. Others go to Cozumel to study the numerous Mayan ruins that are scattered throughout the island, although none have been fully restored to date. Still others go to Cozumel for the solitude that such an island paradise might offer. But for me and my three companions, the island was where we hoped to find two species of birds—Cozumel thrasher and Cozumel vireo—that occur nowhere else.

We reached Cozumel by the ferry boat *Itzam* which three times daily crossed the twelve-mile channel between the mainland port of Playa del Carmen and Cozumel's village-port of San Miguel (population about two thousand). The crossing took just under one hour, but surprisingly it was a trip that did not meet my expectations.

The waters that surround Cozumel are undoubtedly some of the most enticing anywhere. Cozumel is ranked among the world's outstanding areas for diving—along with Australia's Great Barrier Reef, French Polynesia, parts of the Indian Ocean, and the Red Sea. But in spite of the beauty of the waters and their incredible clarity, marine life was scarce. I saw no fish within the crystal clear waters, and the birdlife was minimal. I recorded only a few royal terns during the entire crossing. Later I learned that paucity of birdlife over open tropical waters is fairly typical: warm tropical waters do not support as much plankton (the tiny animals and plants that provide a food base for larger species) as do colder ocean waters. In a sense, the lack of birdlife around the island was in direct contrast to its name.

"Cozumel" is derived from the Mayan word *Cuzamil,* which has been translated to mean "Island of Swallows." Swallows were completely absent during our brief visit, although we did see a number of Vaux's swifts, a swallow-like bird that is more closely related to hummingbirds than to swallows. Vaux's swifts are common in southern Mexico in winter, and breed in forested areas from western Mexico to Alaska. Possibly swallows are more common at other times of year, but more likely the English translation of Cozumel should be "Island of Swifts."

The great Palancar Reef lies just off the southwestern tip of Cozumel, and provides a fascinating underwater wilderness for snorklers and scuba divers. The deep blue to aquamarine of the waters and the pure white of the perfect beaches give the island an almost artificial character. The local Cozumeleaños have capitalized on this allure and provide a wide range of recreational opportunities for visitors who wish to swim, skindive, fish, ride horses, play tennis or golf, or just lie on the beach and soak up the rays. Commercial diving schools are scattered along the coastline near San Miguel, which overlooks the Palancar Reef. Cozumel is called the "Mexican Caribbean" by Mexican travel offices. More than a dozen good to exclusive hotels have been built on the island, and Cozumel's airport offers direct flights from Mexico City, Mérida, and Cancún.

In spite of the local orientation toward tourism, we had a very difficult time finding transportation for the day. Our intention was to find a rental car that we could drive around the island and stop wherever we wished. But upon asking for directions to the nearest rental car office, we were told that rental cars were not available; we could secure a taxi at one of the stores in town.

We hadn't walked very far when we were approached by a gentleman in an old and rather run-down sedan. He informed us that he was willing to take us on a tour of the island. We thanked him and said that we were less interested in a tour than in seeing different parts of the island, and that we were there to find certain kinds of birds. That may have been our first mistake: the driver said his nephew was the local bird expert, having taken many other people out to find birds, and that he would arrange for the nephew to drive the car and be our guide. The 1957 Chevrolet bore lots of dents and scratches, but we decided that a driver who could also act as a guide to the best birding localities would be well worth our while. So we

Downtown San Miguel, Cozumel Island.

gave in, jumped into the car, and off we drove to find our "expert" guide.

We then proceeded to drive from one end of San Miguel to the other and back again looking for the nephew, whom we never did find. At our fourth or fifth stop, we did pick up another relative, however. His name was Juan, and I never was sure about his relation to the original driver. However, Juan became the searcher to enter each place we stopped to find the missing nephew.

In the meantime, we began to realize that the morning and our birding time were fast slipping away. After about a dozen stops we decided it was time to find another taxi. But when we announced this, our driver immediately informed us, without even a glance at Juan, that Juan was to be our driver and was ready to go. The conversation between the two Cozumeleaños that followed was not very clear. We were never sure whether Juan had known this all along or whether he was as surprised as we were. Nevertheless, we decided it would be faster and easier to go ahead with these arrangements than to seek out another taxi and driver in downtown San Miguel.

Although our tour of the town had been somewhat repetitive, it had not been all bad. We had recorded quite a number of birds as we had progressed from stop to stop. One of those was among the Cozumel specialities that we had hoped to find, the black cat-bird. It is known for Mexico only from the Yucatán, but is easily found only on the adjacent islands. We had seen three different in-dividuals at various overgrown, shrubby locations in town. Its habit of utilizing dense shrubby places and being easily attracted by a few squeaks or spishes made it reminiscent of the gray catbird so com-mon in the eastern half of the United States.

During our downtown tour we had negotiated a price of 450 pesos (about five dollars at the time) for the fifty-mile loop trip around the island. We had also intended to take a side trip to the northwest corner of the island, but learned that this route was closed to ve-hicles due to hurricane damage several months earlier. By the time we dropped off the original driver and stopped one more time at Juan's house to collect a paper bag of something or other (his lunch, we later learned), it was close to 10:00 A.M. Not until then did we begin our intended tour of the "Island of Swallows."

Our first stop was at a small but beautiful freshwater lake, called Chancanab Lagoon, only four miles out of town. Juan said the la-goon was connected to the sea by underground channels. The crystal clear water seemed to be moving in no particular direction, and since no outlet was evident, we believed his story. We immediately found the least grebe, tricolored heron, blue-winged teal and common moorhen. And we were attracted to a familiar song emanating from the adjacent vegetation. In no time at all, we coaxed the songster out of its hiding place. It was the first of several golden warblers, one more of the birds we had come to the island to find. Since then, this bird has been lumped with the yellow warbler and is no longer considered a separate species, but at the time, the singing yellow warbler with a chestnut cap was as welcome as any other of our new discoveries. Soon afterwards, however, as we wandered along the lagoon shoreline and admired that unique environment, a party of snorklers arrived and loudly proceeded into the lake. Our chances for finding additional wildlife disappeared. So we moved on toward the beach drive that followed the outer coastline.

Plantlife

Vegetation on the Cozumel beach was rather sparse, although low and dense clumps of plants occurred sporadically. Prominent among these was sea grape with its tree-like trunks and branches; some of those individuals may have been six to eight feet tall. The large circular leaves may be seven inches across and have red veins. Walter Pesman, in his very helpful book, *Meet Flora Mexicana,* stated that "the Spaniards used the leaves of sea grape like paper. Messages were scratched into the leaf surface, the letters resembling white scratches" (p. 163). Sea grape wood is hard and reddish in color; it looks very much like madrone wood of the southwestern U.S. mountains. Other common plants on the Cozumel beach included coconut palm, a palmetto, a date palm-like plant, and trompillo, a small tree that is a member of the borage family.

The dominant habitat along the Caribbean side of Cozumel Island was mangroves, a group of trees that have adapted to living in salt or brackish water, as well as salty mudflats near the shoreline. In fact, most of the outer edge of the island consisted of waterways and lagoons edged with three mangrove species: red, black and white. All are evergreen and some of the taller ones we saw may have been as much as seventy feet in height. The three species form three distinct zones in accordance with their tolerance for moisture.

White mangroves occur furthest inland and prefer drier soils; this species often forms rather dense mangrove thickets. They can be identified by small, rounded leaves that possess a pair of swollen glands on the short stems near the base of the leaves. Black mangroves occur next and can easily be recognized by their dark green, lanceolate leaves and the abundant aeration roots, or "pneumatophores," which project upwards out of the muddy soils for several inches. Carrol Fleming, in writing about mangroves in *Americas* magazine, described a pneumatophore as "an odd woody root that grows upward through the soil in low clusters like soda straws protruding through the mud" (p. 11).

Red mangroves fringe the shorelines and produce aerial or "prop roots" that look like the long tentacles of the strangler fig. Instead of growing up through the mud, these roots grow out and down from the lower portion of the trunks, often forming interlacing networks. Red mangrove leaves are leathery and bluntly pointed, green above and pale below. This species breathes through tiny pores in the prop roots. If these pores become blocked by silt or oil spills, the tree will actually smother. This is the mangrove species that most books on tropical seashores feature. Its name comes from the red wood, which usually is covered with a grayish bark.

The combination of the three mangrove zones performs an important service to both the land and marine ecosystems. The inland plants serve as filters for water runoff so that by the time the flow reaches the sea much of the silt and debris is eliminated. This function not only cleans the runoff; by retaining the debris, it very gradually builds land seaward. The network of prop roots at the edge of the saltwater provides extremely important protection to a myriad of creatures from fish to coral. These protected areas serve as important nurseries for a huge variety of sea life.

A fascinating characteristic of mangroves is their ability to tolerate both salt and fresh water; many are flooded by the daily tides. According to Lugo and Snedaker, the sap of a mangrove can be ten times saltier than the sap of trees found in more temperate habitats. Mangrove seeds are specially adapted to the seashore environment. Most germinate on the tree and are thus immediately ready to take root when they fall or are knocked off the parent plant. They are known to travel hundreds of miles by sea, and a few beached seeds can begin a completely new community at a considerable distance from where they originated.

Mangrove habitats are some of the most productive in the world. Scientists have discovered that a healthy mangrove community may drop as much as four and one-half tons of leaves per acre per year. The leaves decay in about six months, producing nutrients that are four times richer than the leaves. Odum and Heald discovered that the leaf litter undergoes microbial transformation that actually increases the amount of protein available, according to Siddall and colleagues. These nutrients provide food for a multitude of tiny invertebrates on which a wide variety of shrimp, fish, reptiles, birds, and mammals depend.

Worldwide, mangrove habitats dominate coastlines throughout the tropics. But there is good evidence that much of this unique habitat is disappearing, either through direct habitat destruction or pollution by oil spills or other dangerous chemicals. Tropical fisheries often are dependent upon the health of the mangrove habitat: a fishery can be very seriously affected by the loss of its mangroves. "Between 50 and 70 percent of the world's commercial fish catch comes from species which utilize coastal and estuarine area," according to Random DuBois (p. 348). In India, a mangrove-lined estuary produced eighty-eight pounds of prawns per acre annually, while an adjacent estuary, free of mangroves, produced only seventeen pounds of prawns per acre each year.

A healthy Mexican mangrove community can provide excellent habitat for a wide variety of wildlife, including wintering North American songbirds. In a study Fred Sladen and I conducted on the importance of Virgin Islands mangrove habitats to migrant and wintering birds at Salt River, St. Croix, we found that thirty-five bird species utilized the area from October through March. Seventeen of these occurred only during migration and/or in winter. Fifteen species — fourteen warblers and the yellow-throated vireo — actually resided within the mangroves throughout the winter months. The fifteen winter species represented forty-three percent of all the bird species recorded, and thirty-five percent of the total population recorded. The most numerous North American wintering songbirds found, in order of abundance, included: northern waterthrush, black-and-white warbler, American redstart, northern parula, prairie warbler, Cape May warbler, worm-eating warbler, hooded warbler, common yellowthroat, blue-winged warbler, ovenbird, magnolia warbler, and yellow-rumped warbler. The yellow warbler also was common, but a permanent resident. And the blackpoll warbler was a fall migrant only.

The Outer Beach

As we progressed along the outer beach drive, our taxi suddenly died and came to a coasting stop. I guessed that we were almost halfway around the fifty-mile loop drive. At first, Juan insisted that it was a mechanical problem that he could fix, and he spent almost an hour peering under the hood trying to discover the difficulty. Since none of the various dashboard gauges worked, they were of no help. Soon we began to wonder whether or not the vehicle was merely out of gasoline, and after a while someone made that suggestion.

With that, Juan suddenly struck off down the road on his own to find help, and we were left to ourselves. Within the hour he was back. Somehow he had found his "brother," acquired a large can of gasoline, and had returned to save the day. On our way around the other half of the loop, we watched for where he might have found his brother and acquired the gasoline, but saw nothing that could give us a hint of what had occurred. When asked, he simply said that his brother was nearby and they had borrowed some gasoline from a friend. We saw no signs of habitation or another vehicle in the direction he had gone in the next ten or more miles. How he acquired a full can of gasoline will forever remain a mystery.

We had not wasted the two hours that we had been immobile, but had spent the time exploring along the road in both directions and along the beach for several hundred yards. The most abundant bird species we found was the palm warbler, but we also had recorded black-and-white, magnolia and hooded warblers.

But most importantly, we had found a Cozumel thrasher! It was one of the two Cozumel endemics which we had come to the island to find. The lone bird we saw in a field along the outer road was the only thrasher of the day. It struck me as a rather drab and smaller brown thrasher-like bird. Some scientists believe it is an isolated race of the long-billed thrasher and should be lumped with that bird.

A couple of miles before we completed the loop drive and re-entered San Miguel, we discovered a patch of woody vegetation that we decided to explore, hoping to find a Cozumel vireo. We knew that this vireo preferred woodland, but until then had not found any habitat we believed would be appropriate. We had been in the mangrove community and the coastal scrub habitat, and had not seen any of Cozumel's native inland vegetation: thorn forest or tropical deciduous forest. So we climbed out of the taxi to investigate the lone patch of woodland with anticipation. Almost immediately we found a pair of Cozumel vireos. And within the next twenty or thirty minutes we located four others. We had hit the Cozumel vireo jackpot!

This little bird looked very different than its closest relative the white-eyed vireo, although its personality was similiar. Peterson and Chalif described this bird in *A Field Guide to Mexican Birds,* as follows: "A vireo with *cinnamon cheeks and sides* . . . Brown above, white below, washed with cinnamon on sides; 2 conspicuous white or yellowish wingbars and white spectacles" (p. 195). Our birds matched that description remarkably well.

Stripe-headed Tanager

Since we had found both of Cozumel's avian endemics, we decided to spend our remaining time trying to find a stripe-headed tanager. This is a West Indian bird that occurs on Cozumel but nowhere else in Mexico. Our time remaining, before we would be required to board the ferry to return to the mainland, was running short. We tried to explain to Juan that we needed to be taken to a place where there was more native plantlife, preferably a natural thorn forest habitat. We found it impossible to communicate the idea of naturalness. I used what I thought were all the right words to describe a wooded habitat, like *bosque* and *selva baja* and *selva mediana,* but to no avail.

Suddenly, someone use the word jardín, or garden, and Juan was a new man. All the frustration that he had displayed while trying to understand our needs seemed to disappear, and off we flew through the middle of San Miguel toward the northern end of town. Just as suddenly, he turned off the main roadway into a narrow wooded lane that led into a large and very active nursery. We estimated that we could spend about an hour at the nursery and still make the ferry on time.

We all climbed out of the taxi and hurried off in various directions in search for a stripe-headed tanager. I was not even sure if we had come to proper habitat. A nursery was not exactly what I had had in mind but, as late as it was, we had little choice but to try to find the bird there. We lucked out! It took us the better part of an hour. With only fifteen or twenty minutes to spare, I detected bird calls that I could not identify emanating from a few orchard trees in about the center of the nursery grounds. The calls sounded as if they could be the "drawn-out *seep,*" described in Peterson and Chalif. We all gathered around to discover the source. It took us a few more minutes to coax the bird closer. Then a male stripe-headed tanager suddenly flew into the branches of a small fruit tree, and we all had an excellent look at that very colorful bird. The chestnut and yellow breast, boldly striped black and white head, and white striped wings could not be mistaken for anything else. It was indeed a gorgeous bird and a most welcome addition to the day's list.

Twenty minutes later we boarded the ferry and departed Cozumel Island. We all felt a little sad that we had not had time to see other parts of the island. We had missed the experience of the reef and the mysteries available there, not to mention the scattered Mayan ruins, which I had particularly wanted to visit. Cozumel once was an important Mayan center. Hammond, in his 1982 book, *Ancient Maya Civilization,* stated: "At the time of the conquest it was the principal shrine of the goddess Ix Chel, a pilgrim center, and also, not coincidentally, an important trading port. A survey of the island . . . showed that there was a principal center in the middle of the island, called San Gervasio, together with more than thirty other sites, of which many were small coastal shrines that probably doubled as lookouts or beacons" (p. 198). And even after the Mayan empire was conquered by the Spaniards, Cozumel remained a significant place of worship for many years.

Today, however, exotic vegetation dominates much of the island, a fitting climax to human use and abuse of a fragile environment. The birdlife has somehow adapted to the new ecosystem, at least for now. I couldn't help but wonder how much more human abuse Cozumel's endemic birdlife could withstand and yet survive.

Appendix
Common and Scientific Plant Names

Acacia, bullhorn. *Acacia spadicigera*

Agave, Chisos. *Agave glomerfera*

Agave, Shaw's. *Agave shawii*

Agave, sisal. *Agave sisalana*

Alder, Mexican. *Clethra macrocarpa*

Alder, wax. *Alnus jorullensis*

Allthorn. *Koeberlinia spinosa*

Ambrosia. *Ambrosia ambrosioides*

Anthurium. *Anthurium xantho-somifolium*

Apes earring. *Pithecellobium arboreum*

Ash, fragrant. *Fraxinus cuspidata*

Aspen, quaking. *Populus tremuloides*

Balche. *Lonchocarpus longistylus*

Balm tree. *Myroxlon balsamum*

Barreta. *Helietta parvifolia*

Batis. *Batis* spp.

Bee-brush, common. *Aloysia gratissima*

Bird-of-paradise. *Caesalpinia gaumeri*

Blackbrush. *Acacia rigidula*

Blueberry, tropical. *Conostegia xalapensis*

Boojum. *Fouquieria columnaris*

Borderpod. *Lysiloma bahamensis*

Bread-nut tree. *Brosimum aliscastrum*

Brittlebush. *Encelia farinosa*

Buckwheat, flat-topped. *Eriogonum fasiculatum*

Burweed. *Franseria camphorata*

Cactus, barrel. *Ferocactus acanthodes*

Candelilla. *Euphorbia antisyphilitica*

Cardon. *Cereus pringlei*

Ceiba. *Ceiba parvifolia*

Cenizo. *Leucophyllum frutescens*

Century plant. *Agave americana*

Ceriman. *Monstera deliciosa*

Ceron. *Phyllostylon brasiliensis*

Chamise. *Adenostoma fasiculatum*

Charcoal shrub. *Baccharis conferta*

Cherry, wild. *Prunus* spp.

Chicle. *Achras zapota*

Cholla. *Opuntia cholla*

Cholla, cane or tree. *Opuntia imbricata*

Cholla, Christmas. *Opuntia tesajo*

Chuparosa. *Beloperone californica*

Cigarbox tree. *Cedrela mexicana*

Conzattia. *Conzattia* spp.

Copal. *Cyrtocarpa procera*

Corpus. *Magnolia schiedeana*

Creosote bush. *Larrea tridentata*

Cypress, Arizona. *Cupressus arizonica*

Cypress, Montezuma bald. *Taxodium mucronatum*

Cypress, southern. *Cupressus lustanica*

Daisy, sea ox-eye. *Borrichia frutescens*

Desert lavender. *Hyptis emoryi*

Desert willow. *Chilopsis linearis*

Douglas-fir. *Pseudotsuga menziesii*

Dumbcane. *Dieffenbachia* spp.

Eardrop tree. *Enterolobium cyclocarpum*

Ebony, Texas. *Pithecellobium flexicaule*

Elder, Mexican. *Sambucus mexicana*

Elephant tree. *Bursera dicolor* or *B. microphylla*

Fanpalm. *Washingtonia filifera*

Fern, bird's nest. *Asplenium* spp.

Fig, plumleaf. *Ficus padifolia*

Fig, strangler. *Ficus continifolia*

Fig, weeping. *Ficus benjamina*

Fir, Coahuila. *Abies coahuilensis*

Fir, sacred. *Abies religiosa*

Fir, white. *Abies concolor*

Fire dart, giant. *Kochia* spp.

Fish poison tree. *Piscidia piscipala*

Frankenia. *Frankenia palmeri*

Giant dagger. *Yucca carnerosana*

Glasswort. *Salicornia* spp.

Goat-bush. *Castela texana*

Greasewood. *Purshia tridentata*

Guayacan. *Porliera angustifolia*

Guayule. *Parthenium argentatum*

Gumbo limbo. *Bursera simaruba*

Gunnera. *Gunnera insignis*

Hackberry. *Celtis monoica*

Hackberry, desert. *Celtis pallida*

Handflower tree. *Chiranthodendron pentadactulon*

Hawthorn, Mexican. *Crataegus mexicana*

Heliconia. *Heliconia* spp.

Henequen. *Agave fourcroydes*

Hickory. *Carya* spp.

Hop-hornbeam. *Ostrya* spp.

Huisache. *Acacia farnesiana*

Ironwood. *Olneya tesota*

Jaboncillo. *Sapindus saponaria*

Jacquinia. *Jacquinia pungens*

Javelina bush. *Condalia ericoides*

Joint fir. *Ephedra* spp.

Jojoba. *Simmondsia chinensis*

Juniper, California. *Juniperus california*

Juniper, red-berry. *Juniperus pinchotii*

Juniper, weeping. *Juniperus flaccida*

Kapok tree. *Ceiba pentandra*

La coma. *Bumelia celastrina*

Lance pod. *Lonchocarpus lancealatus*

Laurel, Mexican. *Phoebe tampicensis*

Leather stem. *Jatropha* spp.

Lechuguilla. *Agave lechequilla*

Lilac, wild. *Ceonothus* spp.

Kilamache. *Caesalpinia gaumeri*

Lobelia, loose-flowered. *Lobelia laxiflora*

Lomboi. *Jatropha cinerea*

Lysiloma. *Lysiloma candida*

Lysiloma (Oaxaca). *Lysiloma microphylla*

Maculiz prieto. *Tabebuia guayacan*

Madrone, Arizona. *Arbutus arizonica*

Madrone, Texas. *Arbutus xalapensis*

Mahogany. *Sweetenia macrophylla*

Mahogany, mountain. *Cercocarpus montana*

Mallow, wax. *Mavaviscus arboreus*

Mangrove, black. *Avicennia nitida*

Mangrove, red. *Rhizophora mangle*
Mangrove, small button. *Conocarpus erecta*
Mangrove, white. *Laguncularia racemosa*
Manzanita. *Arctostaphylos arizonica*
Maple. *Acer skutchii*
Mariola. *Parthenium incanum*
Mesquite. *Prosopis laevigata*
Mesquite, Honey. *Prosopis grandulosa*
Moradilla. *Chlorophora tinctoria*
Mormon tea. *Ephedra* spp.
Morning glory tree. *Ipomoea murucoides*
Naked indian. *Bursera simaruba*
Needlegrass. *Stipa tenuissima*
Oak, chestnut. *Quercus castanea*
Oak, gray. *Quercus grisea*
Oak, netleaf. *Quercus reticulata*
Oak, Skinner's. *Quercus skinneri*
Ocotillo. *Fouquieria splendens*
Organ pipe. *Cereus thurberi*
Oxhorn bucida. *Bucida buceras*
Palm, coconut. *Cocos nucifera*
Palm, Cohune. *Orbignya cohune*
Palm, Texas. *Sabal texana*
Palmetto. *Sabal* spp.
Palo calabaza. *Beroullia flammea*
Palo totole. *Conzattia multiflora*
Palo verde. *Cercidium floridum*
Papelillo. *Alseis yucatanensis*
Philodendron. *Philodendron* spp.
Phoebe. *Phoebe* spp.
Pimienta. *Pinenta dioica*
Pine, Aztec. *Pinus teocote*
Pine, Bishop. *Pinus muricata*
Pine, Chihuahua. *Pinus leiophylla*
Pine, Hartweg's. *Pinus hartwegii*
Pine, Jeffrey. *Pinus jeffreyi*

Pine, jelecote. *Pinus patula*
Pine, Lawson. *Pinus lawsonii*
Pine, Mexican white. *Pinus ayacahuite*
Pine, Michoacan. *Pinus michoacana*
Pine, Montezuma. *Pinus montezumae*
Pine, ocote. *Pinus oocarpa*
Pine, ponderosa. *Pinus ponderosa*
Pine, southern yellow. *Pinus pseudostrobus*
Pine, southwestern white. *Pinus strobiformis*
Pine, sugar. *Pinus lambertiana*
Pinyon, Mexican. *Pinus cembroides*
Pinyon, Parry. *Pinus quadrifolia*
Pitahaya agria. *Machaerocereus gummosus*
Pochote. *Ceiba aesculifolia*
Podocarp. *Pococarpus reicheri*
Prayer plant. *Maranta* spp.
Pricklenut. *Guazuma ulmofolia*
Pricklypear, Engelmann's. *Opuntia engelmanni*
Pricklypear, Texas. *Opuntia Lindheimeri*
Primavera. *Cybistax donnellsmithii*
Purple heart. *Setcreasea* spp.
Sagebrush. *Artemisia tridentata*
Saguaro. *Cereus giganteus*
Saltbush. *Atriplex* spp.
Sausage tree. *Hymenaea courbaril*
Sea blite. *Suaeda* spp.
Sea grape. *Coccoloba uvifera*
Senna. *Cassia tomentosa*
Seepwillow. *Baccharis emoryi*
Senita. *Cereus schottii*
Silk cotton tree. *Bombax ellipticum*
Sisal. *Agave sisalana*

Sotol. *Dasylirion texanum*
Spanish bayonnet. *Yucca terculeana*
Sugarberry. *Ehretia anacua*
Sumac. *Rhus* spp.
Sumac, evergreen. *Rhus virens*
Sweetbush. *Bebbia juncea*
Sweet gum. *Liquidamber styraciflua*
Sycamore. *Platanus occidentalis*
Tarbush. *Flourensia cernua*
Tasajillo. *Opuntia leptocaulis*
Tepeguaje. *Lysiloma acapulcensis*
Trompillo. *Cordia schestera*

Trumpet tree. *Tabebuia rosea*
Tullidora. *Karwinskia Humboldtiana*
Tzalam. *Lysiloma bahamensis*
Walnut. *Juglans* spp.
Ya-axnix. *Vitex gaumeri*
Yaupon, desert. *Schaefferia* spp.
Yago-lache. *Pseudosmodingium perniciosum*
Yellow trumpet. *Tecoma stans*
Yellowsilk shelltree. *Cochlospermum vitifolium*
Yew, Mexican. *Taxus globosa*
Yucca, Torrey. *Yucca torreyi*

References

Adams, Richard E. W. 1977. *Prehistoric Mesoamerica.* Boston, Mass.: Little, Brown and Co.

Alden, Peter. 1969. *Finding birds in western Mexico.* Tucson: Univ. Ariz. Press.

Alvarez, Ticul. 1963. *The recent mammals of Tamaulipas, México.* Univ. Kansas Publ. Mus. Nat. Hist. 14(15): 363–473.

American Ornithologists' Union. 1983. *Check-list of North American birds.* 6th ed. Lawrence, Kans.: Allen Press.

Andrle, Robert F. 1967. Birds of the Sierra de Tuxtla in Veracruz, Mexico. *The Wilson Bull.* 79, no. 2:163–87.

Andrle, Robert F. 1967. The horned guan in Mexico and Guatemala. *The Condor* 69:93–109.

Anon. 1989. Mexican shoppers return—The border's on the rebound. *The Victoria Advocate* (Dec. 10): 40.

Ayensu, Edward S., 1980. *Jungles.* New York: Crown Publ.

Beard, J. S. 1944. Climax vegetation in tropical America. *Ecology* 25(2): 127–58.

Beard, J. S. 1955. The classification of tropical American vegetation types. *Ecology* 36:89–100.

Belt, Don. 1989. Baja California—Mexico's land apart. *National Geographic* (Dec.): 714–45.

Bennett, F. P., Jr. 1977. Notes on Birds of El Triunfo, Chiapas. *Mexican Birds Newsletter* 2, no. 1:17–21.

Benson, Elizabeth C. 1977. *The Maya world.* New York: Thomas Y. Crowell Co.

Binford, Laurence C. 1980. Avian habitats in Oaxaca. In *Proc. Natl. Audubon Soc. Symp.: The Birds of Mexico: Their ecology and conservation.* Tiburon, Calif.: Natl. Audubon Soc. West Ed. Center, George Whittel Ed. Center—Richardson Bay Wildl. Sanctuary.

Blair, Calvin P. 1977. Mexico—Some recent developments. *Texas Business Review* (May): 98–103.

Blair, Frank W. 1950. The biotic provinces of Texas. *Texas Jour. Sci.* 2:93–117.

Blake, Emmet Reid. 1953. *Birds of Mexico.* Chicago: Univ. Chicago Press.

Bostic, Dennis L. 1975. *A natural history guide to the Pacific coast on North Central Baja California.* San Diego, Calif.: Biology Education Expeditions.

Breedlove, Dennis E. 1973. The phytogeography and vegetation of Chiapas (Mexico). In *Vegetation and vegetational history of northern Latin America,* ed. Alan Graham. New York: Elsevier Sci. Publ. Co.

Brockman, C. Frank. 1968. *A Guide to Field Identification Trees of North America.* Racine, Wis.: Golden Press.

Brodkorb, Pierce. 1943. *Birds from the Gulf lowlands of southern Mexico.* Ann Arbor: Misc. Publ. Mus. Zool., Univ. Mich., no. 55.

Brooks, Paul. 1972. Baja California emergency and opportunity. *Audubon* (Mar.): 12–16, 18, 23.

Brownstein, Richard. 1972. The Cozumel Island, Mexico trip. *Birding* 4, no. 2:97–98.

Burgess, Tony L. 1985. Agave adaption to aridity. *Desert Plants* 7(2): 39–50.

Burleson, Bob, and David H. Riskind. 1986. *Backcountry Mexico: A traveler's guide and phrasebook.* Austin: Univ. Texas Press.

Carr, Archie. 1973. *So excellent a fishe.* Garden City, N.J.: Anchor Natural History Books, Anchor Press/Doubleday.

Carrico, James W. 1988. The proposed Sierra del Carmen National Park. Paper presented at George Wright Society Triennial Conference, Nov. 14–18, Tucson, Arizona.

Clark, Phil. 1972. *A flower lover's guide.* D. F.: Editorial Minutiae Mexicana.

Clover, E. U. 1937. Vegetational survey of the Lower Rio Grande valley, Texas. *Madrono* 41:77–100.

Cobb, David. 1982. Development cuts through jungle. *Not Man Apart,* (Dec.): 11.

Coe, Michael D. 1971. *The Maya.* Middlesex, England: Penguin Books.

Correll, Donovan Stewart, and Marshall Conring Johnston. 1970.

Manual of the vascular plants of Texas. Renner: Texas Research Foundation.

Council on Environmental Quality and Department of State. 1980. *The Global 2000 Report to the President. The Tech. Report. Vol. Two.* Washington, D.C.: GPO.

Critchfield, William B., and E. L. Little, Jr. 1966. *Geographic distribution of the pines of the world.* Washington, D.C.: U.S. Department of Agriculture, Forest Serv. Misc. Publ. 991.

Davis, L. Irby. 1971. *Birds of northeastern Mexico: An annotated checklist.* Austin: Univ. Texas Press.

Davis, L. Irby. 1972. *A field guide to the birds of Mexico and Central America.* Austin: Univ. Texas Press.

Davis, William B. 1966. *The mammals of Texas.* Bull. 41, Tex. Parks and Wildl. Dept., Austin.

Dawson, E. Y. 1944. Some ethnobotanical notes on the Seri Indians. *Desert plant life* 16(9): 133–38.

Deis, Robert. 1981. Again Silent Spring—'Our' birds losing tropical habitat. *Defenders* (Apr.): 6–11.

Diamond, Jared M. 1980. Patchy distributions of tropical birds. In *Conservation biology,* ed. Micael E. Soule and Bruce A. Wilcox. Sunderland, Miss.: Sinauer Assoc.

Dice, Lee R. 1943. *The biotic provinces of North America.* Ann Arbor: Univ. Mich. Press.

DuBois, Random. 1985. Coastal fisheries management lessons learned from the Caribbean. In *Coasts coastal resources management: Development case studies,* ed. John R. Clark, Coastal Publ. no. 3, Renewable Resources Info. Series, Columbia, S.C.: Research Planning Inst.

Eaton, Stephen W., and E. P. Edwards. 1948. Notes on birds of the Gomez Farias region of Tamaulipas. *The Wilson Bull.* 60(2): 109–14.

Edwards, Ernest P. 1968. *Finding birds in Mexico.* Sweet Briar, Va.: Ernest P. Edwards.

Edwards, Ernest P. 1972. *A field guide to the birds of Mexico.* Sweet Briar, Va.: Ernest P. Edwards.

Edwards, Ernest P. 1985. *1985 supplement to finding birds in Mexico.* Sweet Briar, Va.: Ernest P. Edwards.

Ehrlich, Paul R., David S. Dobkin, and Dattyl Wheye. 1988. *The birder's handbook.* New York: Simon and Schuster, Fireside.

Eisenberg, John F. 1980. The density and biomass of tropical mammals. In *Conservation biology*, ed. Michael E. Soule and Bruce A. Wilcox. Sunderland, Miss.: Sinauer Assoc., Inc.

Emmons, Louise H. 1990. *Neotropical rainforest mammals: A field guide*. Chicago: The Univ. of Chicago Press.

Emory, William H. 1857. *Report on the United States and Mexican boundary survey*, vol. 1. 34th Cong., 1st sess. Washington, D.C.: House Exec. Doc. 135.

Felger, Richard S., and Charles H. Lowe. 1976. *The island and coastal vegetation and flora of the northern part of the Gulf of California*. Nat. Hist. Mus. Los Angeles, Cont. Sci., 285.

Fleming, Carrol B. 1983. Life at the water's edge. *Americas* (MAR.–APR.): 9–12.

Flores, M. G., J. Jiménes, X. Madrigal D., F. Moncayo R., and F. Takaki T. 1971. *Memoria del mapa de tipos de vegetación de la república Mexicana*. México, D.F.: Secretaría de Recursos Hidráulicos.

Forshaw, Joseph M. 1977. *Parrots of the world*. Neptune, N.J.: T.F.H. Publications.

Forsyth, Adrian, and Kenneth Miyata. 1984. *Tropical nature*. N.Y.: Charles Scribner's Sons.

Fritts, Thomas H., Jr., and N. J. Scott, Jr. 1984. Final Report: Ecology and Conservation of North American Tortoise (Genus *Gopherus*). Typed report by U.S.F.W.S., Denver Wildl. Res. Cent.

Gallencamp, Charles. 1976. *Maya: The riddle and rediscovery of a lost civilization*. New York: David McKay Co.

Gehlbach, Frederick R. 1981. *Mountain islands and desert seas: A natural history of the U.S.-Mexican borderlands*. College Station, Tex.: Texas A&M Univ. Press.

Gehlbach, Frederick R. 1987. Natural history sketches, densities, and biomass of breeding birds in evergreen forests of the Rio Grande, Texas, and Rio Corona, Tamaulipas, Mexico. *The Tex. Journ. Sci.* 39(3): 241–51.

Gehlbach, Frederick R., D. D. Dillon, H. L. Harrell, S. E. Kennedy, and K. R. Wilson. 1976. Avifauna of the Río Corona, Tamaulipas, Mexico: Northeastern limit of the tropics. *The Auk* 93, no. 1:53–65.

Gilbert, Lawrence E. 1980. Food web organization and the conservation of neotropical diversity. In *Conservation Biology*, ed.

Michael E. Soule and Bruce A. Wilcox. Sunderland, Miss.: Sinauer Assoc.

Gómez-Pompa, Arturo. 1967. Some problems of tropical plant ecology. *Jour. Arnold Arboretum* 48:105–21.

Gómez-Pompa, Arturo. 1977. *Ecología de la vegetación del Estado de Veracruz.* México: Compania Edit. Contin.

Gruson, Edward S. 1972. *Words for birds: A lexicon of North American birds with biographical notes.* New York: Quadrangle Books.

Hall, E. Raymond, and K. R. Kelson. 1959. *The mammals of North America.* New York: Ronald Press Co.

Hall, Henry Marion. 1960. *A gathering of shore birds.* New York: Devin-Adair Co.

Hammond, Norman. 1982. *Ancient Maya civilization.* New Brunswick, N.J.: Rutgers Univ. Press.

Harrell, Byron Eugene. 1951. The birds of Rancho del Cielo: An ecological investigation in the sweet gum forests of Tamaulipas, Mexico. Unpubl. thesis: Univ. Minn.

Harrison, Peter. 1985. *Seabirds: An identification guide.* Boston: Houghton Mifflin Co.

Hartshorn, Gary S. 1980. Neotropical forest dynamics. *Biotropica* 12:23–30.

Humphrey, Stephen R. 1985. How species become vulnerable to extinction and how we can meet the crisis. In *Animal extinctions: What everyone should know,* ed. R. J. Hoage. Washington, D. C. Smithsonian Inst. Press.

IUCN Working Group on Mangrove Ecosystems. 1983. *Global status of mangrove ecosystems.* Commission on Ecology Papers No. 3., ed. Saenger, P., E. J. Hegerl, and J. D. S. Davie. IUCN and Natural Resources, Gland, Switzerland.

Jaeger, Edmund C. 1956. *Desert wild flowers.* Stanford, Calif.: Stanford Univ. Press.

Jaeger, Edmund C. 1957. *The North American deserts.* Stanford, Calif.: Stanford Univ. Press.

Johnson, William Weber. 1972. *Baja California: The American wilderness.* New York: Time-Life Books.

Johnston, Bernice. 1970. *The Seri Indians of Sonora Mexico.* Tucson: Ariz. State Mus. and Univ. Ariz.

Kaufman, Kenn, T. Parker, and M. Robbins. 1976. Notes on the birds of Querto Los Mazos, Sierra de Autlan, Jalisco. *Mexican Birds Newsletter* 1, no. 3:12–15.

Kincey, Herb F. 1978. Climbing Mexico's big three volcanoes. *Summit* (Feb.–MAR.): 3–15.

Kricher, John C. 1989. *A neotropical companion.* Princeton, N.J.: Princeton Univ. Press.

Krutch, Joseph Wood. 1961. *The forgotten peninsula: A naturalist in Baja California.* New York: W. Sloane Assoc.

Lasley, Greg. 1987. A location for finding maroon-fronted parrots south of Monterrey, Mexico. Photocopied report.

Leigh, Egbert Giles, Jr. 1975. Structure and climate in tropical rain forest. *Annual Review of Ecology and Systematics* 6:67–86.

Leopold, A. Starker. 1950. Vegetation zones of Mexico. *Ecology* 31, no. 4:507–18.

Lugo, Ariel E., and Samuel C. Snedaker. 1974. The ecology of mangroves. *Annual Review of Ecology and Systematics* 5:39–64.

MacArthur, Robert H. 1972. *Geographic Ecology.* New York: Harper & Row.

McGee, W. J. 1896. *The Seri Indians.* Washington, D.C.: Smithsonian Inst. Bur. Amer. Ethnol. Ann. Rept. 17(1): 1–344.

Marsh, Ernest G., Jr. 1936. Biological survey of the Santa Rosa and del Carmen mountains of northern Coahuila, Mexico. Typed report to Natl. Park Serv.

Martin, Paul D. 1958, *A biogeography of reptiles and amphibians in the Gomez Farias region, Tamaulipas, Mexico.* Ann Arbor: Misc. Publ. Mus. Zool., Univ. Mich., no. 101.

Martinez y Ojeda, Enrique, and F. Gonzales Medrano. 1977. Vegetation of the southeastern part of Tamaulipas, Mexico. *Biotica* 2, no. 2:1–45.

Mason, Charles T., Jr., and Patricia B. Mason. 1987. *A handbook of Mexican roadside flora.* Tucson: Univ. Ariz. Press.

Miller, Alden H. 1955. The avifauna of the Sierra del Carmen of Coahuila, Mexico. *The Condor* 57, no. 3:154–78.

Miranda, Faustino. 1952. *La vegetación de Chiapas.* 2 vols. Ediciónes del Gobierno del Estado, Tuxtla Gutierrez.

Miranda, Faustino. 1958. Estudios acerca de la vegetación. In *Los recursos naturales de sureste y su aprovechamiento.* Edic. Inst. Mex. Rec. Nat. Renov. México, D.F. vol. 2:215–71.

Mirov, N.T. 1967. *The genus pinus.* New York: Ronald Press.

Morley, Sylvanus Griswold: rev. George W. Brainerd. 1956. *The ancient Maya.* Stanford, Calif.: Stanford Univ. Press.

Mountfort, Guy. 1988. *Rare birds of the world: A Collins/ICBP handbook.* Lexington, Mass.: The Stephen Greene Press.

Muller, Cornelius H. 1939. Relations of the vegetation and climatic types in Nuevo Leon, Mexico. *Am. Midland Nat.* 21:687–729.

Muller, Cornelius H. 1947. Vegetation of Coahuila, Mexico. *Madrono* 9:1–32.

Myers, Norman. 1979. *The sinking ark.* Oxford: Pergamon Press.

Nadkarni, Nalini M. 1985. Roots that go out on a limb. *Natural History* (Feb.): 43–48.

National Audubon Society. 1975. 1983. Catemaco, Vera Cruz, Mex. *American Birds* 29(2): 591–93.

Orme, William A., Jr. 1982. Mexico leads world in export of salt. *R&D Mexico* (Apr.): 5–10.

Orme, William A., Jr. 1982. The watch on Mexico's most violent volcano. *R&D Mexico* (Apr.): 5–10.

Palmer, Ralph S. 1962. *Handbook of North American birds.* vol. 1, *Loons through flamingos.* New Haven, Conn.: Yale Univ. Press.

Pesman, M. Walter. 1962. *Meet flora Mexicana.* Globe, Ariz.: Dale S. King.

Peterson, Roger Tory, and Edward L. Chalif. 1973. *A field guide to Mexican birds.* Boston: Houghton Mifflin Co.

Pfeiffer, John E. 1980. The mysterious rise and decline of Monte Alban. *Smithsonian* (Feb.): 62–75.

Pritchard, P. C. H., and Rene Marquéz M. 1973. *Kemp's ridley turtle or Atlantic ridley Lepidochelys kempi.* Monog., Intern. Union Conser. Natural Res. 2:1–30.

Puig, H. 1970. Etude phytogéographique de la Sierra de Tamaulipas (Mexique). *Bull. Soc. Hist. Nat. Toulouse* 106:59–79.

Puig, H. 1974. Phytogéographie et écologie de la Huasteca (NE du Mexique). Thesis. Université Paul Sabatier. Toulouse.

Richards, P. W. 1969. Speciation in the tropical rain forest and the concept of the niche. *Biol. Journ. Linn. Soc.* 1:149–53.

Rowley, J. Staurt. 1966. Breeding records of birds of the Sierra Madre del Sur, Oaxaca, Mexico. *Proc. West. Found. Vert. Zool.* 1(3), Oct.

Rudolph, James D. 1984. *Mexico: A country study.* Washington, D.C.: GPO.

Ruz, Alberto L. 1953. The mystery of the Temple of the Inscriptions. *Archeology* 6(1).

Rzedowski, Jerzy. 1983. *Vegetación de México.* México, D.F.: Editorial Limusa.

Rzedowski, Jerzy, and R. McVaugh. 1966. *La vegetación de Nueva Galicia.* Ann Arbor: Contr. Univ. Mich. Herb. 9:1–123.

Sada, Andres M. 1987. Locations for finding Worthen's sparrow (*Spizella wortheni*) in Nuevo Leon [correction: Coahuila]. *Mex. Birding Assoc. Bull. Board* 1, no. 87:3.

Scammon, Charles Melville. 1874. *The marine mammals of the northwestern coast of North America, described and illustrated together with an account of the American whale-fishery.* San Francisco, Calif.: John H. Carmany.

Schaldach, W. J., Jr. 1963. *The avifauna of Colima and adjacent Jalisco, Mexico.* Los Angeles, Calif.: Proc. West. Found. Vert. Zool.

Schaldach, W. J., Jr. 1969. Further notes on the avifauna of Colima and adjacent Jalisco, Mexico. *An Inst. Biol. Univ. Nat. Auton. Mexico* 40, Ser. Zool. (2): 299–316.

Schaldach, W. J., Jr., and Allan R. Phillips. 1961. The eared poorwill. *The Auk,* 78:567–72.

Schmidt, Robert H., Jr. 1976. *A geographical survey of Sinaloa.* Southw. Studies, Monog. no. 50, Univ. Texas El Paso, Texas West. Press.

Schmidt, Robert H., Jr. 1986. Chihuahuan climate. In *Invited papers from the second symposium on the Chihuahuan desert region United States and Mexico, 20–21 October 1983,* ed. Jon C. Barlow, A. Michael Powell, and Barbara N. Timmermann, Alpine, Tex.: Chihuahuan Desert Res. Inst.

Schmidt, Robert H., Jr. 1989. The arid zones of Mexico: Climatic extremes and conceptualization of the Sonoran Desert. *Journ. Arid Environments* 16:241–56.

Schmidly, David J. 1977. Factors governing the distribution of mammals in the Chihuahuan Desert Region. In *Trans. symp. biol. resources Chihuahuan desert region, U.S. and Mexico.* Natl. Park Serv. Ser. Trans. Proc. no. 3., ed. R. H. Wauer and D. H. Riskind. Washington, D.C.: U.S. Department of Interior, GPO.

Secretaría de Agricultura y Recursos Hidráulicos. 1977. *Peninsula de Yucatán.* Comisión Técnico Consultiva para la Determinación Regional de los Coeficientes de Agostadero.

Sharp, A. J., E. Hernandez X., H. Crum, and W. B. Fox. 1950. Nota florística de una asociación importante del suroestre de Tamaulipas. *Bol. Soc. Bot. Méx.* 11:1–4.

Shreve, Forrest. 1942. The desert vegetation of North America. *The Botanical Review* 8(4): 195–246.

Siddall, Scott E., J. A. Atchue III, and R. L. Murray, Jr. 1985. Mariculture development in mangroves: A case study of the Philippines, Ecuador and Panama. In *Coasts coastal resources management: Development case studies,* ed. John R. Clark. Coastal Publ. no. 3, Renewable Resources Info. Series, Columbia, S.C.: Research Planning Inst.

Simon, Kate. 1965. *Mexico places and pleasures.* Garden City, N.Y.: Doubleday & Co.

Smith, Alan P. 1973. Stratification of temperate and tropical forests. *The American Naturalist* 107:671–83.

Snedaker, Samuel C., and Charles D. Getter. 1985. *Coastal resources management guidelines.* Renewable Res. Info. Ser. Coastal Mgt. Publ. 2, Washington, D.C.: Natl. Park Serv.

Snyder, Noel F. R., and Eric V. Johnson. 1985. Photographic Censusing of the 1982-1983 California Condor Population. *The Condor* 87:1–13.

Standley, Paul S. 1961. *Trees and shrubs of Mexico, Parts 1–3* and *Parts 4–5.* 2 vols. USNM, Cont. U.S. Natl. Herbarium, Washington, D.C.: Smithsonian Inst.

Steinbeck, John. 1945. *The pearl.* New York: Viking Press.

Steinbeck, John. 1975. *The log from the Sea of Cortez.* New York: Penguin Books.

Stephens, John L. 1949. *Incidents of travel in Central America, Chiapas, and Yucatan.* New Brunswick, N.J.: Rutgers Univ. Press.

Sumichrast, Francis. 1882. Enumeración de las especies de reptiles observados en la parte meridional de la República Méxicana. *La Naturaleza* 6:31–45.

Sutton, George Miksch. 1951. *Mexican birds: First impressions.* Norman: Univ. Okla. Press.

Sutton, George Miksch. 1972. *At a Bend in a Mexican river.* New York: Paul S. Eriksson.

Sutton, George Miksch, and O. S. Pettingill, Jr. 1942. Birds of the Gomez Farias region, southwestern Tamaulipas. *The Auk* 59(1): 1–34.

Taylor, Walter P., W. B. McDougall, C. C. Presnall, and K. P. Schmidt. 1946. The Sierra del Carmen in northern Coahuila, a preliminary ecological survey. *Texas Geogr. Mag.* 10, no. 1:11–22.

Terborgh, John. 1989. *Where have all the birds gone?* Princeton, N.J.: Princeton Univ. Press.

Thompson, J. Eric S. 1966. *The rise and fall of Maya civilization.* Norman: Univ. Okla. Press.

Titchmarsh, Alan. 1982. *The Larousse guide to house plants.* New York: Larousse & Co.

Tompkins, Peter. 1976. *Mysteries of the Mexican pyramids.* New York: Harper & Row.

UNESCO and UNEP. 1974. *Programme on Man and the Biosphere (MAB) Task Force on: Criteria and guidelines for the choice and establishment of biosphere reserves Final Report.* Paris: UNESCO.

Urban, Emil K. 1959. *Birds from Coahuila, México.* Univ. Kan. Publ. Mus. Nat. Hist. 11(8): 443–516.

U.S. Department of State. 1984. *June 1984 Mexico post report.* Dept. State Publ. 9128. Washington, D.C.: GPO.

U.S. Fish and Wildlife Service. N.d. *The wildlife corridor.* Info. Brochure for the Lower Rio Grande Valley National Wildlife Refuge Land Acquisition Program, U.S.F.W.S.

U.S. Fish and Wildlife Service. 1979. Last-ditch contingency plan seen as only hope for California condor. *Endangered Species Tech. Bull.,* May, Washington, D.C.: U.S. Department of Interior.

U.S. Interagency Task Force on Tropical Forests. 1980. *The world's tropical forests: A policy, strategy, and program for the United States.* Washington, D.C.: Dept. of State. Publ. 9117.

Vines, Robert A. 1960. *Trees, shrubs and woody vines of the Southwest.* Austin: Univ. Texas Press.

Voss, Golbert L. 1976. *Seashore life of Florida and the Caribbean.* Miami, Fla.: Banyan Books.

Wallace, Alfred Russell. 1878. *Tropical nature and other essays.* London: MacMillan.

Wauer, Roland H. 1978. The breeding avifauna of Isla Tiburon, Sonora, Mexico. Typed report to Natl. Park Serv.

Wauer, Roland H. 1979. "Head Start" for an endangered turtle. *Natl. Parks & Conserv. Mag.* (Nov.): 16–20.

Wauer, Roland H. 1980. Great blue heron and osprey nest on cardon cactus on Tiburon Island, Sonora, Mexico. *The Southwestern Naturalist* 25:103–104.

Wauer, Roland H., and J. D. Ligon. 1977. Distributional relations of breeding avifauna of four southwest mountain ranges. In *Trans. symp. biol. resources Chihuahuan desert region, US and Mexico.* Natl. Park Serv. Ser. Trans. Proc. no. 3., eds. R. H. Wauer and D. H. Riskind. Washington, D.C.: U.S. Department of Interior, GPO.

Wauer, Roland H., and Fred Sladen. (In press.) Importance of Virgin Islands mangrove habitats to wintering birds.

Webster, A. Marie, and M. Deshayes. 1965. 17. Oak-sweet gum cloud forest. *Audubon Field Notes* (Dec.): 599–600.

Webster, A. Marie, and M. Deshayes. 1966. 46. Oak-sweet gum cloud forest. *Audubon Field Notes* (Dec.): 648–49.

Webster, Fred S., Jr. 1974. Resident birds of the Gomez Farias region, Tamaulipas, Mexico. *American Birds* (Feb.): 3–10.

Wells, Philip V. 1966. Late Pleistocene vegetation and degree of pluvial climatic change in the Chihuahuan Desert. *Science* 153:970–75.

Wells, Philip V. 1977. Post-glacial origin of the present Chihuahuan Desert less than 11,500 years ago. In *Trans. symp. biol. resources Chihuahuan desert region, US and Mexico.* Natl. Park Serv. Ser. Trans. Proc. no. 3., ed. R. H. Wauer and D. H. Riskind, Washington, D.C.: U.S. Department of Interior, GPO.

Westcott, Cynthia. 1973. *The gardener's bug Book.* Garden City, N.J.: Doubleday & Co.

Wiggins, Ira L. 1980. *Flora of Baja California.* Stanford, Calif.: Stanford Univ. Press.

Wilbur, Sanford, R. 1978. *The California condor, 1966–76: A look at its past and future.* No. Amer. Fauna, no. 72, USFWS, Washington, D.C.: GPO.

Williams, Sartor O. III. 1977. A search for the azure-rumped tanager. *Mexican Birds Newsletter* 2, no. 1:14–16.

Wilson, E. O. 1971. *The insect societies.* Cambridge, Mass.: Belknap Press.

Wilson, Larry David., and J. R. Meyers. 1985. *The snakes of Honduras.* Milwaukee Wis.: Milw. Public Museum.

Wright, Ronald. 1989. *Time among the Maya.* New York: Weindefeld & Nicolson.

Zwinger, Ann. 1983. *A desert country near the sea.* Tucson: Univ. Ariz. Press.

Index

(Illustrations are indicated in bold type)